Learning to Teach

Learning to Teach

Curricular and Pedagogical Considerations for Teacher Preparation

Edited by Patrick M. Jenlink

ROWMAN & LITTLEFIELD
Lanham • Boulder • New York • London

Published by Rowman & Littlefield
An imprint of The Rowman & Littlefield Publishing Group, Inc.
4501 Forbes Boulevard, Suite 200, Lanham, Maryland 20706
www.rowman.com

6 Tinworth Street, London SE11 5AL, United Kingdom

British Library Cataloguing in Publication Information Available

Library of Congress Cataloging-in-Publication Data

Names: Jenlink, Patrick M., editor.
Title: Learning to teach : curricular and pedagogical considerations for teacher
    preparation / edited by Patrick M. Jenlink.
Description: Lanham : Rowman & Littlefield, [2021] |
    Includes bibliographical references.
Identifiers: LCCN 2021010330 (print) | LCCN 2021010331 (ebook) |
    ISBN 9781475860184 (cloth) | ISBN 9781475860207 (paperback) |
    ISBN 9781475860191 (ebook)
Subjects: LCSH: Teachers—Training of. | Teaching—Methodology.
Classification: LCC LB1707 .L436 2021 (print) | LCC LB1707 (ebook) |
    DDC 370.71/1—dc23
LC record available at https://lccn.loc.gov/2021010330
LC ebook record available at https://lccn.loc.gov/2021010331

♾️™ The paper used in this publication meets the minimum requirements of American National Standard for Information Sciences—Permanence of Paper for Printed Library Materials, ANSI/NISO Z39.48-1992.

Learning to Teach: Curricular and Pedagogical Considerations for Teacher Preparation is dedicated to present and future generations of preservice teachers preparing to enter the teaching profession.

Praise for *Learning to Teach: Curricular and Pedagogical Considerations for Teacher Preparation*

"*Learning to Teach: Curricular and Pedagogical Considerations for Teacher Preparation* is a 'must read' for faculty and staff in teacher education programs across the nation. The chapters in this book explore fundamental connections between teacher preparation and P–12 classrooms. Research-supported topics on pre-service teacher perceptions, preparation to practice, preparing to teach in diverse settings, and preparation of depth in content knowledge are the focus of this book. Are we making the connections for our teachers to meet the needs of an ever-changing society? That is the question we should be asking ourselves as we reflect on these chapters."

—**Sandra Stewart,** associate dean for educator preparation,
Sam Houston State University

"*Learning to Teach: Curricular and Pedagogical Considerations for Teacher Preparation* is a great book for educators interested in making teacher preparation more meaningful. Each chapter provides a unique look into one aspect of teacher preparation, with an emphasis on the interactions between clinical practice and coursework. This book is helpful for educators and programs interested in making stronger connections between theory and practice for teacher candidates."

—**Christina Yuknis,** professor and EdS and PhD program director
professor, Department of Education, Gallaudet University

"Teacher preparation is more significant now than ever as teachers are adapting to extraordinary complexities in the context of schooling. In *Learning to Teach: Curricular and Pedagogical Considerations for Teacher Preparation*, Patrick Jenlink weaves together expertise from current scholars who are examining the ways that teacher preparation programs can cultivate the knowledge, skills, and dispositions of the next generation of teachers so that they are ready to guide students and families through current and future challenges. There is no profession more critical and no time more crucial for this examination."

—Julie Henry, professor and chair, Elementary Education, Literacy and Educational Leadership, Buffalo State College

"How to effectively support preservice teachers to connect what they learn in program courses to what they do in classrooms meaningfully has been one of the persistent and predominant challenges facing scholars, teacher educators, and policymakers in teacher preparation. *Learning to Teach: Curricular and Pedagogical Considerations for Teacher Preparation* contributes to an extensive and deep understanding of the challenge and offers useful approaches to addressing it using studies featuring research-based conceptualization, systematic literature review, qualitative and quantitative examination, and theory-based intervention in different content areas and fields. A resourceful and inspiring read for researchers, policymakers, teacher educators, and teachers interested in the issues of teacher preparation and learning to teach."

—Jian Wang, professor and Helen DeVitt Jones Chair in Teacher Education, Texas Tech University

"*Learning to Teach: Curricular and Pedagogical Considerations for Teacher Preparation* masterfully argues that effective teacher preparation programs include classroom-based instruction complemented by relevant clinical experiences. In teacher preparation classes, pre-service teachers 'learn to teach' by discussing educational theories and cases studies and by observing and analyzing models of effective teaching. Integrated, systematic, and progressive clinical experiences then provide opportunities for pre-service teachers to 'teach to learn' through practical application and reflection of their theoretical knowledge bases. The authors also effectively identify variables that influence pre-service teachers during their professional development journeys. These variables include backgrounds, experiences, and beliefs of pre-service teachers and their university professors, clinical educators, and mentor teachers. Supporting pre-service teachers as they 'learn to teach' and 'teach to learn' is truly a shared responsibility. Given this, *Learning to Teach: Curricular and Pedagogical Considerations for Teacher Preparation* is a must-have resource for teacher educators, P–12 teachers, curriculum specialists, and school/district administrators, all of whom will appreciate reaffirmation of their roles in, and influences upon, the lives of pre-service teachers."

—Annette D. Digby, dean, Thayer School of Education, Wingate University, Wingate, NC

Contents

Preface

"Learning to teach" is complex, made so because of the roles and responsibilities of teachers, compounded by the nature of schools and classrooms in today's ever-changing culture and climate, and the diversity of students. Equally important is the demand of different disciplines on teacher preparation, that is, elementary versus secondary levels, mathematics versus social students, language arts, English as a foreign language (EFL), and special education. Learning to teach is dynamic because there are influences from students, curriculum, policy, leadership, school environments, and preservice teacher's personal beliefs about teaching and learning.

More recently, over the past decade, research on how preservice teachers learn to teach has indicated that individual differences in learning to teach can be distinguished. Research has indicated that teachers' conceptions of learning are influenced by their personal and professional experiences. Related research has indicated that teachers have specific conceptions about how students should learn.

Current research has described teachers' beliefs as being represented in an integrated system, critical for guiding perception, interpretation, and prediction. Belief systems are defined as constantly evolving structures that cover a domain of knowledge. Such belief systems are activated depending on the context and are used to interpret incoming information. Concerns center on preservice teachers' educational belief systems and more specifically their belief systems about learning and teaching.

The "teaching to learn" aspect of symmetry is important to the preservice teacher "learning to teach" as is the relationship that is established in clinical or practicum settings between the preservice teacher and the cooperating or mentoring teacher in order to foster the learning of teaching. There are potential tensions that result from philosophical differences and an intolerance of uncertainty, as well as issues of power as they affect the student teacher-cooperating teacher pair.

The "learning to teach" experiences in preparation programs and the "teaching to learn" experiences in clinical settings foster a dynamic interplay between knowing and doing in which teachers are decision makers who consistently face pedagogical dilemmas and employ professional judgment. "Learning to teach" that embodies pedagogical reasoning concerns those moments when teachers face equally reasonable alternatives while teaching that require reasoned arguments with oneself. These dilemmas occur for teachers in a steady stream (e.g., who to call on, when to offer input, and when to hold back).

Teacher preparation, in particular preparation experiences that emphasize the symmetry in "learning to teach–teaching to learn" enables the preservice teacher to develop an understanding that their expertise stems from their ability to engage with those problems as they arise in ways that are contextually appropriate, ethically considered, humane, nurturing, and consistent with disciplinary inquiry.

Researchers have noted that the influence of mentor teachers who differed from their assigned student teachers in terms of their beliefs in reform-minded practices creates tensions in the "learning to teach" process. Researchers have also reported that the personal, contextual, and professional aspects of preservice teachers have influenced "learning to teach." The complexities of "learning to teach" for preservice teachers is significant and requires continued research.

Learning to Teach: Curricular and Pedagogical Considerations for Teacher Preparation introduces the readers to a collection of thoughtful research-based works by the authors. The chapters reflect the personal and professional experiences, based on field research, of the contributing authors. The research study presented in each chapter offers different perspectives and approaches to "learning to teach." Bridging theory and research in preservice teacher preparation programs are examined. Each study reflects the findings on how the components and experiences of teacher preparation are addressed in diverse contexts and disciplines as well as the prevalent challenges for preservice teacher preparation.

Chapter 1 by Patrick M. Jenlink focuses on learning to teacher and the importance of symmetry in preparation and practice. Anna E. Bargagliotti, in chapter 2, examines the importance of learning trajectories in teacher learning. In chapter 3, Courtney Shimek et al. focus on connecting curricular contexts and bridging coursework and fieldwork. Marie Tejero Hughes, Gina Braun, and Courtney Lynn Barcus, in chapter 4, focus on preparing special educators for inclusive classes. In chapter 5, Rory P. Tannebaum focuses on experiential learning and experiences in context. Amanda A. Olsen and

Roberta J. Scholes, in chapter 6, present research coping strategies for preservice teachers. In chapter 7, Chyllis E. Scott et al. draw attention to preparing teachers for literacy instruction. Amanda L. Nolen and Karina R. Clemmons, in chapter 8, examine the impact of duration and quality of field experiences. In chapter 9, Patricia Paulson et al. present research on professional development days. Burcu Ates et al., in chapter 10, examine EFL Teaching Experience. Finally, in chapter 11, Patrick M. Jenlink offers an epilogue for the book that focuses on the importance of first lessons in learning to teach.

Acknowledgments

The initial idea for this book began as a conversation among colleagues focused on a concern for how preservice teachers learn to teach to preparation programs and the complexities of learning in preparation programs responsible for each new generation of teachers. Specifically, we focused on concerns evident in current teacher preparation programs and the importance of understanding how preservice teachers engage in *learning to teach* in both classroom and clinical experiences designed to prepare teachers.

The concern we fostered was the need to ensure that each generation of teachers leaving preparation programs and entering school classrooms demonstrate an understanding of the integral role of learning as a cognitive reasoning process and in relation to the many dilemmas that preservice and early career teachers face upon entering the classroom. Equally important was a concern for pedagogical reasoning and instruction that is guided by the teacher and that are instrumental to student learning.

In our conversations, we examined "learning to teach" in relationship to "teaching to learn"; focusing on the relationship and the importance for teacher preparation to consider the deep relation one has with the other. We also noted that "learning to teach" is different in terms of disciplines and the importance that "teaching to learn" has in shaping the teacher's understanding of teaching as a profession. We recognized that using a subject-specific framework for examining teacher educators' focus on "learning to teach" in relation to teacher preparation was vey important. Importantly, such a focus could give researchers, teacher educators, and teacher practitioners insight into the importance of increasing the emphasis on evolving forms of "learning to teach", in relationship to "teaching to learn". This emphasis would significantly influence teachers' teaching and students' learning in the classroom.

Acknowledgment and thanks goes to the contributing authors whose research offers insight and thoughtful considerations for understanding the need to examine the meaning of "learning to teach" related to teacher preparation and practice, and the need for a deep understanding of the complexities of preservice teacher learning.

The authors bring the welcomed perspective of theorists and researchers as well as their own field-based research to the discourses presented in the book. Without the contributing authors, this book would not have been possible. The authors of the chapters examining the complexities of preservice teacher learning bring their considerable experience to bear on interpreting the challenges and problems associated with preparing each new generation of teachers, bringing a depth of understanding concerning the integral role that "learning to teach" and the cognitive, pedagogical, and literacy considerations play in the preparation and practice of teachers.

Gratitude is extended to the external reviewers who took time out their busy schedules to review and provide comments and suggestions on the chapters. Acknowledging the value of the chapters and offering constructive feedback were invaluable, as was the affirmation by reviewers for both of the need and importance of a book examining how preservice teachers learn to teach in preparation programs guided by the teacher educators in those programs.

Likewise, gratitude is extended to Tom Koerner and the editorial staff at Rowman & Littlefield Education for their vision in seeing the value of a book on preservice teacher learning that draws into specific relief the need to advance an understanding of how focusing on the complex nature of teacher learning and "learning to teach" is quintessential to teacher preparation and how teachers entering public school classrooms engage with their students.

As well, thanks to the production staff at Rowman & Littlefield is in order for their ever-vigilant efforts to move the book through to completion. Working with a quality publisher and the folks that do the work to translate a manuscript into a completed book is a rewarding experience.

Finally, gratitude goes to Stephen F. Austin State University for supporting this project and enabling the realization of a work that will shape educator preparation for years to come.

Chapter 1

Learning to Teach, Teaching to Learn: The Importance of Symmetry in Preparation and Practice

Patrick M. Jenlink

Learning to teach and teaching to learn are two halves of a larger symmetry[1] of preparation and professional experiences for preservice teacher education. Implicit in this symmetry is an evolving set of questions concerned with the relationship between teacher learning, knowledge, and practice. Naylor, Campbell-Evans, and Maloney (2015), in a study on preservice teachers learning to teach, noted that "the pre-service teachers' approaches to learning to teach were pivotal to what they learned from their teacher education experiences and to their vision of teaching" (p. 123).

The *learning to teach* experiences in teacher preparation, when considered as one aspect of symmetry that connects with *teaching to learn*, presents a complexity in relationships that is instrumental to understand for successful teacher preparation. As Naylor, Campbell-Evans, and Maloney (2015) explained in their research, "pre-service teachers' approaches . . . to learning to teach influenced what was taken from their campus and practicum-based experiences and what they had learnt about their profession" (p. 123). Bound in the complexity of this symmetry are emergent questions and ongoing tensions.

Ball (2000), focusing on bridging practices and the importance of intertwining content and pedagogy in learning to teach, noted:

> The prevalent conceptualization and organization of teachers' learning tends to fragment practice and leave to individual teachers the challenge of integrating subject matter knowledge and pedagogy in the contexts of their work. We assume that the integration required to teach is simple and happens in the course of experience. In fact, however, this does not happen easily, and often does not happen at all. (p. 242)

Importantly, teacher educators should, as they engage the preservice teacher in learning to teach, necessarily recognize that the tension Ball (2000) identified in terms of bridging practices persists and there is a continuing struggle for a proper relationship.

Learning to teach, that is, learning to engage in teaching practice:

> in substantially different ways than one has ever before experienced can occur neither through theoretical imaginings alone nor through unguided experience alone. Instead it requires a tight coupling of the two. (Darling-Hammond, 1997, p. 319)

Within the theory and practice tension in learning to teach emerge important questions that have dominated the discourse of teacher preparation and professional practice variously for decades, conceptualized as the personal, epistemological, contextual, and professional aspects of learning to teach (Bloomfield, 2010). These questions are for teacher educators, given the rapidly changing cultural, political, and ideological context of education and the need to reimagine teacher preparation (Darling-Hammond, 2006; Darling-Hammond & Bransford, 2005; Grossman, Hammerness, & McDonald, 2009).

LEARNING TO TEACH—QUESTIONS TO CONSIDER

The professional preparation teachers has been researched and reported in relevant literature concerning the learning to teach experience (Ball & Forzani, 2009; Brew & Saunders, 2020; Brownlee, 2004; Cochran-Smith et al., 2012; Edwards-Groves & Hoare, 2012; Eilam & Poyas, 2009; Hastings, 2010; Hattie, 2012; McDonald, Kazemi, & Kavanagh, 2013; Naylor, Campbell-Evans, & Maloney, 2015; Opfer, Pedder, & Lavicza, 2011).

Equally researched and reported in relevant literature is the recognition of importance for understanding the teaching to learn aspect (Adoniou, 2013; Avalos, 2011; Edwards-Groves & Hoare, 2012; Girvan, Conneely, & Tangney, 2016; Grossman et al., 2009; Kavanagh, Conrad, & Dagogo-Jack, 2020; Kennedy, 2016; Klette, Hammerness, & Jenset, 2017; Lampert et al., 2013; Orchard & Ellis, 2014).

Importantly, always at the center of these research endeavors to understand preservice teacher preparation is the understanding that preservice teacher preparation is concerned, first and foremost, with "teachers learning, learning how to learn, and transforming their knowledge into practice for the benefit of their students' growth" (Avalos, 2011). What follows in the remaining sections is a series of questions, derived from the previously cited research that extends the discussion of learning to teach—teaching to learn in preservice teacher preparation and practice.

What Types of Knowledge Are Needed for Pre-Teachers to Mediate the Theory and Practice Tension and Be Prepared to Address Diverse Student Populations?

Within the learning to teach process, the question concerned with knowledge is one focused on subject matter, theoretical, and pedagogical knowledge. This question also focuses on the origin of knowledge. More specifically, recent state and national discourses around standards and accountability have fostered tensions between knowledge-for-practice (or codified knowledge) versus knowledge-in-practice and knowledge-of-practice (Cochran-Smith & Lytle, 1999). Long-standing in this tension is a concern for whether teachers entering the classroom will be able to bridge theory and practice, particularly within increasingly diverse classrooms.

Concerning the address of ethnically, cultural, socially, and linguistically diverse student populations in classrooms, learning to teach that addresses social justice, as Kavanagh, Conrad, and Dagogo-Jack (2020) noted in their research, teaching for educational justice concerns "textural practices to support novices in engaging in pedagogical reasoning informed by knowledge about historical and ongoing structures of oppression, or students' cultural funds of knowledge and linguistic resources in their teaching context" (p. 9).

The preservice teacher entering a clinical setting for the first time, or entering the first formal teaching assignment as a teacher, will necessarily require an understanding of "the affordances and constraints of a variety of responses calling on knowledge about privilege and power and how they operate in classroom spaces" (p. 9). The teaching to learn experiences of a clinical or practicum nature afford opportunity to examine the nature of diversity and how it is witnessed among the students in a classroom. The importance of practice-based and experiential knowledge that informs pedagogical reasoning and concern for social justice is or paramount concern (Dutro & Cartun, 2016; MacPherson, 2010).

Most often this concern focuses on the skill and understanding needed to integrate content knowledge and pedagogical knowledge in the contexts of the teacher educator's work. The types of knowledge and understanding necessary to address this tension should be a part of the intellectual environment of the preparation program and should move beyond the dangerous assumption that the integration necessary to teach is simple. Unless students of teaching are grounded in a tight coupling of theory and practice, teaching to learn in classrooms and schools is often a complex challenging experience, fragmenting rather than connecting theoretical, pedagogical, and content knowledge.

Learning to teach as well as engaging in teaching to learn requires a high level of pedagogical reasoning to address the learning needs of a diverse student population (Loughran, 2019; Philip et al., 2019). For the preservice teacher learning to teach as well as teaching to learn, a tight coupling of theory and practice offers important considerations for establishing symmetry in the professional learning experiences of educators. Working to achieve symmetry makes visible the tension between theory and practice, drawing the tension to the foreground of discourses on teacher education.

What Stands as Appropriate Contexts for Teacher Preparation and Practice?

Within the tension of theory and practice, symmetry in professional learning acknowledges the need to rethink what stands as appropriate contexts for teacher preparation and practice. Specifically, preservice teacher preparation that is concerned with learning to teach reflects carefully designed activities. These activities connect the college classroom where the learning to teach experience begins, and often where theory is introduced. Equally important is presenting activities for students engaged in learning to teach wherein the theory-to-practice connection may be situated contextually, i.e., in the space of the real-time classroom in schools.

Concerning the contextual nature of preservice teacher preparation, Grossman (2010) noted that the challenges of designing experiences for preservice teachers requires "bridging a number of divides: between professional knowledge and skilled practice; between universities and PK-12 schools; and between the settings in which prospective teachers learn and the contexts of their early years of teaching" (p. 1). Given the context-specific nature of learning to teacher and teaching to learn, recognizing the various contexts that influence preservice teacher preparation is crucial.

Learning and teaching, in relationship to preparation and practice are contextual and consequential in nature; they are not isolated from reality of the world around, including the personal, the university, and the clinical or practicum contexts associated with preparation (Adoniou, 2013; Higgs & McAllister, 2007; Klette, Hammerness, & Jenset, 2017). The symmetry of learning to teach is equally contextual and consequential in the preservice teacher's learning to teach.

Contexts wherein learning is situated relate to bringing forth knowledge that "is personal, context-bound, and gained through experience" (Swennen & Klink, 2009, p. 12) and the kind of implicit knowledge "that is embedded within action that cannot be separated from that action" (Swennen & Klink, 2009, p. 12). The nature of context and design of learning experiences within and/or related to contexts are consequential in terms of how the preservice teacher experiences learning and making sense of the experiences.

What Is the Place of Discourse in Learning to Teach and Teaching to Learn?

Teaching by its very nature is a discursive act, engaging in conversation and dialogue with students. Therefore, in preservice teacher preparation, focused learning to teacher is concerned with dialogic and interactional practices of classrooms and how these practices shape not only knowledge and learning practices concerned with learning to teach but also teacher-student relationships that are deeply embedded in teaching to learn. The symmetry quintessential to connecting learning to teach with teaching to learn reflects "teaching and learning as an interactive practice whereby the sociality of classrooms visibly influences classroom life" (Edwards-Groves & Hoare, 2012, p. 85).

The learning to teach experience takes place in the college classroom as well as the clinical site or school classroom. The role of dialogue for learning to teach, and teaching to learn, is to engage the preservice teacher in formalizing social discourse as means of interacting with others and learning from the discursive or dialogic interaction. Through engaging in dialogue, preservice teachers, both in the college classroom and clinical site, find a space for mediation through dialogue, conversations and interactions centered on materials and situations.

Similarly, teaching to learn often "involves horizontal sharing of ideas and experiences, active participation in projects or becoming aware of problems that need solutions" (Avalos, 2011, p. 16). How individuals mediate teaching to learn through dialogue is a form of "talking to learn." Edwards-Groves and Hoare (2012) focus on preservice teachers' experiences of learning to teach. Importantly, for preservice teachers, "talking to learn" creates "opportunities for pre-service teachers to examine the development of the language of teaching . . . through a dialogic pedagogy" (p. 83).

In particular, when pre-service teachers engage in a dialogue guided by classroom observations as well as actual teaching to learn practice and mentoring experiences, this form of dialogic discourse informs the learning to teach experience, which in turn contributes to a symmetry in preparation. There is, as Edwards-Groves and Hoare (2012) noted, "inherent and far-reaching value and impact for pre-service teachers studying interaction, for in it lies its contribution to the efficacy of pedagogy—a central concern for education globally" (p. 98).

What Is Needed to Ensure that Learning to Teach Embraces the Development of Aesthetic Qualities in Prospective Teachers?

Aesthetics in teaching reflects an important aspect of symmetry. Preparing to teach as well as teaching in the classrooms of schools brings with it important issues related to an increasing awareness of violence, struggle, hate, and ugliness that is reflective of the larger society. Symmetry in professional learning also denotes an aesthetic quality that fosters creativity, beauty, and morality in the teacher and his or her practice. Symmetry in this sense seeks to bring balance to the world of teaching and prepare teachers for the work before them in the schools. Understanding teaching as an art does not reify the arguments across nearly a century for at the expense of practice.

Rather, symmetry in professional learning seeks to grow within the prospective teacher and the practicing teacher alike, a sense of moral wisdom woven into the fabric of creativity that fosters spiritual and cultural beauty. The aesthetic qualities of symmetry provide a balance in teacher preparation and practice, a balance focused on the artistry of teaching. Dewey (1934) explained art as a:

> quality of doing and what is done. . . . When we say that tennis-playing, singing, acting, [teaching], and a multitude of other activities are arts, we engage in an elliptical way of saying that there is art in the conduct of these activities, and that this art so qualifies what is done and made as to induce activities in those who perceive them in which there is also art. (p. 214)

Dewey's explanation of art, when translated to preservice teacher preparation provides an elliptical way of saying that there is symmetry in learning to teach, and that the aesthetic of symmetry is reflected in teaching to learn.

Learning to teach experiences in preparation, carefully designed, inculcate in prospective teachers the desire to create "intellectual activities" that will in turn stimulate the desire for learning in students (Eilam & Poyas, 2009). Preservice preparation programs enriched with "intellectual activities" provide the first context in which the student of teaching may develop and/or grow the epistemological understanding and creative dimensions of teaching practice (Eilam & Poyas, 2009). This creative dimension enables the teacher in his or her work of translating theory into practice as well as connecting knowledge with pedagogical knowledge. For Dewey, the artistry of teaching was in the conduct of teaching and learning activities.

What Is the Challenge to Symmetry in Learning to Teach and Teaching to Learn?

Symmetry always exists in relationship to the possibility of or struggle with asymmetrical manifestations in teacher preparation and practice. The complexities of teacher learning are made apparent as the ideologies, politics, and cultural patterns that shape and are shaped by teacher preparation and practice challenge teachers. Finding symmetry in the learning to teach–teaching to learn experience will necessarily call colleges of education to rethink the purpose of preparation programs (Ball & Forzani, 2009; Grossman, Hammerness, & McDonald, 2009; Klette, Hammerness, & Jenset, 2017).

The challenge to symmetry, as it relates to preservice teacher preparation practice, is ensuring a sense of harmonious proportionality and balance, wherein the nature of learning to teach, in order to be successful, requires the experiential nature of teaching to learn to complete the whole. The more aligned the two are (learning to teach and teaching to learn), the more symmetry there is in the preservice teacher's teaching upon entering the classroom. Where the relationship between the two is not well developed, that is, when it is more asymmetrical, then teacher preparation falls short of meeting the needs of the preservice teacher to develop a balanced relationship with self and students as learners upon entering the classroom.

As an example, a tight coherence and integration among courses and between coursework and clinical work in schools present a symmetry in the knowledge and experience of learning to teach. Strong coherence as a pattern in symmetry helps to form almost seamless experience of learning to teach (Darling-Hammond, 2014). When core ideas are reiterated across courses and the theoretical frameworks animating courses and assignments are aligned with the experiential nature of learning to teach, a consistent pattern exists across the program supporting learning to teach.

Extensive and intensely supervised clinical work shapes the teaching to learn aspect of symmetry in preservice teacher preparation, when tightly integrated with coursework, enables preservice teachers to learn from expert practice in schools that serve diverse students (Darling-Hammond, 2014). Recent studies of learning to teach suggest that immersing teachers in the materials of practice and working on particular concepts using these materials can be particularly powerful for teachers' learning (Eilam & Poyas, 2009; Girvan, Conneely, & Tangney, 2016; Grossman et al., 2009; Naylor, Campbell-Evans, & Maloney, 2015).

CONCLUSION

Symmetry in teacher preparation and practice that bridges the learning to teach and teaching to learn motifs of preservice teacher preparation is perhaps the most important attention needed in professional educator preparation today. Where the lack of symmetry in courses and content, practicum and clinical settings, and epistemological and pedagogical content knowledge lends to asymmetrical experiences in learning to teach, the preservice teacher is deprived a rich and quality preparation experience.

Teacher professional learning is a complex process that draws attention to the contextual and consequential aspects of learning to teach as well as the relational dynamics that reside within all preparation programs. There is need, based on a large body of research, to focus on symmetry so that the quality and the integrity of teacher preparation are ensured. Understanding the symmetry, between and within both learning to teach and teaching to learn, is important to the quality and integrity of teacher preparation. The greatest challenge teacher educators face is examining the asymmetrical nature of teacher preparation and then setting about to implement change that brings a high level of symmetry to the foreground.

NOTE

1. Symmetry as related to mathematics, art, nature, and across many disciplines is defined as a balanced and proportional relationship between two parts of a whole. In the case of the learning to teach and teaching to learn experiences, one-half is the mirror image of the other half. That is, the epistemological, pedagogical, theoretical, and related aspects of learning to teach are mirrored in teaching to learn. Symmetry as used in this chapter reflects the relationship between learning to teach and teaching to learn as related to preservice teacher preparation and practice.

REFERENCES

Adoniou, M. (2013). Preparing teachers: The importance of connecting contexts in teacher education. *Australian Journal of Teacher Education, 38*(8), 47–60. http://dx.doi.org/10.14221/ajte.2013v38n8.7

Avalos, B. (2011). Teacher professional development in teaching and teacher education over ten years. *Teaching and Teacher Education, 27*, 10–20. doi:10.1016/j.tate.2010.08.0 07

Ball, D. L. (2000). Bridging practices: Intertwining content and pedagogy in teaching and learning to teach. *Journal of Teacher Education, 51*(3), 241–247. https://doi.org/10.1177/0022487100051003013

Ball, D. L., & Forzani, F. M. (2009). The work of teaching and the challenge for teacher education. *Journal of Teacher Education, 60*(5), 497–511. doi: https://doi.org/10.1177/0022487109348479

Bloomfield, D. (2010). Emotions and getting by: A pre-service teacher navigating professional experience. *Asia-Pacific Journal of Teacher Education, 38*(3), 221–234. http://dx.doi.org/10.1080/1359866X.2010.494005

Brew, A., & Saunders, C. (2020). Making sense of research-based learning in teacher education. *Teaching and Teacher Education, 87*, 1–11. https://doi.org/10.1016/j.tate.2019.102935

Brownlee, J. (2004). Teacher education students' epistemological beliefs: Developing a relational model of teaching. *Research in Education, 72*, 1–17. Retrieved from http://www.manchesteruniversitypress.co.uk/cgi-bin/scribe?showinfo=ip018 http://dx.doi.org/10.7227/RIE.72.1

Cochran-Smith, M., & Lytle, S. L. (1999). Relationships of knowledge and practice: Teacher learning in communities. In A. Iran-Nejad & P. D. Pearson (Eds.), *Review of research in education*, vol. 24 (pp. 249–305). Washington, DC: American Educational Research Association.

Cochran-Smith, M., Cannady, M., McEachern, K. P., Viesca, K., Piazza, P., Power, C., et al. (2012). Teachers' education and outcomes: Mapping the research terrain. *Teachers College Record, 114*(10), 1–49.

Darling-Hammond, L. (1997). *The right to learn: A blueprint for creating schools that work.* San Francisco, CA: Jossey-Bass. Inc.

Darling-Hammond, L. (2006). Constructing 21st-century teacher education. *Journal of Teacher Education, 57*, 300–314. http://dx.doi.org/10.1177/0022487105285962

Darling-Hammond, L. (2014). Strengthening clinical preparation: The Holy Grail of teacher education. *Peabody Journal of Education, 89*(4), 547–561. doi: 10.1080/0161956X.2014.939009

Darling-Hammond, L., & Bransford, J. (Eds.). (2005). *Preparing teachers for a changing world: What teachers should learn and be able to do.* San Francisco, CA: Jossey-Bass.

Dewey, J. (1934). *Art as experience.* New York: Capricorn Books.

Dutro, E., & Cartun, A. (2016). Cut to the core practices: Toward visceral disruptions of binaries in practice-based teacher education. *Teaching and Teacher Education, 58*, 119–128. https://doi.org/10.1016/j.tate.2016.05.001.

Edwards-Groves, C. J., & Hoare, R. L. (2012). "Talking to learn": Focusing teacher education on dialogue as a core practice for teaching and learning. *Australian Journal of Teacher Education, 37*(8), 82–100. http://dx.doi.org/10.14221/ajte.2012v37n8.8

Eilam, B., & Poyas, Y. (2009). Learning to teach: Enhancing pre-service teachers' awareness of the complexity of teaching—learning processes. *Teachers and Teaching, 15*(1), 87–107. doi: 10.1080/13540600802661337

Girvan, C., Conneely, C., & Tangney, B. (2016). Extending experiential learning in teacher professional development. *Teaching and Teacher Education, 58*, 129–139. http://dx.doi.org/10.1016/j.tate.2016.04.009

Grossman, P. (2010). *Learning to practice: The design of clinical experience in teacher preparation.* Policy Brief. Retrieved from citeseerx.ist.psu.edu/viewdoc/summary?doi=10.1.1.178.4088

Grossman, P., Hammerness, K., & McDonald, M. (2009). Redefining teaching, re-imagining teacher education. *Teachers and Teaching: Theory and Practice, 15*(2), 273–290. Retrieved from http://www.tandfonline.com/doi/pdf/10.1080/13540600902875340

Grossman, P., Compton, C., Igra, D., Ronfeldt, M., Shahan, E., & Williamson, P. W. (2009). Teaching practice: A cross professional perspective. *Teachers College Record, 111*(9), 2055–2100.

Hastings, P. (2010). Expectation of a pre-service teacher: Implications of encountering the unexpected. *Asia-Pacific Journal of Teacher Education, 38*(3), 207–219. Retrieved from http://www.tandfonline.com.ecu.edu.au/toc/capjzo/VCulCck5DGg#.VCchlMkSDGg http://dx.doi.org/10.1080/1359866X.2010.493299

Hattie, J. (2012). *Visible learning for teachers: Maximizing impact on learning.* London, UK: Routledge.

Higgs, J., & McAllister, L. (2007). Educating clinical educators: Using a model of the experience of being a clinical educator. *Medical Teacher, 29*(2–3), e51-e57. doi: 10.1080/01421590601046088

Kavanagh, S. S., Conrad, J., & Dagogo-Jack, S. (2020). From rote to reasoned: Examining the role of pedagogical reasoning in practice-based teacher education. *Teaching and Teacher Education, 89*, 1–11. https://doi.org/10.1016/j.tate.2019.102991

Kennedy, M. (2016). Parsing the practice of teaching. *Journal of Teacher Education, 67*(1), 6–17. https://doi.org/10.1177/0022487115614617.

Klette, K., Hammerness, K., & Jenset, I. S. (2017). Established and evolving ways of linking to practice in teacher education: Findings from an international study of the enactment of practice in teacher education. *Acta Didactica Norge, 11*(3), 1–22. https://doi.org/10.5617/adno.4730

Lampert, M., Franke, M. L., Kazemi, E., Ghousseini, H., Turrou, A. C., Beasley, H., & Crowe, K. (2013). Keeping it complex: Using rehearsals to support novice teacher learning of ambitious teaching. *Journal of Teacher Education, 64*(3), 226–243. https://doi.org/10.1177/0022487112473837.

Loughran, J. (2019). Pedagogical reasoning: The foundation of the professional knowledge of teaching. *Teachers and Teaching, 25*(5), 523–535. https://doi.org/10.1080/13540602.2019.1633294.

MacPherson, S. (2010). Teachers' collaborative conversations about culture: Negotiating decision making in intercultural teaching. *Journal of Teacher Education, 61*(3), 271–286. https://doi.org/10.1177/0022487109353032.

McDonald, M., Kazemi, E., & Kavanagh, S. S. (2013). Core practices and pedagogies of teacher education: A call for a common language and collective activity. *Journal of Teacher Education, 64*, 378–386. https://doi.org/10.1177/0022487113493807

Naylor, D. A., Campbell-Evans, G., & Maloney, C. (2015). Learning to teach: What do pre-service teachers report. *Australian Journal of Teacher Education, 40*(11), 120–136. http://dx.doi.org/10.14221/ajte.2015v40n11.7

Opfer, V., Pedder, D., & Lavicza, Z. (2011). The role of teachers' orientation to learning in professional development and change: A national study of teachers in England. *Teaching and Teacher Education, 27*, 443–453. http://dx.doi.org/10.1016/j.tate.2010.09.014

Orchard, J., & Ellis, V. (2014). *Learning teaching from experience: Multiple perspectives and international contexts.* London, UK: Bloomsbury.

Philip, T. M., Souto-Manning, M., Anderson, L., Horn, I. S., Andrews, D. C., Stillman, J., et al. (2019). Making justice peripheral by constructing practice as "core": How the increasing prominence of core practices challenges teacher education. *Journal of Teacher Education, 70*(3), 251e264. https://doi.org/10.1177/0022487118798324.

Swennen, A., & Klink, M. v. d. (2009). *Becoming a teacher educator: Theory and practice for teacher educators.* Dordrecht, London: Springer.

Chapter 2

Developing Learning Trajectories for Teacher Learning

Anna E. Bargagliotti

Learning trajectories (LTs) in mathematics education have been often cited as effective ways to model student learning. While the term "learning trajectory" is widely used, several definitions and interpretations of LTs exist (see special issue of *Mathematical Thinking and Learning* [2004], for different descriptions and conceptualizations of LTs). Initially, the term hypothetical LT was introduced by Martin Simon (1995) and described as "the learning goal, the learning activities, and the thinking and learning in which students engage" (p. 133).

Grounded in constructivist theory, LTs connect students' thinking and learning for specific mathematical content with a conjectured pathway to move students through a developmental progression (Clements & Sarama, 2004). LTs offer both structure and responsiveness to students by outlining a sequence of concepts, sample problems, and teaching tasks (Simon & Tzur, 2004).

While the LT construct has been conceptualized as a model for student learning, the development of LTs as a model for *teacher* learning is under-explored. In teacher preparation programs and professional development, teachers are learners themselves; thus, it is natural to extend LTs to teacher learning. While this extension seems obvious, this extension is not straight-forward in practice.

The purpose of this commentary is to argue that teacher learning trajectories (TLTs) are empirically different than LTs for students. In particular, this chapter discusses three considerations that emerged while developing the TLTs: (1) existing teacher knowledge frameworks can be incorporated into TLTs; (2) teachers themselves can be active participants in the development of TLTs; and (3) it is useful for TLTs to allow for pedagogy transfer moments to emerge.

PROJECT-SET TLTS

The basis of this chapter comes from experiences in the National Science Foundation (NSF)-funded Project-Statistics Education of Teachers (SET). Project-SET developed two TLTs and designed a professional development program around the TLTs. The goal of the project was to enhance teachers' content knowledge of two fundamental statistics topics—sampling variability and regression.

Project-SET used Clements and Sarama's (2004) conceptualization of an LT as a "learning goal, developmental progression of thinking and learning, and sequence of instructional tasks" to guide the TLT development. The learning goal of the Project-SET TLTs centered on teachers' content knowledge of sampling variability and regression. This learning goal was manifested through three design principles: (1) teacher learning should adhere to widely accepted models of statistics practice; (2) teacher learning should progress from informal notions of the content to formal understandings; and (3) teacher learning in statistics should incorporate the use of technology. These design principles guided the development of the progression and the instructional tasks.

Several papers and reports in the statistics education literature discuss models for statistical practice (Franklin et al., 2007; Gould, Bargagliotti, & Johnson, 2017; Wild and Pfannkuch, 1999). Project-SET used the model presented by Franklin et al. (2007) in the Guidelines for Assessment and Instruction in Statistics Education (GAISE). The GAISE model articulates the process in four components: formulate questions, collect data, analyze data, and interpret data (see figure 2.1). The progression of the TLT was then organized around the components of this statistical process.

With respect to the notion that teacher learning should progress from informal thinking about the content to formal procedures and ideas related to the content, much literature in statistics education has presented the case for focusing on statistical reasoning and steering away from procedures and calculations (Bakker & Gravemeijer, 2004; Makar & Rubin, 2009; Zieffler et al., 2008). As informal reasoning helps construct intuition, it develops conceptual understanding that would later be beneficial when learning formal procedures.

Figure 2.1.   Model for the Statistical Investigative Process Used by Project-SET

Formulate Question	Collect Data	Analyze Data	Interpret Results
a. Set up a statistical question to explore a population parameter of interest by either (1) a teacher bringing in a claim to explore, or (2) a student making a claim or posing a question to explore	a. Describe methods to obtain repeated samples of the same size b. Take repeated samples of the same size "by hand" (e.g., collect packs of M&Ms and find the proportion of green in each pack, roll a die twenty times and find the number of times an even number is rolled in each set of twenty rolls)	a. Notice that different samples will give different summary statistics b. Notate the "pattern" with which the summary statistic varies by making a dot plot	a. Informally relate the sample statistic to the population parameter where (1) the population parameter is known, and (2) the population parameter is not known

Loop 1[4]

Figure 2.2. Loop 1 of the Sampling Variability LT

This design principle was conceptualized in the developmental progression as a "loop," where a loop would work through each of the four components—formulate, collect, analyze, and interpret. The sampling variability TLT consisted of six loops and the regression TLT consisted of five. As a result, teachers moving through the progression had to "loop through" the investigative process multiple times—six times for sampling variability and five times for regression. For example, for sampling variability, teachers proceeded through loop 1 content, then loop 2 content, then loop 3 content, and so on. Figure 2.2 provides an example loop, Loop 1 of the sampling variability developmental progression.

The loop structure in each TLT represented the increased levels of sophistication in statistical investigations the teacher would experience, with the loops progressing from more informal ideas and the ending loops being more formal. The sampling variability TLT begins with teachers being introduced to repeated sampling, takes them through the Central Limit Theorem, and ends with formal inference. The regression LT begins by plotting data on scatterplots and informally examining the association between two variables and ends with constructing sampling distributions for the regression parameters. In other words, aligned with the design principles, the loops progressed from informal statistical reasoning to formal statistical ideas.

The third guiding principle used in the TLT design was the incorporation of technology in the teaching and learning of statistics. Technology has changed the manner in which statisticians work and in turn has had a tremendous impact on how statistics is taught (Chance et al., 2007; Moore, 1997; Moore et al., 1995). Given the prevalence of technology in statistics education, Project-SET employed the incorporation of technology as a guiding principle for the instructional tasks of the TLTs.

The TLTs were refined over the course of three years through three professional development implementations and two refinement phases (see figure 2.3).

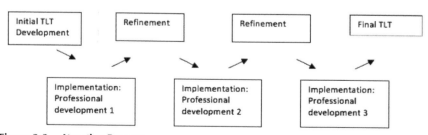

Figure 2.3.   Iterative Process

Throughout the iterative process, three interesting considerations repeatedly surfaced that highlighted how TLTs are empirically different from LTs for students. In the next three sections, each of these considerations are discussed and we argue that TLT development manifests different deliberations than student LT development.

Consideration #1: Teacher Knowledge Frameworks Can Be Explicitly Incorporated in TLTs

Much research has noted that teacher understanding of statistics is similar to that of their students (Groth & Bergner, 2006; Jacobbe & Horton, 2012; Leavy & O'Laughlin, 2006). For example, Hammerman and Rubin (2004) found that teachers' statistical knowledge is not substantially different from students' statistical knowledge. Teachers have gaps in their understanding of several basic concepts in statistics such as measures of center and variation (Callingham, 1997; Greer & Ritson, 1994) as well as more complex concepts such as covariation and regression (Casey & Wasserman, 2015; Engel & Sedlmeier, 2011). Jacobbe and Horton (2010) documented that while teachers were successful at reading data from graphical displays, they were not able to answer questions that assessed higher levels of graphical comprehension requiring them to interpret the information on a graph and answer questions about the data.

Because of this literature base, it seemed logical that a teacher LT focused on developing teacher statistical knowledge would be similar to a student LT developing similar content knowledge. It was only after the first refinement that evidence emerged to support the fact that, even if teacher and student knowledge was similar, the development and design of a teacher LT might be different from a student LT. It became clear that an LT aiming to model teacher knowledge should not only include content knowledge but also include specific knowledge geared toward teaching. In this sense, the learning goal of a TLT is not the same as a learning goal for a student LT.

Instead, TLTs require different learning experiences for teachers, with attention being paid to different types of knowledge to achieve these goals. In other words, TLTs are not trajectories for the same learning, even if the content is the same.

This shift in the learning goal is centered on that fact that while applying LTs to teachers, one is in fact intersecting LTs with frameworks of teacher knowledge. In the case of statistics and Project-SET, Groth's (2013) hypothetical Statistical Knowledge for Teaching (SKT) is the relevant teacher knowledge framework. Using the Mathematical Knowledge for Teaching (MKT) framework, Groth (2013) outlined a framework of teachers' knowledge for teaching statistics. The framework interweaved the MKT framework by Ball et al. (2008) with the notion of Key Developmental Understandings (KDUs) introduced by Simon (2006) and pedagogically powerful ideas outlined by Silverman and Thompson (2008).

Groth mirrored the MKT framework by characterizing SKT into two overarching categories (subject matter knowledge and pedagogical content knowledge) and six subcategories of MKT: common content knowledge, specialized content knowledge, horizon content knowledge, knowledge of content and students, knowledge of content and teaching, and knowledge of content and curriculum. While student LTs might focus solely on common content knowledge, TLTs shift the learning goal to include other types of knowledge. In this manner, a TLT can explicitly account for the multiple dimensions of knowledge outlined in Groth's SKT.

Shifting the learning goal from content-only to the inclusion of other dimensions of SKT called for adjustments to the initial TLT. During the first professional development and first refinement phase, we made two critical observations that led to the explicit inclusion of SKT in the progression. They were as follows:

1. Teachers had difficulties formulating statistical questions and connecting the question to the scope of a loop. This blocked the teachers from seeing the big picture, understanding how to progress from one loop to the next, and made it difficult for the "Formulate Questions" component of the GAISE framework to be addressed. Additionally, the ability to ask good investigative statistical questions is a fundamental statistical skill for teachers. Teachers need be able to ask and understand good statistical questions since they pose questions to lead discussions with their own students. This type of knowledge was identified as specialized content knowledge in SKT.

2. Teachers had difficulties transferring their content knowledge to what they would do in the classroom. As noted in SKT, content knowledge of a topic is not enough for teachers. Instead, SKT incorporates other types of knowledge as well. While working through a TLT, teachers needed multiple opportunities to develop their content knowledge into pedagogy. Some of these transferable opportunities were identified as potential KDUs leading to pedagogically powerful moments in SKT.

To adjust our initial TLT, we added several features and reorganized several aspects of the progression. Our main shifts included giving an explicit title to each loop, restructuring the formulate questions column to be more guided, introducing key benchmarks for each loop, and changing our activities to be adaptable to teachers' own classrooms. Figure 2.4 illustrates these changes for the example Loop 1 of the Sampling Variability TLT.

Project-SET Sampling Variability Final Learning Trajectory [1,2]

GAISE Framework[3]

	Formulate Question	Collect Data	Analyze Data	Interpret Results	Key Understandings
Loop 1[4] Concept of a Sampling Distribution	a. How can we discover how a summary statistic varies from random sample to sample from a population of interest? b. My friend and I just collected data from the same population. Can I expect my friend's summary statistic to be close to mine? c. Are some values of the statistic more common than others? d. How can we describe the variation of a statistic from one sample-to-another sample?	a. Describe methods that generate repeated samples of the same size from a population. b. Take repeated samples of the same size "by hand" and compute the summary statistic for each sample (e.g., collect packs of Skittles and find the proportion in each pack that are orange) *It should be noted that "by hand" simulations of this type are solely for pedagogical purposes in order to help understand computer simulations. c. Construct an approximate sampling distribution using computer-aided simulation	a. Notice that different samples give different summary statistic values for the population characteristic of interest. b. Record the distribution of the summary statistic from the different random samples by making a dot plot c. Summarize the simulated sampling distribution using shape, center, and variability also looking for potential outliers	a. Informally relate the summary statistic to the population parameter; that is, a single statistic is an estimate of the population parameter b. Link the variability in the summary statistic from sample to sample to the variability in the constructed sampling distribution and make conjectures about what might affect this variability. c. Distinguish between the population distribution, distribution of a sample, and the sampling distribution	The sampling distribution is a distribution that describes how a statistic varies for repeated samples from the same population. An approximate sampling distribution can be constructed, using simulation. This approximate sampling distribution can be described by its shape (typically symmetric or skewed), center (mean or median), and variability (typically, standard deviation).

Figure 2.4. Loop 1 of Sampling Variability LT—Refined

Although some of these changes appear to be minor (i.e., giving a title to a loop), they gave the TLT progression a cohesive structure through which teachers in the following implementations were more successful in accessing the multiple dimensions of SKT.

The key benchmarks column in the refined TLT progression represents the desired teacher content understandings the loop strived to develop. The benchmarks articulated reflect statistical concepts that are noted as important by the statistics education community for understanding sampling variability and regression. In addition, some of the key benchmarks were identified as KDUs. As defined by Simon (2006), KDUs involve conceptual advances that "change students' ability to think about and/or perceive particular mathematical relationships" (pp. 362). Simon highlights the distinction between formal definitions of concepts, like the key benchmarks and KDUs—as KDUs represent pivotal developmental issues that shape understanding. However, Project-SET found evidence that some of the key benchmarks were in fact also KDUs. For a discussion about three such KDUs, see Bargagliotti and Anderson (2017).

The potential for teacher pedagogical knowledge for teaching was also represented explicitly in the TLT through the key benchmarks column and specialized content knowledge was well defined for each loop in the formulate questions column.

In addition to what can be seen in the loop adjustments, pedagogical knowledge was represented through the accompanying instructional tasks (see Consideration #3, for more discussion about the instructional tasks). The explicit incorporation of multiple aspects of SKT in the TLT thus aligned with the newly recognized learning goal of the TLT.

Consideration #2: Teachers Can Be Active Participants in the Development Process

Because teachers are adults, they clearly have a maturity level much greater than their students. After our first implementation, we realized that because of this cognitive maturity level, teachers themselves should be given the opportunity to adjust and adapt the TLTs. This realization came at the completion of the first implementation of the professional development.

During the last meeting of the first implementation of professional development, we introduced and presented participating teachers to the two TLTs. At that time, we believed that after the extensive work teachers had spent on each of the loops, the teachers would connect how everything covered in the TLT fit together. Before this presentation of the TLTs, the teachers were not aware of their existence. In other words, their learning had been limited to that within each loop without knowing the larger structure of the TLTs.

Teachers turned in culminating projects that required them to demonstrate their full understanding of the topics of sampling variability and regression.

The projects assessed whether teachers were able to connect the content covered throughout the loops. This was identified as horizon knowledge in SKT. Horizon knowledge, as originally defined by Ball, Thames, and Phelps (2008), is "an awareness of how mathematical topics are related over the span of mathematics included in the curriculum."

For the TLTs, the content covered in the loops was the curriculum that teachers needed to draw on to make connections on how the topics cohesively merged. For example, the final project relating to sampling variability asked teachers to pose a statistical question, take a single sample from a population of interest and use the knowledge about sampling distributions they had built in the loops to make inferences about the population. In a class discussion of the process of drawing an informal inference from a single sample, one of the teachers asked about the data she had collected for her project:

> If I don't know the mean of the population, how do I know what the sampling distribution looks like? How do I know that 10 [the sample mean] is close or not close to the population mean?

Notably, the concept of inference was just beyond the last loop of the LT. Our team originally designed the TLT in such a way that formal inference would be understood if teachers were able to connect all the ideas in the TLT; thus, formal inference was the horizon knowledge of the TLT. Formal inference necessitated that teachers connect the loop content together. However, the final projects made clear that the horizon knowledge of the TLT was problematic, as the teachers remained unsure of what conclusions could be drawn about a population from a single sample. For example, one of the questions on the project asked, "Why were you able to make inferences about the population when you have only have one sample?"

Several teachers expressed discomfort with having only one sample. A typical conclusion was that "because it is only one sample of relatively small size, we are limited in the conclusions we can make." Several other teachers explicitly described the need for taking multiple samples, not knowing that, in fact, it was possible to draw conclusions about the population from a single sample.

Another difficulty that we found was that the teachers' knowledge of inference was not as conceptually grounded as their understanding of the earlier loops of the TLT. For example, Teacher 3 asks if she could read an answer that she wrote in response to the project questions.

Teacher 3 (reading answer): "I believe the sample mean of 26.92 is within two standard deviations about the population mean." Do I need to go back and add something about 95% sure? . . . I tried when I was answering the question to use what we had [talked about in the course]. . . .

Teacher 7: We didn't really talk about the confidence intervals. I think #7 was
   leading there when it was like "how certain can you be."

These teachers recognized the boundaries of the content that had been
addressed in the TLT; however, they were unable to fully access the horizon
knowledge even though they had worked for several weeks on the loops in
the TLT that led them to formal inference.

During the first implementation when teachers had not been told about the
TLTs ahead of time, *none* of the participating teachers was able to demonstrate an understanding of the horizon knowledge. Due to this result, in the
next iteration, teachers became active participants in the redesign of the TLTs
in order to further engage teachers with this aspect of SKT and adjust the
TLT accordingly. This active participation included being presented with the
progression while working through the loops and asking teachers to reflect on
their progression through the content.

During our second and third implementations, teachers were told on the
first day that TLTs were constructed that mapped out benchmarks to be mas-
tered that ultimately would connect to overall mastery of sampling variability
and regression. During every meeting, teachers were reminded of this fact
and asked if they saw the structure of how the last concepts connected to the
current concepts. In addition, we incorporated an assessment of this structure
by presenting teachers with the TLT at the completion of their progression
through it.

We then asked teachers to reflect on the LT and to audio record their
answers to the following questions: (1) What are the big takeaway ideas
of what you have done so far? Are there any open questions that you want
answered immediately? (2) Do you feel like you progressed through the
trajectory in the manner outlined or do you feel you acquired the knowledge
following a different pathway?

The results were impressive.

Teachers had fifteen minutes to think and audio record themselves reflecting on their learning and progression through the LT. Here are representative
excerpts from two of the teachers from the second iteration of professional
development (PD) recordings on sampling variability:

Teacher A: Some of the big takeaways, for me, from the sampling variability
   learning trajectory was the different distributions . . . so sampling distribution vs. sample distribution vs. population distribution. Also, the idea of
   using one sample to make a formal conclusion. I originally thought this
   was crazy when we were first doing the M&M activity. . . . How you use
   one sample . . . so that was a major take away for me. Also the central limit
   theorem . . . that all sampling distributions are basically the same shape,

just centered around the population mean. . . . The learning trajectory . . .
I think that I progressed through it in how it's outlined here. At first,
I didn't really see where we were going, but now that we went through the
whole trajectory, I feel like it is a whole circle and that made sense to me.

Teacher A demonstrates not only an accurate and broad picture description of
sampling variability (e.g., the Central Limit Theorem that sampling distributions are the same shape) but also capitalizes on the potential difficulties and
misunderstandings that often occur when learning about sampling variability
(e.g., how you use one sample). By saying that "I didn't really see where we
were going, but now that we went through the whole trajectory, I feel like it
is a whole circle and that made sense to me," this teacher notes how the TLT
progression enabled her to connect all of the concepts toward horizon knowledge. A second teacher during the second implementation responded similarly:

Teacher B: I feel that I progressed through the trajectory in the manner outlined. I followed right along and I really liked how it built up the theories,
so that when we actually got to where we were going, it was clear why we
did it. So in other words, using samples to estimate population parameters
and the whole flow from population parameter down to sampling statistics
and then the inference going back up to population parameter. It was very
clear and I liked how we built it. Then we actually moved away from taking a bunch of samples, because we already understood what the sampling
distribution looked like and then we were able just to use one sample. With
the confidence intervals, we moved completely away from that after calcu-
lating our confidence interval, without knowing what we were doing, with
just estimating a range. Then moving to formal confidence intervals and
from there actually just using the software. So once we had calculated by
hand and understand what we were doing, we then moved to the software.

Again, this teacher observes how the TLT progression allowed her to "followed right along and I really liked how it built up the theories, so that when
we actually got to where we were going, it was clear why we did it." This
teacher also moved toward formal inference by noting the potential of using
only one sample to draw inferences.

These examples, representative of the other reflections for sampling variability recorded, offer insights on how actively engaging with the TLT and
knowing that they were progressing through a TLT allowed teachers to access
horizon knowledge. The active engagement was characterized by being given
the TLT progression and asking the teachers to reflect and comment on the
progression. In other words, instead of merely using the TLT in the background of the professional development, teachers were explicitly told about

the progression and used it throughout the professional development as a means to connect their learning into a bigger picture.

In addition, by asking teachers if they progressed in the manner outlined in the progression or whether they took a different pathway, it enabled our research team to make necessary adjustments to the TLT progression to better match teacher learning. In this sense, teachers not only became active participants in their own progression development, but they also were asked to contribute to the overall TLT development process.

As with the first implementation of the PD, culminating projects were given to the teachers in implementations two and three after having seen and reflected on the TLTs. *All* teachers in the second and third iterations of the professional development completed the culminating projects successfully for sampling variability and regression.

Consideration #3: It Is Useful for TLTs to Allow for Pedagogy Transfer to Emerge

Groth's (2013) SKT includes the notion for the development of pedagogically powerful ideas. These ideas can be described as moments in which teacher knowledge and understanding gives rise to a change in teaching and classroom practice. In order for such ideas to develop within the context of TLTs, I argue that it is useful for teachers to be given opportunities to work through activities as students and subsequently be asked to view the same activities through the lens of teaching. This realization ultimately urged us to specifically incorporate pedagogical transfer into the TLT instructional tasks.

During the first implementation, for example, the first regression activity focused on the placement of the line of best fit on a scatterplot. Teachers used spaghetti to place a line on a scatterplot in such a way that they believed best fit the plot. Teachers were then asked to articulate how they made their decision of where to place the line. For example, one teacher stated: "I placed the line to start at the origin and then near all of the points." Interestingly, this activity had been given in a prior study to middle-school students (Casey, 2015). Teachers offered *all* of the same responses the students had in the prior study. To encourage pedagogical content knowledge, we asked the teachers to determine whether the reasons the students had provided would work for all types of scatterplots.

Teachers struggled with viewing the same activity they had just completed under the pedagogical lens. They were to sketch scatterplots to illustrate situations in which the students' reasoning would not lead to the placement of the line of best fit. For example, the teacher who stated that she placed the line of best fit so that the line would start at the origin and then proceed near all of the points was unable to sketch a scatterplot for which her rule would not work. Figure 2.5 illustrates such a scatterplot where clearly the rule of

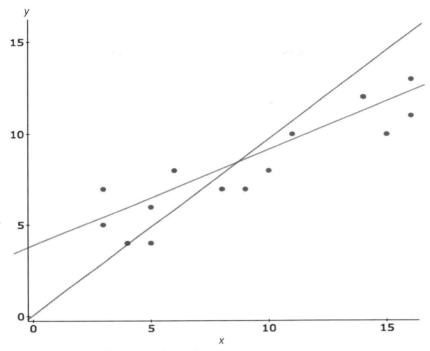

Figure 2.5.   Scatterplot Comparing Rules

starting at the origin and going toward the point would not place the line of best fit the blue line. Instead, the line with the y-intercept at approximately y = 4 would be the line of best fit.

While the original task of placing the spaghetti line motivated teachers to think about the content as a learner, it was only when teachers were pushed to think about the same task through a pedagogy lens that the potential for shifts in practice might occur.

In subsequent loops of the regression TLT, teachers demonstrated pedagogically powerful ideas. For example, one teacher after loop 3 of the regression TLT stated:

So he (referring to another teacher) brought up a good point about, he said explicitly made me think maybe we should teach the line of best fit differently in the way they match this up. It has to go through the point of *x*-bar—*y*-bar. It has to go through the average *x* and the average *y*. There is an ordered pair. The regression line has to go through there. So we should have the spaghetti or something there that will turn on that point somehow and they would actually fit it from there. Does that make sense how we could do it. I never thought how we could use technology to do that is my thought I would never thought of doing that way.

The teacher then explained: "Anchoring it there. It is kind of an interesting way of thinking about the line of best fit. Which I have never thought of before just now." This teacher connected the ideas discussed through the specialized content knowledge to how he would potentially change his teaching. In addition, he points to technology as a means to achieve this teachable moment in his own classroom. We submit that since teachers had the opportunity to work through several activities as learners prior to translating to teaching, they began moving beyond trying to understand how what they were learning and how it could map onto what they did in the classroom but instead had them focus on *how* what they were learning would connect to their pedagogy.

Another example of a pedagogically powerful idea was while working through the sampling variability TLT and developing the Central Limit Theorem. A focus of several of the tasks accompanying the loops of the TLT was to understand how the size of the sample affected the shape and variability of the sampling distribution. The opportunities while working through the LT to visualize the effect of different sample sizes on the sampling distributions led to "Aha" moments for the teachers, particularly when comparing sampling distributions of samples drawn from very different populations. In one activity, the teachers compared sampling distributions of samples of different sizes drawn from the same skewed population (the year of pennies still in circulation).

The goal of this activity (associated with loop 4 of the TLT) was to derive the Central Limit Theorem. As such, the teachers not only created the distributions, but they also found the standard deviation of the population and the standard deviations of the approximate sampling distributions and used these information to derive the formula for the standard error. At the conclusion of this lesson (hereafter referred to as the Pennies Activity), Teacher 8 noted that he had never before understood where the formula for the standard error came from. Instead, he thought it was "just something that you memorized."

Several weeks later, Teacher 8 demonstrated how he used TI-Nspire graphing calculators to implement the Pennies Activity with this Algebra 2 class. He used the TI-Nspire calculators and the Navigator to demonstrate for other teachers how he was able to quickly collect all of the information on the penny population by aggregating the data from individual students. He was then able to quickly share that population data with the students so that they could explore it individually. His description of how he implemented the activity with technology reflected a pedagogically powerful approach to "seeing" the effect of the sample size.

Teacher 8: I got the penny data right here. Actually do you know what this is? I made it take 100 samples of 1 of size 1. With $n = 1$. Make sense? It is not very normal at all. Because n is not very large. . . . [Demonstrates how to change the sample size and shows the associated sampling distribution] And it goes $n = 2$. Look at that! Even with a sample size of 2 my standard deviation is getting a little smaller, it is becoming a little more normal. . . . [Again shows how to change the sample size and see the effect on the sampling distribution.] Look at that! Sample size 3. We are starting to look a little bit more normal. . . . Click up a little more times, then see how it goes [indicating a change in the sample size]. Notice it is random every time. Because I made this so that it is random. So yours may not look exactly the same as this. It is randomly sampling 100 samples of size whatever n is. That is what it looks like. It is kind of cool. . . . It is kind of cool everyone looks a little bit different. But if you click up a few more times, it starts getting taller, the standard deviation gets smaller it is a little bit more normal. . . .

Teacher 2: Is this the Central Limit Theorem?

Teacher 8: That is the Central Limit Theorem. The standard deviation is getting smaller.

Teacher 2: And how cool that they [students] can watch it happen!

Teacher 8: How cool is that? I thought it was very cool we can experience that and watch it. We can experiment and ask what would happen if it was 1,000. What would happen if it was whatever. We can make predictions and so forth, I thought it was pretty neat.

In this extended segment, Teacher 8 demonstrated how he took the original activity used with the TLT to develop the Central Limit Theorem and translated it, using technology, into a dynamic experience of the effect of the sample size for his students. The teacher recognized the need for students to be able to visually compare multiple examples of approximate sampling distributions of increasing sample sizes. Moreover, the pedagogical power of this translation is captured by the reaction of Teacher 2 ("How cool that they can watch it happen?").

Pedagogically powerful ideas emerged as teachers had the opportunity to engage with materials first as learners and then pushed toward thinking about classroom practice. In the third round of the professional development, we explicitly asked teachers at the end of each loop to connect their knowledge of the loop to their classroom through the tasks they had encountered in the loop. In this implementation of the professional development, teachers reflected on whether the specific activity they had just worked through would be applicable in their classroom and if so how it could be adapted.

This adjustment appeared successful as teachers in the third professional development actively adjusted several of the tasks to use in their own classes. For example, one teacher adjusted and developed a regression activity based on finding the relationship between crime rates and poverty rates in the United States. Another teacher used data that she had collected on her class to explore whether students' use of questioning techniques during test-taking impacted her students' test scores. This teacher not only used the task with her class, but she also used her analyses in a district-level professional development where teachers were asked to evaluate features of their own teaching.

CONCLUSION

The development of TLTs to help guide and design coursework for teachers and professional development for teachers offers an appealing extension of the literature surrounding LTs for students. However, in undertaking developing TLTs, I argue that some specific considerations should be attended to: (1) teacher understanding about a topic includes accessing several different types of knowledge about the topic; (2) teachers are mature learners and thus can reflect deeply on their understanding about a topic; and (3) teachers should be given the opportunity to apply their developed knowledge to their classroom practice.

While reflecting on these considerations, two important questions naturally emerge: what affordances do TLTs provide for teacher preparation, and how can the considerations discussed in this commentary inform future development of TLTs? I argue that TLTs are worthwhile to develop because they offer a means to model teacher learning within a bigger contextual picture that in turn fosters deeper engagement with different aspects of teacher knowledge. The considerations noted in this research commentary can be used both explicitly and implicitly in the development process.

Often times professional development or other opportunities in which teacher educators work with teachers lead to, at best, small shifts in teacher knowledge. Constructing LTs and using the trajectories to structure professional development can provide a coherent big picture that teachers often need and seek. Having TLTs to provide a structure for the development of teacher knowledge can lead to increased teacher content understanding (Bargagliotti et al., 2014) and pedagogical knowledge (Bargagliotti & Anderson, 2017). These affordances suggest that the development of TLTs is not only worthwhile but in fact may lead to shifts in practice through teacher preparation.

To undertake the development of a TLT, the Project-SET team first hypothesized content TLTs and then through teaching experiments refined the TLTs. While the refinement process led to the considerations discussed earlier, if I were to develop a TLT for a new mathematical or statistical concept, I would structure the development process differently. First, the initial conceptualization of a TLT would be aligned with relevant existing teacher knowledge constructs. For example, the initial conception of a TLT would highlight where different types of pedagogical knowledge would be referenced and thought to emerge. Second, teachers would be presented with the TLT at the beginning of an implementation in order to garner teacher feedback of how the concept developed for them.

While with students this process might be done through classroom observations, in the case of teachers, this process can be explicitly done by asking teachers to reflect and organize the concepts in a progression in a way they deemed appropriate. This active engagement of teachers in the TLT development process is different from what is possible with students. Last, it is useful for TLT tasks to push teachers to not only understand the content but also apply their knowledge to their own teaching. Our ultimate goal in professional development is to increase teacher knowledge and ultimately change teacher practice. TLTs offer a potential promising way to engage teachers in this process that should be developed and studied further.

REFERENCES

Bakker, A., & Gravemeijer, K. P. (2004). Learning to reason about distribution. In D. Ben-Zvi & J. Garfield (Eds.), *The challenge of developing statistical literacy, reasoning and thinking* (pp. 147–168). Netherlands: Springer.

Ball, D. L., Thames, M. H., & Phelps, G. (2008). Content knowledge for teaching: What makes it special? *Journal of Teacher Education, 59*(5), 389–407.

Bargagliotti, A., & Anderson, C. R. (2017). Using learning trajectories to structure professional Development. *Mathematical Thinking and Learning: An International Journal, 19*(4), 237–259. https://doi.org/10.1080/10986065.2017.1365222

Bargagliotti, A. E., Anderson, C., Casey, S., Everson, M., Franklin, C., Gould, R., Groth, R., Haddock, J., & Watkins, A. (2014). Project-SET materials for the teaching and learning of sampling variability and regression. In K. Makar, B. de Sousa, & R. Gould (Eds.), *Proceedings of IASE's Ninth International Conference on Teaching Statistics (ICOTS9): Sustainability in Statistics Education,* Voorburg, The Netherlands: International Statistical Institute. Retrieved from http://icots. info/9/proceedings/pdfs/ICOTS9_3E2_WATKINS.pdf

Callingham, R. (1997). Teachers' multimodal function in in relation to the concept of average. *Mathematics Education Research Journal, 9*(2), 205–224. https://doi. org/10.1007/BF03217311

Casey, S. (2015). Examining student conceptions of covariation: A focus on the line of best fit. *Journal of Statistics Education, 23*(1), 1–32.

Casey, S., & Wasserman, N. (2015). Teachers' knowledge about informal line of best fit. *Statistics Education Research Journal, 14*(1), 8–35.

Chance, B., Ben-Zvi, D., Garfield, J., & Medina, E. (2007). The role of technology in improving student learning of statistics. *Technology Innovations in Statistics Education, 1*(1), 1–26.

Clements, D. H., & Sarama, J. (2004). Learning trajectories in mathematics education. *Mathematical Thinking and Learning, 6,* 81–89. https://doi.org/10.1207/s1532 7833mtl0602_1

Engel, J., & Sedlmeier, P. (2011). Correlation and regression in the training of teachers. In C. Batanero, G. Burrill, & C. Reading (Eds.), *Teaching statistics in school mathematics—Challenges for teaching and teacher education: A joint ICMI/IASE study* (pp. 247–258). New York: Springer.

Franklin, C., Kader, G., Mewborn, D., Moreno, J., Peck, R., Perry, M., & Scheaffer, R. (2007). *Guidelines for assessment and instruction in statistics education (GAISE) report: A pre-K–12 curriculum framework.* Alexandria, VA: American Statistical Association. Retrieved from www.amstat.org

Gould, R., Bargagliotti, A. & Johnson, T. (2017). An analysis of secondary teachers' reasoning with "Big Data." *Statistics Education Research Journal, 16*(2), 305–334.

Greer, B., & Ritson, R. (1994). Readiness of teacher in Northern Ireland to teach data handling. In *Proceedings of the Fourth International Conference of Teaching Statistics* (pp. 49–56). Rabat, Morocco: The National Institute of Statistics and Applied Economics.

Groth, R. E. (2013). Characterizing key developmental understandings and pedagogically powerful ideas within a statistical knowledge for teaching framework. *Mathematical Thinking and Learning, 15,* 121–145. https://doi.org/10.1080/1098 6065.2013.770718

Groth, R., & Bergner, J. (2006). Preservice elementary teachers' conceptual and procedural knowledge of mean, median, and mode. *Mathematical Thinking and Learning, 8*(1), 37–63. https://doi.org/10.1207/s15327833mtl0801_3

Hammerman, J. & Rubin, A. (2004). Strategies for managing statistical complexity with new software tools. *Statistics Education Research Journal, 3*(2), 17–41.

Jacobbe, T., & Horton, R. (2010). Elementary school teachers' comprehension of data displays. *Statistics Education Research Journal, 9*(1), 27–45.

Jacobbe, T., & Horton, B. (2012). The importance of sustained professional development for teaching statistics—an example involving the mode and range. *International Journal of Statistics and Probability, 1*(1), 138–147. doi:10.5539/ijsp. v1n1p138

Leavy, A., & O'Laughlin, N. (2006). Preservice teachers' understanding of the mean: Moving beyond the arithmetic average. *Journal of Mathematics Teacher Education, 9*(1), 53–90.

Makar, K., & Rubin, A. (2009). A framework for thinking about informal statistical inference. *Statistics Education Research Journal, 8*(1), 82–105.

Moore, D. S. (1997). New pedagogy and new content: The case of statistics. *International Statistical Review, 65*(2), 123–137.

Moore, D. S., Cobb, G. W., Garfield, J., & Meeker, W. Q. (1995). Statistics education fin de siecle. *The American Statistician, 49*(3), 250–260.

Silverman, J., & Thompson, P. W. (2008). Toward a framework for the development of mathematical knowledge for teaching. *Journal of Mathematics Teacher Education, 11*(6), 499–511.

Simon, M. (2006). Key developmental understandings in mathematics: A direction for investigating and establishing learning goals. *Mathematical Thinking and Learning, 8*(4), 359–371.

Simon, M. A. (1995). Reconstructing mathematics pedagogy from a constructivist perspective. *Journal for Research in Mathematics Education, 26*(1), 14–145.

Simon, M. A., & Tzur, R. (2004). Explicating the role of mathematical tasks in conceptual learning: An elaboration of the hypothetical learning trajectory. *Mathematical Thinking and Learning, 6*(2), 91–104. https://doi.org/10.1207/s15327833mtl0602_2

Wild, C. J., & Pfannkuch, M. (1999). Statistical thinking in empirical enquiry. *International Statistical Review, 67*(3), 223–248. https://doi.org/10.1111/j.1751-5823.1999.tb00442.x

Zieffler, A., Garfield, J., Delmas, R., & Reading, C. (2008). A framework to support research on informal inferential reasoning. *Statistics Education Research Journal, 7*(2), 40–58.

Chapter 3

Connecting Curricular Contexts: A National Survey and Two Exemplary Cases of Teacher Educators Bridging Coursework and Fieldwork

Courtney Shimek, Marliese R. Peltier,
Elizabeth M. Bemiss, Ann Van Wig,
Laura J. Hopkins, Stephanie G. Davis,
Roya Q. Scales, and W. David Scales

At a national literacy conference in 2016, we, a group of teacher education researchers/instructors, described the difficulties we had in connecting our undergraduate courses to the local literacy curricular contexts our teacher candidates experienced in the field. We use the term *literacy curricular contexts* to refer to policies and resources that guide literacy curriculum and instruction (e.g., core reading programs, supplemental programs, pacing guides, fidelity mandates, accountability structures, and professional development on curriculum programs) (Peltier et al., 2019a).

We were struck by our discovery that we each experienced similar difficulties bridging coursework and fieldwork contexts, despite teaching in six universities located in different states. Other education scholars (e.g., Ahmed, 2019; Barnes & Smagorinsky, 2016; Clark et al., 2013; Young et al., 2017) echoed our frustrations with the divide between teacher preparation programs' pedagogical foundations and PK–12 curricular contexts. For example, researchers have argued that teacher preparation programs promote varying sociocultural theories and student-centered pedagogies, whereas K–12 contexts tend to emphasize teacher-centered and transmissional approaches to teaching (Anderson & Stillman, 2011; Smagorinsky, Rhym, & Moore, 2013).

Given the Council for Accreditation of Educator Preparation's (CAEP) call for close connections between coursework and fieldwork, we wondered if and how other literacy teacher educators were experiencing and overcoming the pedagogical differences that existed between their teacher preparation programs and local literacy curricular contexts. More specifically, we sought to understand how other teacher educators perceived the alignment between their coursework and fieldwork contexts and how they worked to help teacher candidates navigate and learn from these two entities throughout their respective programs.

We embarked upon a longitudinal study to understand teacher educators' bridging of coursework and fieldwork by designing and disseminating a national survey of elementary literacy teacher educators' perceptions of alignment of coursework and fieldwork (phase 1), conducting a content analysis of assignments uploaded during that survey (phase 2), and interviewing survey respondents to inform a multicase study of teacher educators' contexts and practices (phase 3). Throughout this endeavor, our overarching research question has been as follows: How do elementary literacy teacher educators perceive and enhance alignment between coursework and fieldwork contexts?

THEORETICAL GROUNDING AND LITERATURE REVIEW

This research was undergirded by sociocultural theory, which theorizes that individuals are shaped by their interactions with others and by the culture in which they live. Vygotsky (1978) determined that "every function in the child's cultural development appears twice: first, on the social level, and later, on the individual level. . . . All the higher functions originate as actual relationships between individuals" (p. 57). Within the context of our research, this assertion framed all teaching and learning as contextually situated practices (Cole, 1996) and established that all experiences and interactions are influential in shaping the beliefs, actions, and understandings of teacher candidates, teacher preparation programs, and teacher educators.

As Scales et al. (2018) and Young et al. (2017) argued, teacher preparation programs must prepare candidates to understand and interrogate the curricular contexts they encounter in their field placements. This preparation equips candidates to develop practical knowledge and professional judgment through their field experiences that equip them to flexibly navigate the complexities and constraints of teaching while maintaining a focus on student learning rather than on compliance. Teacher educators, then, ought to provide scaffolded opportunities for candidates to experience and learn to navigate the complexity and tensions inherent to teaching (Smagorinsky et al., 2004).

This approach necessitates that teacher educators understand the curricular contexts candidates encounter in relation to the educational theories and approaches espoused by their preparation program. Presently, there is a dearth of research examining how teacher educators perceive fieldwork curricular contexts and how that intersects with their courses. Thus, we sought to develop an understanding of how teacher educators engage and support candidates to navigate and bridge discrepancies between differing curricular contexts.

Tensions in Navigation

Although teacher educators are responsible for the design and implementation of their courses, ultimately it is the teacher candidates who are required to navigate these disparate systems. Some scholars have argued that teacher attrition is a result of a lack of support in negotiating these contradictory ideals (Kennedy, 2006; Sydnor, 2017). Candidates and novice teachers, alike, have desired more direct connections between theory and practice, as well as explicit instruction on literacy curricular materials (Clark et al., 2013; Kosnik & Beck, 2009). Further, some candidates have criticized teacher preparation instructors for not addressing teaching practices observed in the field (Ahmed, 2019; Bainbridge & Macy, 2008; Ellis & Maguire, 2017).

These criticisms of teacher preparation programs have exacerbated the discrepancies between course and field contexts. Burnett et al. (2015) reported that candidates frequently valued the literacy practices perpetuated in schools over those encouraged by their programs, which suggests that teacher educators need to reframe or adjust their pedagogies to better align with local contexts. Although some researchers have contradicted this finding (e.g., Roberts-Harris, 2014; Scales et al., 2018), candidates' reliance upon the practices of field contexts continues (Ball & Forzani, 2009; Barnes & Smagrinsky, 2016; Castañeda-Trujillo & Aguirre-Hernández, 2018).

Based upon the candidates' reliance on field context practices in shaping their own pedagogies, it becomes even more important that teacher educators learn to adapt their course content to reflect, and even critically examine, the pedagogies of the field contexts to assist candidates in navigating these varying spaces. The challenge of bridging course and field contexts and assisting candidates in navigating these spaces to provide responsive instruction focused on student learning is exacerbated by educational policies and mandates that center on compliance (Cobb, 2012; Vaughn et al., 2019). Cobb (2012) surveyed and interviewed twenty-eight inservice teachers and found that they often abandon engaging instructional practices emphasized by their preparation programs for the teacher-centered mandated curriculums.

Vaughn et al. (2019) interviewed nine principals from across the United States and found that top-down accountability practices limited teachers' autonomy in curriculum decisions, which makes tensions between teacher preparation programs and field contexts even more disparate. Hence, teacher educators are positioned to assist candidates in navigating not only the curricular contexts of their field placements but also the state mandates and policies. Despite these complex challenges, scholars of teacher preparation urge teacher educators to support candidates in navigating the tensions between course and field contexts and to bridge these contexts (Ahmed, 2019; Cochran-Smith et al., 2016).

Bridging the Divide

Previous research has shown that there are inconsistent opportunities for teacher educators to connect coursework and fieldwork contexts (Symcox, 2012). There is a growing consensus in contemporary research that teacher preparation programs and teacher educators should intentionally connect preparation programs with fieldwork experiences (AACTE, 2018; CAEP, 2018; Canrinus et al., 2017). Presently, there is a breadth of scholarship examining how preparation programs can approach connecting with field contexts at the programmatic level (e.g., Burroughs et al., 2020; Canrinus et al., 2017; McDonald et al., 2011).

However, few studies examine how teacher educators engage and support teacher candidates in connecting coursework and fieldwork. Teacher educators face the realities of how to engage and support candidates in the assimilation of new knowledge while connecting coursework to fieldwork (Peltier et al., 2019a). Educators can design field experiences to be educative (Dewey, 1938). That is, field experiences can be designed to foster opportunities for candidates to share with one another, with practicing teachers, and with teacher educators about their observations and learning across course and field contexts. Within these contexts, candidates can engage in learning how to navigate differing views of learning and experience different varying pedagogies.

A few studies have identified how educators can use educative approaches to bridge the divide between coursework and fieldwork. First, educators can learn about the fieldwork context to remain abreast of changes in these contexts and then use this knowledge to design course-based learning experiences that incorporate pedagogical practices or curricula from the fieldwork context (Bricker & Tracy, 2017; Hoge & Jenks, 2000). For example, Ahmed (2019) found that his teacher educator participant was able to share field-based realities with candidates since the educator was knowledgeable of the fieldwork context. Second, teacher educators can design intentional fieldwork components such as scaffolded learning experiences.

Brannon and Fiene (2013) determined that candidates who engaged in scaffolded field experiences, namely structured participation experiences, had an increased understanding of child development, teaching strategies, and the role of the teacher. Third, teacher educators can attend field placements alongside teacher candidates to model how to bridge coursework and fieldwork. Illustratively, Ahmed's (2019) study described a teacher educator modeling how to integrate pedagogical practices taught in her course with the fieldwork's mandated literacy curricula. While numerous teacher educators have worked individually to bridge these divides, few studies have investigated how teacher educators nationwide perceive these divisions and assist their candidates in navigating the differences. Similarly, few studies have closely examined differing approaches for bridging fieldwork and coursework contexts.

LONGITUDINAL STUDY METHODS AND FINDINGS

This longitudinal study occurred in three phases. In phase 1, we surveyed elementary literacy teacher educators for perceptions of alignment of curricular contexts between coursework and field placements. This forty-six-item survey consisted of a mix of multiple-choice, Likert scale, and open-ended questions. We collected data through a nationwide survey with twenty-eight completed responses. Participants represented public and private institutions ranging in size (5,000–25,000+ undergraduates) and from fifteen states (Georgia, Indiana, Maryland, Michigan, Minnesota, Nevada, New York, North Carolina, Pennsylvania, Rhode Island, South Carolina, Texas, Utah, Washington, and Wisconsin).

Quantitative analysis involved descriptive statistics (e.g., frequency counts, percentages), while we relied on Miles, Huberman and Saldaña's (2014) qualitative methods of thematic analysis to analyze short answers and open-ended responses. Four research team members then reconvened to complete our first cycle of coding using descriptive and *in-vivo* codes. The same four researchers completed a second cycle coding to finalize pattern coding and determine themes. Upon completion of the first and second cycles of coding, all team members individually reviewed codes and then came to complete agreement.

As part of the phase 1 survey, we asked participants to share teaching documents that demonstrated the types of learning activities that connected coursework and field placements to support curricular navigation. Teacher educators provided a variety of assignments with nineteen submitted descriptions. These descriptions became the focus of our content analysis in phase 2. We developed inclusion and exclusion criteria to refine the number of descriptions so that we could conduct a content analysis, and eleven descriptions met our inclusion criteria.

We then sorted these descriptions into two distinct categories that included descriptions addressing principles and practices of literacy instruction ($n = 8$); and/or explicit descriptions about curricular context ($n = 4$). These activities created opportunities for candidates to (1) make comparisons among coursework, field theories, and practices; (2) examine how to transfer coursework practices to the field; and (3) apply practices introduced in coursework.

Phase 1 and Phase 2 Findings

Phase 1 data suggested that teacher educators perceived that their candidates encountered varied curricular contexts in terms of materials, policies, and supports (e.g., field supervision, mentor teachers). Teacher educators further explained that the types of curricular and instructional materials commonly found in practice included basal or core reading programs, guided reading materials, and computer-assisted core and supplemental programs. The most commonly mentioned materials were guided reading materials ($n = 16$) and basal/core programs ($n = 14$).

Teacher educators responded that curricular alignments and disconnects created "confusion, stress, and added complexity" when shaping teacher candidates learning experiences. Teacher educators addressed this dissonance through purposeful planning which included (1) building relationships with candidates' mentors; (2) supporting teacher candidates in navigating constraints (finessing, addressing time constraints, planning district-appropriate instruction, etc.); (3) addressing theory, best practices and how to connect these to practice; and (4) discussing and incorporating contextual factors (programs, policies, practices).

Phase 2 content analysis of learning activities descriptions revealed themes of how coursework *engaged* students, how students were *supported* in navigating curricular contexts, and how curricular contexts *connected* to field experiences. Teacher educators uploaded descriptions ranging from very specific class activities, such as critically examining literacy curricular contexts such as Accelerated Reader, to uploading their entire syllabus. Many of the descriptions did not explicitly explain how they assisted candidates in navigating fieldwork curricular contexts; however, descriptions that did include explanations mentioned opportunities to identify specific literacy practices, critically consider how to implement these practices in the field, and engage in application of these practices.

After collecting and analyzing survey responses (phase 1) and descriptions (phase 2), we were left with more questions than answers. While we were intrigued to see that teacher educators recognized and desired to bridge the divide between coursework and fieldwork contexts, we needed to better understand the context of each teacher educator to situate their descriptions and better understand how they supported candidates in navigating the tensions between course and fieldworks (Smagorinsky, 2018). This information provided a foundation for phase 3, the interview of teacher educators.

INTERVIEW STUDY METHODS AND FINDINGS

For phase 3, we conducted semi-structured interviews with six survey respondents to hear, in their own words, how they address curricular contexts within their undergraduate literacy courses. The interviews became the final data source for our phase 3 case studies, providing crucial insights into six teacher educators' reflections on how these descriptions provided opportunities for candidates to learn to navigate curricular contexts.

Of the 119 survey respondents, nineteen elected to describe or upload descriptions of *learning experiences* that bridged coursework and fieldwork contexts. We defined a learning experience as an intentionally designed learning opportunity within a course that addressed the content which the candidates were exposed to or engaged with and/or how they engaged with the content (Peltier et al., 2019b). Of the nineteen who submitted learning experiences, nine also provided their information to be interviewed. Ultimately, six of the nine who provided their information were scheduled for interviews. To maintain continuity of the data collection, two team members conducted all six interviews. During the interviews, two participants submitted further descriptions and, thus, were interviewed twice.

Once the interviews had been conducted and transcribed, the transcripts were then divided between two coding teams (three members each that did not conduct the interviews) for analysis. Each team open-coded the descriptions in one category and then, using the codes created during the initial open coding, phase 1 data, and phase 2 data, two members from each coding team created an agreed-upon master codebook. Each coding team applied the descriptive and in vivo codes from the master codebook to the interview transcripts and the submitted descriptions per unit of thought (Miles, Huberman, & Saldaña, 2014); thus, applying codes that identified how educators engaged and supported candidates in relevant learning experiences, as well as how they connected course learning with field placements.

We used an analytic software (Dedoose) to identify frequency counts for each subcode. After the initial round of coding, the teams switched participants for inter-rater reliability. Consensus among the research team on the coding and the evolution of the master codebook was established during the bimonthly meetings.

After the codes were agreed upon, we then determined patterns across the participants. Discussion of this cross-participant analysis can be found in Peltier et al. (2019b). For this chapter, we focus on what our research team learned from exemplary cases. In particular, we wondered how exemplary teacher educators were bridging their coursework and fieldwork through course learning experiences. In the findings, we present two cases of teacher educators who intentionally designed learning experiences that supported and engaged candidates in connecting coursework and fieldwork contexts.

Phase 3 Findings

Phase 3 interview data added depth to phase 2 findings, because conversations with participants about their learning experiences provided insights into their reasoning behind the activities and how they implemented them. Across the interviews of the six participants, teacher educators *engaged* candidates in their literacy method courses by making instructional decisions, enacting curricular context with peers and faculty, and familiarizing/identifying candidates to curricular contexts they might experience in their fieldwork. Teacher educators *supported* their candidates through providing concrete resources, prompting candidates to use professional knowledge when making decisions, and providing time to interact with faculty or their peers.

Finally, teacher educators created opportunities to *connect* curricular contexts to fieldwork and coursework by making explicit connections to fieldwork through lesson planning, administering assessments, and using curricular materials from the field. Our purpose for sharing these two exemplary cases in this manner is to engage our fellow teacher educators into thinking about how to make connections between coursework and fieldwork contexts more explicit. We encourage our fellow educators to consider how these two cases might inform their teaching in the immediate and present design to enhance bridging coursework and fieldwork.

Mia

At the time of her interview, Mia had been teaching for five years at a small (fewer than 5,000 undergraduate students) university in the rural Southeastern United States. She taught juniors and seniors the two literacy courses required for initial teacher certification: one focused on teaching methods and the other on literacy assessments. Both courses contained a field placement, but Mia's candidates were placed in four to six different school districts. In her initial survey, Mia did not describe the demographics of any of the school districts.

The initial assignment Mia uploaded during the phase 1 survey was a project that required candidates to focus their attention on the actions of one student from their field placements. Candidates were expected to select one student from their field placement to "Kidwatch," which consisted of conducting interviews with a child, designing, creating, and implementing eight sessions of one-on-one literacy instruction based upon the elementary student's needs, and writing a parent letter that detailed the child's literacy strengths and needs.

However, during her interview, Mia explained that there were challenges in getting candidates to work with children one-on-one during their field placements. During class discussions with candidates, some would report never seeing one-on-one or small group instruction, which began to alarm Mia and made her Kidwatching assignment difficult to implement for her candidates. Additionally, Mia shared that she felt her candidates needed extra support in addressing core reading programs, guided reading instruction, and "non-negotiable" or "must-do" elements in policies more critically.

Mia described how she purposefully enhanced her course to scaffold candidates' experiences with these curricular contexts. She engaged candidates by designing experiences where they familiarized themselves with core reading programs and evaluated and discussed what curricular contexts they encountered. Mia found it beneficial for candidates to share what they were seeing in terms of curricular contexts since they were placed in at least five different school districts.

She also stressed the importance of helping candidates think critically about the curriculum materials and programs they were experiencing in their field placements. In the interview, she explained, "I think if we don't scaffold them (teacher candidates) to think like this now, then they'll just get in the classroom and they won't have that foundation for critical thinking."

Mia also provided candidates with curricular contexts she anticipated they would encounter once they fully entered the profession. For example, she believed that candidates needed more support with guided reading because many did not experience this kind of instruction in their placements. Thus, Mia purposefully incorporated guided reading into her course and provided resources for candidates to use in their future classrooms.

In addition to incorporating curricular contexts as a central component of her course, Mia enhanced candidates' learning experiences by purposefully designing a field experience with a local after-school program. This eliminated the challenge some candidates experienced in completing the Kidwatching project during their field component. After securing a common field placement that she could oversee, Mia created a course requirement where candidates worked with children in an after-school program over a series of sixteen sessions, each forty-five-minutes long. Mia shared:

> My hope is that . . . they will actually do small group and one-on-one work and because they've had that experience, they won't be as hesitant to try it, or they'll see the benefits of it and they'll say, well I don't care if you're not doing it to another team member in nice words. I see the benefits of this.

By incorporating this field component as a part of her course, Mia designed a scaffolded experience for candidates where they engaged in making instructional decisions, enacted their decisions directly with elementary students, and reflected upon the experience. By using an after-school program as the field component, Mia and her candidates had more freedom to meet the needs of individual students and fewer curricular requirements. It also provided Mia opportunities to support candidates' development as literacy teachers through modeling and verbal interactions.

Because Mia was able to directly oversee her candidates' teaching as they designed lesson plans, implemented the lessons with children, and reflected upon their experiences, she supported candidates with instantaneous feedback and assisted them in their instructional decision-making. Mia highlighted, "I feel like I'm able to maybe intervene more than it is, more than I could just in class when I'm circulating that way." Due to her presence during this field component, Mia experienced the field context and elementary students as often as her candidates, which gave her insider knowledge into the children's cultures, expectations, and abilities. With this knowledge, Mia could better support candidates in their attempts at situating their literacy practices to meet the needs of their elementary students.

When asked about what she continues to work on as a teacher educator, Mia described her efforts in designing experiences for candidates that focus on and emphasize the language of teaching. She shared, "My goal was to have them think about the type of words of agency or naming that they were specific within the terms of what they specifically wanted the student to engage in." Mia explained how she works with candidates to become more specific in their feedback with students but admitted that this is a continued goal for her courses.

Mia also described how she works to incorporate assignments where candidates learn to design and implement curriculum cooperatively, as this is a requirement for many classroom teachers. Ultimately, Mia continued to reflect upon and incorporate learning experiences with candidates where they enacted as teachers. "I think it gives them a direct correlation to what they need to be doing," she said.

Mia's purposeful design of her literacy course supplements what she perceived as lacking in the field. She bridged the divide between the two entities by incorporating curricular contexts candidates were experiencing into her courses and expected candidates to critically examine these practices. Further, Mia connected her course with a field component by finding a partnership where she could design an experience that supported and scaffolded candidates' experiences as literacy teachers.

When Mia noticed that candidates needed extra support with one-on-one literacy instruction and guided reading, she supplemented her curriculum with curricular contexts she felt were important for candidates to experience. Mia's case demonstrated that it is not enough for candidates to bring learning from the field context into a course or to ask candidates to implement course content into their field placements. Rather, the two contexts should work together to provide a wide variety of opportunities and experiences for teacher candidates.

Charles

At the time of his interview, Charles had been teaching for three years at a university (5,000–10,000 undergraduate students) in the Midwestern United States. He taught a literacy course for juniors that builds on their previous course focused on foundations of reading and reading processes. The course was a literacy-focused one that provided a holistic approach to teaching literacy, with writing instruction and assessment embedded throughout. Both courses required field components. Charles planned learning experiences for candidates to prepare them for the varying contexts they could enter as future teachers due to the statewide school of choice program, which included public charter schools within the public school system, as well as private charters and private schools.

As a part of the initial survey, Charles uploaded an assignment that supported candidates to develop a whole-group literacy lesson from the teacher's manual for the basal reading series *Journeys* by Harcourt Houghton Mifflin. In this assignment, candidates were required to use the text from the basal reading series as their core text in the lesson and they were required to adapt and include their own "teaching voice" (e.g., materials, extension activities) when delivering the lesson.

Charles chose to share this assignment as an example of how he taught candidates to "balance the affordances and constraints of curricula that they're [candidates] going to encounter with all the things they're learning in the university coursework, the best practices and the research-based decision making around literacy." In this assignment, candidates planned and taught a whole-group literacy lesson with integrated reading and writing.

Charles supported candidates so they could become familiar with the teacher's manual for the basal reader in this task because he knew from experience and from research (Pardo, Highfield, & Florio-Ruane, 2011; Valencia et al., 2006) that novice and veteran teachers will resort to using the teacher's manual without problematizing how it aligns with best practices or reflecting on how it supports students' learning needs.

In the interview, Charles emphasized the need to help candidates become critical consumers of the materials with which they will be provided as teachers, while also considering the current learning needs of children when planning instruction. He emphasized that "it's getting them to understand that kind of dance that we do as educators using the materials we're provided, but being respondent to the learners sitting in front of us." He taught candidates to view students holistically as learners (e.g., not just an assessment score or "above" or "below" grade level) and taking in "individual-to-class-wide dynamics of the learner."

It is through this lens that he engaged and supported teacher candidates with evaluating and determining what pieces of the lesson in the teachers' manual were appropriate for the students in the fieldwork placement. Charles described the mentor teachers' and teacher candidates' frustrations in looking through the overwhelming amount of information and determining how to choose what was best to teach. Navigating this experience with teacher candidates prepared them to connect foundational knowledge, research, and materials they were expected to use in the field.

Beyond incorporating curricular contexts as a central part of his coursework, Charles also had candidates read several articles from *The Reading Teacher* and *Language Art*s to understand what it meant to be an exemplary literacy teacher based on what we know from literacy research. Additionally, candidates reviewed position statements about effective reading teachers from the International Literacy Association.

Candidates also read about challenges they will face when entering school systems, such as required curriculum or assessment misaligned from student needs. Charles shared that he hoped that the course assignments, coupled with powerful conversations surrounding research and literature will, "empower my candidates to be ready for the world when they leave and that the world is not perfect, but we make it more perfect by doing good work within it."

DISCUSSION

We chose these specific cases to illustrate the ways two teacher educators deliberately engaged teacher candidates in ways that enhance their understanding of teaching contexts. Both Mia and Charles had the benefit of teaching literacy courses connected to field placements for teacher candidates. This scenario provided them the affordance to develop relationships with mentor teachers, evaluate specific curriculum materials, and understand the field contexts where teacher candidates will implement lessons planned in their courses.

Although there is a breadth of research examining these connections from a programmatic level (e.g., Burroughs et al., 2020; Canrinus et al., 2017; McDonald et al., 2011), both case studies exemplify how teacher educators too can structure and design their courses to bridge these divides (Peltier et al., 2019b). Equipped with this deep knowledge of field contexts, Mia and Charles understood what they needed to do to better support their candidates' learning as they provided different ways of engaging candidates in teaching while connecting those experiences to the field or to future teaching.

Thus, Mia and Charles created bridges from coursework to fieldwork by intentionally addressing discrepancies they noticed from the literacy curriculum contexts. For instance, Mia described specific ways she connected one-on-one and guided reading experiences in her course as a response to the absence of this kind of differentiated instruction in field placement contexts.

Similarly, Charles utilized his cooperating district's curriculum materials to help teacher candidates evaluate and adapt these to meet the needs of students in field placement classrooms. Given the dearth of scholarship examining how teacher educators support candidates' navigation (Peltier et al., 2019a), we hope these practical examples demonstrate for teacher educators how they can adjust their coursework to include and supplement the curricular contexts candidates experience in the field.

We acknowledge that these two cases are ideal because of the affordances and we recognize that many teacher educators' literacy courses do not have these immediate teaching connections for their teacher candidates (Symcox, 2012). Without field placements, it becomes even more important for teacher educators to somehow help bridge coursework to the curricular contexts that candidates will experience in their future teaching. We noticed that both Charles and Mia emphasized intentional course connections to field placements.

The benefits of this intentionality for candidates' growth are echoed in other academic literature (e.g., Clark et al., 2013; Scales et al., 2018; Young et al., 2017). Intentional connections can still be made without a field placement, but these connections may need to be broader to address multiple potential materials that candidates may encounter.

From this research, we recognize a need to develop strong relationships with teacher educators who supervise field placements. Given candidates' propensity for adopting the practices they witness in the field (Barnes & Smagorinsky, 2016; Burnett et al., 2015; Castañeda-Trujillo & Aguirre-Hernández, 2018), developing relationships with and knowledge of the field placements are paramount.

By collaborating throughout the course with individuals who support teacher candidates in the field, teacher educators can help candidates discuss and contemplate their field placement contexts in relation to course goals. In turn, conversations with field placement supervisors can help teacher educators better understand the field contexts, which could influence how teacher educators plan their courses. For instance, teacher educators may provide more deliberate responses to candidates when issues arise about how learning from their course could be implemented in field placements because conversations with field placement supervisors could result in teacher educators gaining deeper knowledge of materials teachers are required to use.

Teacher educators' voices are important in the field placement decision-making process (Roberts-Harris, 2014). We know that some teacher educators have the ability to decide and develop relationships within the field placements, while others have no say (Kosnick & Beck, 2009). However, developing deep knowledge and understanding of the schools and classrooms our candidates experience for fieldwork helps teacher educators better engage candidates in learning experiences that bridges learning from coursework to their teaching (Bricker & Tracy, 2017; Hoge & Jenks, 2000).

Being explicit with teacher candidates in how coursework is relevant to the real world of teaching ultimately supports them in their teaching journey. Charles shared the benefits of getting candidates to consider how their learning from coursework fits with what they witness in their field placements. He said:

> Things we learn about and talk about in course we immediately can see in perfect and non-perfect ways in the field. I think that helps them to start to build their own sense making of what the possibilities are and some of the challenges.

Despite the exemplary cases of Mia and Charles' bridging of coursework and fieldwork, this research has demonstrated to our team that a call to action is needed for teacher educators. Although we work to intentionally design course assignments, readings, and activities that respond to and supplement the curricular contexts candidates experience in the field, this longitudinal study has revealed that we do not always articulate this intentionality well to the said candidates. Research has shown that both candidates and novice teachers wish teacher educators would address curricular contexts explicitly in their teacher preparation programs (Ahmed, 2019; Bainbridge & Macy, 2008; Ellis & Maguire, 2017).

CONCLUSION

Our longitudinal study provided critical insight into how elementary literacy teacher educators perceive and enhance alignment between coursework and fieldwork contexts. Phase 1 data helped us identify that teacher educators perceive their candidates encounter varied curricular contexts (e.g., materials, policies, and supports such as field supervision and mentor teachers). Phase 2 revealed how teacher educators engaged students through coursework, how teacher educators supported candidates in navigating curricular contexts, and how curricular contexts connected to field experiences.

Phase 3 provided additional depth to the ways teacher candidates engage candidates in literacy methods coursework (e.g., familiarizing candidates with curricular contexts they may experience in fieldwork, making instructional decisions, enacting curricular contexts with peers/faculty), how teacher educators support candidates (e.g., via concrete resources, opportunities for collaborative reflection on instruction), and how teacher educators connected curricular contexts to fieldwork and fieldwork to coursework (e.g., lesson planning with field materials, administering assessments).

The findings from this survey, document analysis, and interview study suggest that teacher educators perceive their courses as aligning with the needs of the field, but that we struggle to explicitly name this alignment for candidates and to each other. As teacher educators, then, we should ask ourselves: How can we design our courses to connect to a field placement if this is not already incorporated into the program? How can we communicate regularly with the supervisors of the field placements? And, how do we support and engage candidates to connect coursework and fieldwork contexts?

Our research suggests that teacher educators are asking themselves these questions, but often fail to illuminate this decision-making process to candidates or peers, which undermines our design. In making these connections more explicit for candidates, perhaps they too will begin to see the connections between the coursework of their preparation program and their fieldwork. In sharing these explicit connections with one another, we continue to strengthen and develop our practices as teacher educators to better bridge coursework and fieldwork. We must engage in continued practice in such work and support one another through the process because "Learning to teach—like teaching itself—is always the process of becoming; a time of formation and transformation, a scrutiny into what one is doing, and who one can become" (Britzman, 2003, p. 31).

REFERENCES

Ahmed, K. S. (2019). Being a "bridge builder": A literacy teacher educator negotiates the divide between university-promoted culturally responsive pedagogy and district-mandated curriculum. *Literacy Research and Instruction, 58*(4), 211–231. https://doi.org/10.1080/19388071.2019.1655683

American Association of Colleges for Teacher Education (AACTE) Clinical Practice Commission. (2018). *A pivot toward clinical practice, its lexicon, and the renewal of educator preparation.* Retrieved from https://aacte.org/professional-development-and-events/clinical-practicecommission-press-conference.

Anderson, L., & Stillman, J. (2011). Student teaching for a specialized view of professional practice? Opportunities to learn in and for urban, high-needs schools. *Journal of Teacher Education, 62*(5), 446–464. https://doi.org/10.1177/0022487111412052

Bainbridge, J. M., & Macy, L. (2008). Voices: Student teachers link teacher education to perceptions of preparedness[sic] for literacy teaching. *Teacher Education Quarterly, 35*(2), 65–83.

Ball, L. D., & Forzani, F. M. (2009). The work of teaching and the challenge for teacher education. *Journal of Teacher Education, 60*(5), 497–511. doi:10.1177/0022487109348479

Barnes, M. E., & Smagorinsky, P. (2016). What English/language arts teacher candidates learn during coursework and practica: A study of three teacher education programs. *Journal of Teacher Education, 67*(4), 338–355. https://doi.org/10.1177/0022487116653661

Brannon, D., & Fiene, J. (2013). The effect structured participation experiences have on pre-service teachers' preparedness to teach reading. *Education, 134*(2), 185–194.

Bricker, P., & Tracy, K. N. (2017). Elementary teachers leading from the classroom. In C. Rogers, K. Lomotey & A. Hilton (Eds.), *Innovative approaches to educational leadership: Selected cases* (pp. 95–104). New York: Peter Lang.

Britzman, D. P. (2003). *Practice makes practice: A critical study of learning to teach.* Albany, NY: State University of New York Press.

Burnett, C., Daniels, K., Gray, L., Myers, J., & Sharpe, S. (2015). Investigating student/teachers presentations of literacy and literacy pedagogy in a complex context. *Teacher Development, 19*(3), 275–293.

Burroughs, G., Lewis, A., Battey, D., Curran, M., Hyland, N. E., & Ryan, S. (2020). From mediated fieldwork to co-constructed partnerships: A framework for guiding and reflecting on P-12 school-university partnerships. *Journal of Teacher Education, 71*(1), 122–134. https://doi.org/10.1177/0022487119858992

Canrinus, E. T., Bergem, O. K., Klette, K., & Hammerness, K. (2017). Coherent teacher education programmes: Taking a student perspective. *Journal of Curriculum Studies, 49*(3), 313–333. https://doi.org/10.1080/00220272.2015.1124145

Castañeda-Trujillo, J. E., & Aguirre-Hernández, A. J. (2018). Pre-service English teachers' voices about the teaching practicum. *HOW, 25*(1), 156–173.

Clark, S. K., Jones, C. D., Reutzel, D. R., & Andreasen, L. (2013). An examination of the influences of a teacher preparation program on beginning teachers' reading instruction. *Literacy Research and Instruction, 52*(2), 87–105.

Cobb, J. B. (2012). Navigating mandates: Teachers face "troubled seas." *Language and Literacy, 14*(3), 112–132. doi: https://doi.org/10.20360/G20P4W

Cochran-Smith, M., Villegas, A. M., Abrams, L., Chavez Moreno, L., Mills, T., & Stern, R. (2016). Research on teacher preparation: Charting the landscape of a sprawling field. In D. Gitomer & C. Bell (Eds.), *Handbook of research on teaching* (5th ed.) (pp. 439–547). Washington, DC: American Educational Research Association.

Cole, M. (1996). *Cultural psychology: The once and future discipline.* Cambridge, MA: Harvard University Press.

Council for the Accreditation of Educator Preparation (CAEP). (2018). CAEP 2018 K-6 elementary teacher preparation standards [initial licensure programs]. Retrieved from http://www.ncate.org/accreditation/caepaccreditation/caep-k-6-elementaryteacher-standards

Dewey, J. (1938). *Experience and education*. New York, NY: Collier Books.

Ellis, V., & Maguire, M. (2017). Teacher education pedagogies based on critical approaches: Learning to challenge and change prevailing educational practices. In D. J. Clandinin & J. Husu (Eds.), *The SAGE handbook of research on teacher education* (pp. 594–609). Los Angeles, CA: Sage Publications.

Hoge, J. D., & Jenks, C. (2000). *Professors in K-12 classrooms: Rewards, risks, and recommendations*. Paper presented at the Annual Conference of the National Council for the Social Studies. San Antonio, Texas.

Kennedy, M. M. (2006). Knowledge and vision in teaching. *Journal of Teacher Education, 57*(3), 205–211. https://doi.org/10.1177/0022487105285639

Kosnik, C., & Beck, C. (2009). *Priorities in teacher education: The 7 key elements of pre-service preparation*. New York, NY: Routledge.

McDonald, M., Tyson, K., Brayko, K., Bowman, M., Delport, J., & Shimomura, F. (2011). Innovation and impact in teacher education: Community-based organizations as field placements for preservice teachers. *Teachers College Record, 113*(8), 1668–1700.

Miles, M. B., Huberman, A. M., & Saldaña, J. (2014). *Qualitative data analysis: A methods sourcebook* (3rd ed.). Thousand Oaks, CA: Sage.

Pardo, L., Highfield, K., & Florio-Ruane, S. (Eds.). (2011). *Standing for powerful literacy: Teaching in the context of change*. New York, NY: Hampton Press.

Peltier, M. R., Bemiss, E. M., Hopkins, L. J., Van Wig, A., & Davis, S. (2019b, December). *Comparing contextual cases: Examining learner experiences designed to help teacher candidates navigate diverse curricular contexts*. Paper presented at the annual conference of the Literacy Research Association. Tampa, Florida.

Peltier, M. R., Scales, R. Q., Bemiss, E. M., Shimek, C., Van Wig, A., Hopkins, L. J., Davis, S. G., & Scales, W. D. (2019a). A national survey of literacy teacher educators' perceptions of alignment across coursework and fieldwork. *Literacy Practice and Research, 44*(2), 27–39.

Roberts-Harris, D. (2014). What did they take away?: Examining newly qualified U.S. teachers' visions of learning and teaching science in K-8 classrooms. *Teaching & Learning Inquiry, 2*(2), 91–107.

Scales, R. Q., Wolsey, T. D., Lenski, S., Smetana, L., Yoder, K. K., Dobler, E., Grisham, D. L., & Young, J. (2018). Are we preparing or training teachers?: Developing professional judgment in and beyond teacher preparation programs. *Journal of Teacher Education, 69*(1), 7–21. https://doi.org/10.1177/0022487117702584

Smagorinsky, P. (2018). Literacy in teacher education: "It's the context, stupid." *Journal of Literacy Research, 50*(3), 281–303. https://doi.org/10.1177/1086296X18784692

Smagorinsky, P., Rhym, D., & Moore, C. (2013). Competing centers of gravity: A beginning English teacher's socialization process within conflictual settings. *English Education, 45*(2), 147–183. https://doi.org/10.1177/1541344620909444

Smagorinsky, P., Cook, L. S., Moore, C., Jackson, A. Y., & Fry, P. G. (2004). Tensions in learning to teach: Accommodation and the development of a teaching identity. *Journal of Teacher Education, 55*(1), 8–24. https://doi.org/10.1177/0022487103260067

Sydnor, J. (2017). "I didn't realize how hard it would be!": Tensions and transforma-
tions in becoming a teacher. *Action in Teacher Education, 39*(2), 218–236. https://
doi.org/10.1080/01626620.2016.1226202

Symcox, L. (2012). Forging new partnerships: Collaboration between university
professors and classroom teachers to improve history teaching, 1983–2011. *The
History Teacher, 45*(3), 359–382.

Valencia, S. W., Place, N. A., Martin, S. D., & Grossman, P. L. (2006). Curriculum
materials for elementary reading: Shackles and scaffolds for beginning teachers.
Elementary School Journal, 107, 93–120.

Vaughn, M., Scales, R. Q., Stevens, E. Y., Kline, S., Barrett-Tatum, J., Van Wig,
A., Yoder, K. K., & Wellman, D. (2021). Understanding literacy adoption policies
across contexts: A multi-state examination of literacy curriculum decision making.
Journal of Curriculum Studies. DOI: 10.1080/00220272.2019.1683233

Vygotsky, L. S. (1978). *Mind in society: The development of higher psychological
processes*. Cambridge, MA: Harvard University Press.

Young, J. R., Scales, R. Q., Grisham, D. L., Dobler, E., Wolsey, T. D., Smetana, L.,
Chambers, S., Ganske, K., Lenski, S., & Yoder, K. K. (2017). Student teachers'
preparation in literacy: Cooking in someone else's kitchen. *Teacher Education
Quarterly, 44*(4), 74–97.

Chapter 4

Preparing Special Educators for Inclusive Classes: Focusing Experiential Learning Experiences on Content and Disciplinary Literacy Instruction

Marie Tejero Hughes, Gina Braun,
and Courtney Lynn Barcus

Well prepared special educators make an impactful difference in their students with disabilities development of literacy and content area achievement. One way that special educators can enhance their students' achievement and skills in these areas is to incorporate literacy strategies within content area instruction (Alger, 2007). Yet determining what preservice special educators need in their teacher education programs in order to become effective teachers in content area classes is challenging, given the complexities of teaching in inclusive content classes, as well as the wide range of needs students with disabilities may have (Parker-Katz, Hughes, & Lee, 2017).

We know that often general educators see themselves as either a content area teacher or a literacy teacher and do not receive adequate preparation to build strong knowledge and skills in both areas, leaving them ill-prepared (Ness, 2016). This dilemma is compounded for special educators who teach in content area classes, but also face additional challenges as they work to meet the individual needs of students with disabilities in these inclusive settings.

Scholars in special education talk about these challenges, including the special educator's role ambiguity in these inclusive environments (Rock et al., 2016), but how best to prepare preservice special educators for the multiple roles and responsibilities they will encounter has been more difficult to identify (Shepherd et al., 2016). Therefore, given special educators' roles and responsibilities in these settings, they first require a deep knowledge base of both the general education curriculum and how to adapt the curriculum to meet the multiple needs of learners (Leko et al., 2015).

Thus, successful teacher education programs not only must offer opportunities for the preservice special educators to gain knowledge of the theories behind best practices across all of these areas (Spear-Swerling, 2009), but they should also provide preservice special educators with multiple opportunities. That is, opportunities to both design and implement instruction in the field while receiving feedback and reflecting on their instruction and student learning (Bohon et al., 2017; Lacina & Block, 2011).

Providing these experiential learning opportunities that are embedded into all classwork, rather than structured primarily in their student teaching experience, is a recommended component of special educators' teacher preparation programs. However, little to no research has been done examining the impact these early experiences have on the development of preservice special educators teaching of literacy in content areas to adolescent students with disabilities (Leko et al., 2015).

Teaching Literacy in the Content Areas

Teaching literacy in a content area requires a complex set of knowledge and skills. First and foremost, special educators must have knowledge of both content and literacy development. Second, they require a set of skills to enable them to integrate and implement effective practices in these areas. Finally, special educators must also determine the unique set of needs each student with disabilities has and then select effective and appropriate supports that will provide the students with access to the general education curriculum.

Literacy is naturally connected to content area classes (e.g., science and social studies), since it is a critical component of the instruction in these classrooms. Literacy skills such as vocabulary and comprehension are core components for a successful understanding of the content in these classes. Thus, special educators need general knowledge on literacy strategies that support both developing understanding and building word knowledge (Fisher & Frey, 2015).

Because of the tight connection between the two, the idea that all teachers are literacy teachers is a mindset that should be instilled in preservice special educators, especially those pursuing positions in middle and high schools (Fang, 2014). In doing so, these novices not only build strong background knowledge in their content area, but they also develop a strong/knowledge base on literacy strategies to support the development of this content such as the use of concept maps and engaging in discussions related to primary sources (Kane, 2017).

Embedding literacy into content instruction requires a set of unique skills beyond the knowledge of these two areas. Research shows that there is a lack of knowledge among educators on how to take what they know related to literacy development and successfully embed it into their content area classes (Fenty & Brydon, 2017). To facilitate teachers' preparation for the successful implementation of developing content through literacy practices, teacher preparation courses must be grounded in both a strong literacy knowledge base and effective strategies for integrating the practices into content area classes (Castles, Rastle, & Nation, 2018).

The development of content knowledge for preservice special educators is thus grounded in research-based theories and practices that increase their background knowledge on the evidence-based practices for instructing literacy (Rock et al., 2016). Therefore, an effective literacy course focused on literacy in the content areas needs to lay out a foundation of knowledge that includes an overview of literacy development, information on evidence-based literacy practices, integration of literacy and content (Fang, 2014), and discussion of effective instructional strategies to support the diverse needs of students with disabilities (Lacina & Block, 2011). In addition, preparation courses designed to develop teacher's knowledge and skill in content area literacy should also develop a deep understanding and practice using the skills connected to assessing students in these areas (Mandinach, 2012).

Beyond the basic knowledge and skills connected to literacy and content area, preservice special educators also are expected to know the common characteristics of diverse struggling students and how to select and implement the appropriate supports in these inclusive content area classes (Brownell et al., 2010). Scholars in the field have provided a variety of suggestions for strategies that work for content area classrooms, including teaching adequate notetaking (Boyle, Forchelli, & Cariss, 2015), pre-teaching skills (Berg & Wehby, 2013), comprehension strategies such as anticipatory guides (Poch & Lembke, 2018), incorporating technology (Ciampa, 2017), and using adapted texts (Roberts et al., 2019).

Experiential Learning in Content Areas

To develop effective special education teacher preparation and classroom practice, teacher educators focus on models that reflect experiential learning theories for teacher education (DeGraff, Schmidt, & Waddell, 2015). Thus, to successfully prepare special educators to teach in content areas, novices need rich experiences in the field, coupled with the strong development of content through coursework (Helfrich & Bean, 2011).

Furthermore, components such as observation of explicit modeling of instructional practices; opportunities for application through field experience;

and immediate feedback from instructors, mentor teachers, and peers, support this experiential model for learning (Hughes & Braun, 2019; Leko et al., 2015). While several frameworks exist supporting experiential learning for preservice educators, few have focused specifically on how to incorporate this type of learning to prepare special educators to meet the literacy needs of students with disabilities in content area classes.

An experiential-based model, based on the science of learning, which specifically considers special education teachers, has been proposed by researchers in special education (Leko et al., 2015). In this model, the coursework is grounded in research and paired with opportunities for novices to practice both in the university classroom and in the field to enhance their knowledge and skill, gain feedback from others, as well as reflect both individually and collaboratively, on their practices to make informed decisions related to their instructional practices and student success and continued need (DeGraff, Schmidt, & Waddell, 2015).

When specifically considering the impact of experiential learning and developing content area literacy, Fenty and Brydon (2017) examined the impact of these experiences on preservice elementary special educators' feelings of self-efficacy, beliefs, and practices. Findings showed that through experiential learning opportunities, the novices saw the value in teaching literacy in content areas, and they had increased knowledge on integrating the two into planning. While this provides the field insight into the impacts of experiential learning for elementary special educators, it does not examine preservice special educators working in an adolescent (grades 6–12) classroom.

Another study completed by Bohon et al. (2017) examined high school content area teachers increase in knowledge of supporting students after participating in experiential learning opportunities. The results from a pre- and post-survey demonstrated that teachers gained knowledge and understanding in supporting their students. Although this research examined high school teachers, the participants were current teachers who took part in a professional development opportunity, which did not focus on students with disabilities.

Continuing to look at the impact of experiential learning opportunities when instructing students with disabilities, Wozencroft, Pate, and Griffiths (2015) demonstrated a positive impact on preservice educators and their knowledge and attitudes toward working with students with disabilities. However, their study did not specifically examine the impact of knowledge and skills of experiential learning on preservice special educators in teaching in content area classes.

Building off on the positive impacts that experiential learning has demonstrated to have on preservice educators, Hughes and Braun (2019) investigated how preservice special educators enhanced their knowledge, shifted beliefs, and modified practice for working with elementary students with disabilities while participating in a literacy course with an experiential learning component. Results demonstrated that the novices made large growth in their knowledge around literacy and shifted their beliefs from initially blaming students for not learning, to holding themselves accountable for the instructional outcomes of students.

This study demonstrated the positive impact that experiential learning had on preservice special educators, though it only examined elementary literacy practices. Thus, this current study expands on the former to look at experiential learning opportunities in a special education preparation program with a focus on meeting the literacy needs of adolescent learners with disabilities in content area classrooms.

Purpose of Study

Providing preservice special educators with experiential learning experiences that focus on literacy instruction not only increases their instructional knowledge of literacy, but novices can also learn to adapt their instruction and utilize more evidence-based practices as they engage with students with disabilities during these experiences (Hughes & Braun, 2019). However, there is a dearth of research available that examines how these experiential learning experiences influence preservice special educators' teaching of literacy within inclusive science and social studies classes.

Given that the majority of students with high-incidence disabilities (e.g., specific learning disabilities, emotional and behavioral disorders) receive instruction in these inclusive content area classes (Scruggs, Mastropieri, & Okolo, 2008), we need to take a closer look at how special education teacher education programs are incorporating early experiences in these settings and the impact these practice-based activities have on the development of the preservice special educator. Since we had recently revised our literacy course that focused on literacy practices for students with disabilities in content area classes, we decided to look closely at how an experiential learning experience (middle and high school content area teaching) that was integrated into the course influenced the planning and instruction of the novices enrolled in the course.

We were especially interested in learning how this experience may have influenced the preservice special educators' integration of literacy practices, planning for instructional supports, and reflections of their instruction. In addition, we wanted to document how preservice special educators navigated the complexity of planning interdisciplinary lessons for students with disabilities in their lessons.

METHODOLOGY

This study used a qualitative content analysis method of research to examine the experiential learning experiences of special education preservice educators. The participants and procedures are discussed in the following sections.

Participants

Preservice special educators ($n = 59$) in a large, urban university in the Midwest of the United States participated in this study, which was approved by the university's Institutional Review Board. The educators were in a special education master's program designed to prepare them to obtain an initial special education teaching endorsement and were enrolled in a literacy course. The department offered the course once a year, and all educators in the three sessions offered during this investigation participated. The educators in the program are overwhelmingly females (79 percent), and their racial and ethnic background includes white 77 percent, Hispanic/Latinx 15 percent, black/African American 3 percent, Asian 3 percent, unknown 2 percent, and multiracial 1 percent.

Procedures

The procedures used in the study reflect those related to the literacy course, experiential learning experience, and data collection and analysis. These procedures are further discussed in the following sections.

Literacy course

As part of the special education program requirement, the educators were taking a required literacy methods course, which the first author taught. The focus of the course was on developing preservice special educators' knowledge and skills around evidence-based practices for content area literacy for middle and secondary aged students with high-incidence disabilities. The course is the second course of two required literacy courses in the program, which consists of eleven courses along with an internship and student teaching and is typically taken prior to their student teaching semester.

The course emphasizes the components of planning, instructing, and monitoring literacy for students with disabilities in grades five to twelve within the content areas, particularly science and social studies classes. The educators are also introduced (e.g., videos, modeling) to evidence-based practices that are effective for a variety of students with disabilities to enhance their comprehension of content area materials. They were required to complete several assignments related to the topics of the course, such as demonstrating in-class lessons that integrate literacy strategies within content areas instruction.

Experiential learning experience

A fifteen-hour experiential learning experience was a required component of the course, which allowed the educators an opportunity to work directly in a fifth- to twelfth-grade science or social studies classroom that included at least two students with disabilities. The experiential learning experience primarily took place in local public schools, but a few were in specialized settings (e.g., a private school for students with disabilities). As is typical with most of the early field experiences in the program, educators could make their own field placements and identify a content area teacher at the school to serve as their cooperating teacher, or they could request that the special education university supervisor place them with a teacher at schools that regularly host special education student teachers.

In the end, approximately half the educators identified their own placement for the course. All educators worked with general education students and students identified with a disability who were identified by the schools as receiving services for a range of disabilities, but mostly for learning disabilities, emotional and behavioral disabilities, and autism spectrum disorder.

Overwhelmingly, educators were in inclusive content area classes with forty-three in social studies classes (e.g., history, world history, and civics) and sixteen in science classes (e.g., environmental, physics, and biology). During the first part of the experience, the educators worked alongside their cooperating teacher in a supportive capacity as they began to get to know the students and the content of the class. They were required to plan an integrated unit related to the topics that their cooperating teacher was focusing on and then teach at least three of the lessons to the students in the class. This fifteen-hour experiential learning experience was conducted primarily over the latter half of the semester.

Course assignments relating to the experience included planning the unit, designing lesson plans, and writing reflections. Educators were provided with a lesson plan template, which included highlighting the learning standards and lesson outcome, describing the lesson activities, outlining the materials used, and identifying the assessments. They were also provided with questions to facilitate their reflections (e.g., How did you build connections between student's prior learning and new content? What did you do to support students who required additional assistance to meet the lesson outcome?).

The educators designed content area lessons that integrated literacy strategies that they then implemented with either the whole class or groups of students to assist students in developing their content knowledge and literacy skills. Educators also identified the two focus students with disabilities in their class and paid particular attention to their individual needs in the lesson plan by identifying any additional adaptations or modifications they may require. Following each of the three lessons, they wrote a reflection of their instruction and met individually with their cooperating teacher, who, after observing the lesson, provided explicit feedback on how to enhance it and guided the educator to think critically about their instruction.

The cooperating teacher also provided written feedback for the educator that was shared with the course instructor. In addition, they digitally recorded one lesson and shared the video with their peers and the instructor, thus receiving feedback about their instruction based on the videos as well as during the experience.

Data sources and analysis

All the lesson plans and reflections that educators submitted were downloaded from the course website at the end of the semester and de-identified before analysis. In total, there were 177 lesson plans and reflections included in the analysis. To examine the lesson plans and reflections and determine how the course may have enhanced educators' knowledge and skills related to literacy in the content area for students with disabilities, we utilized qualitative content analysis (Mayring, 2014). The methodology of qualitative content analysis allows the data to be analyzed step by step. It began by developing a category system directly on the data sources employing a theory-guided procedure (Kohlbacher, 2006).

We used an inductive analysis as we reviewed all the data collected and developed common categories across the data source. First, we began with the purpose of the investigation and worked through the first few lesson plans and then some reflections. As we went through this process, we summarized and reorganized notes, read data sources, drafted memos, coded data, compared and contrasted codes, negotiated codes, developed themes from codes, and created matrices of the identified themes. To complete this process, we used collaborative online documents and scheduled regular research meetings. We continued to negotiate as a team until we came to a final agreement on the major themes. Once established, two of us independently coded the remaining lesson plans and reflections, and then we went back and reviewed each other's coding for reliability and negotiated any items that we disagreed on (Mayring, 2014).

FINDINGS

After participating in an experiential learning experience as part of a literacy course, the preservice special educators demonstrated knowledge and ability to (1) integrate literacy practices to develop content areas; (2) plan for instructional supports; (3) reflect on instruction, and (4) understand the complexity of planning interdisciplinary lessons. These primary findings are described, along with represented examples and quotations.

Integrating Literacy Practices to Develop Content Areas

In general, the educators planned for several strategies to help support their students learning the new content while engaging in literacy activities. Based on the planning templates used, the educators considered both the content and literacy standards. Though they often provided a description of a strategy in the beginning, less frequently seen was the integration of it in the instructional sequence. Overall, they planned or selected to use a wide variety of evidence-based strategies to develop an understanding of content and enhance the students' literacy skills: this often included explicit instruction, graphic organizers, activation of prior knowledge, vocabulary development, and discussions.

Explicit instruction

Across educators, there was substantial evidence of explicit instruction utilized. In most cases, they used it as a way to introduce a literacy strategy, specifically focusing on modeling. For example, one educator stated, "My teaching was explicit in that I modeled an example of a good summary before instructing the students to write. I identified the important components of a summary." Similarly, another educator stated, "I modeled the pyramid summary organizer before presenting students with their copies." Comments such as these in which they included a model of the literacy strategy were prevalent across many of the preservice special educators; however, there was less evidence of scripted modeled metacognitive thinking planned.

An additional component of explicit instruction that frequently appeared across lesson plans was the opportunities to practice, eventually leading to gradually releasing students to independence. Missing was specifics on how the educators provided specific feedback. Comments were more general, such as they would plan to "circulate and provide feedback during partner and group work."

Graphic organizers

One of the most utilized strategies across the educators was the use of graphic organizers. They were often planned to be utilized by all students in the class to support the organization of new learning. As one educator stated, "I will use the graphic organizer to help students keep all information organized and neat." Another educator said, "The graphic organizer will help to scaffold new learning and assist in notetaking."

Educators planned to introduce new social studies or science content through literacy, for example, articles, short texts, or videos. Because most of the educators taught social studies versus science, the graphic organizers were used primarily as "notetaking" tools or ways to help organize and make sense of their thinking. For example, many educators planned for the use of concept maps for their social studies class. However, in some cases, for science courses, the graphic organizers were used to help students organize their original ideas to design experiments. One educator expressed her use of the strategy as follows: "Students utilize a 'reasoning tool' to aid them in structuring a scientific argument that includes a claim, evidence, and reasoning."

The educators planned for graphic organizers that would support comprehension of the text and encourage students to dig deeper into the content, allowing them to "read to learn." For example, several educators used an organizer known as a "History Change Frame." One of the educators explained that its use was meant to "help students understand how historical events impacted a specific group of people from the time." Other educators used various compare and contrast organizers to help students make sense of the new content they were learning. In their plans, one educator noted, as did several others, "A graphic organizer will help students compare and contrast how the textbook presents the same information about three different cultures."

Across most of the educators, they also planned to use graphic organizers as a way to "pre-assess" or gain an understanding of what information their students knew about the given topics. One of the most commonly used graphic organizers for this purpose was the KWL (Know, Want to learn, Learned) chart. The preservice special educators would often start with the K (prior knowledge) and sometimes the W (want to learn) at the beginning of their lesson. For example, the educators would either have students write down everything they know about a topic by posing a question such as, "What do you know about the great migration?" Other times, the educators would allow the students to discuss what they know with a partner.

There was less evidence of the W being completed; however, sometimes, they would model asking new questions related to the topic. It was less evident that educators planned to return to this tool to discuss new learning on the chart and compare across it. Similar to a KWL chart, many of the preservice special educators often chose to use anticipatory guides as introductions to the content of the lessons. When discussing the purpose of planning to use it, one educator stated, "The purpose of this strategy is to connect the students to the lesson. It gives them an interest and helps them connect with the lesson. It also helps them predict what the reading will be about."

Activation of prior knowledge

Activating student's prior knowledge was regularly planned by beginning the lesson with a general discussion question. Sometimes they answered them on graphic organizers as mentioned earlier, and sometimes they completed "do now's" or "bell-ringers," and other times, they planned for small or whole group discussions.

When planning, most educators asked broad questions relating to the content, for example, "Where did the first people in America come from?" "What is the great migration? Who was involved?"; or "Provide a few examples of living things and nonliving things." Some of the questions were more specific and encouraged students to make connections. For example, "How do rumors get started? Why might lies and myths about people persist even after they have been proven wrong? Have you ever helped to spread a rumor that you doubted or knew wasn't true? Why?"

While much of the questions and prior knowledge activities related to the content, there were occasions where the preservice special educators focused on literacy skills, mostly related to vocabulary and comprehension. As one educator stated, "I wanted to use the students' prior knowledge by having them think about the type of strategies that they use when they come across a word that they do not know." Another educator stated that they "will lead a discussion about the previous class' reading, asking students to identify main ideas of the passage."

Vocabulary development

At the same time, educators used a lot of literacy-based strategies to teach new content through vocabulary instruction. Educators often mentioned that they would begin their lessons with vocabulary development. This often was done through various graphic organizers. One of the most commonly selected was the use of the Frayer Model, as this educator noted, "The purpose of this strategy is to help students become familiar with new vocabulary that they will see in their readings and throughout the unit."

The educators used the Frayer Model to help students develop a personal understanding of new content area vocabulary by considering examples and non-examples. It was evident that the educators had a clear understanding of the purpose of this strategy and how to introduce it to students. One educator stated, "It requires students to define target vocabulary and apply their funds of knowledge by generating examples and non-examples, giving characteristics, and using visuals to illustrate the meaning of the word." At times, educators also encouraged their students to use vocabulary in group or partner work. For example, an educator stated, "During partner work, the students will use the ten most important word strategy while reading an excerpt to help identify content vocabulary."

Oral discussions

Many of the educators also planned to engage students in oral discussions related to the topic of the content. Across most educators, it was evident that they wanted to ensure the students felt comfortable engaging in the discussions; thus, they would set them up for success in a variety of ways. For example, some educators had the students first write down their ideas before discussing with partners or the whole group. As this educator said, "The students will have time to write down their thoughts before sharing out loud to the whole group." Similarly, another educator stated, "The students will share their ideas with partners before sharing out loud with the whole group to boost confidence."

Also, many of the educators implemented explicit routines and expectations related to discussions both in whole group and partner work. One such example highlights the expectations used for small groups to share out with the larger class, "Each group will spend a minute presenting their image to the class and going over what they discussed and filled out in their graphic organizer."

Planning for Instructional Supports

The educators considered various evidence-based instructional supports to provide access to all learners. They implemented a variety of supports that were either differentiated for various groups of students or specific accommodations for individual students. Whether whole or small group differentiation or individualized accommodations, the educators went beyond practices and strategies described earlier to include supports that would help literacy development and general access to the lessons.

Differentiated supports and strategies

Differentiated strategies were evident in two ways across the educators' lesson plans and reflections. First, many educators considered supports embedded in the instructional design of the lessons. Second, educators considered various supports that students could use throughout their work to give them access to the texts and content. Most educators considered instructional design in order to differentiate and provide adequate supports to all learners during their lessons.

One of the most commonly used differentiated strategies seen across the educators was small group instruction. The use of small groups was evident in lesson plans; however, the purpose and type of small groups varied. For example, some educators grouped students in an effort to ensure student engagement in the work and based this on student personality and considered who would work best together. This particular educator stated:

> Deciding how to group students ahead of time is a strategy that can markedly affect students' participation in this lesson. Thinking carefully about which students work well together and which do not can make today's lesson and the series of lessons to follow work more smoothly.

Though they did not have extensive knowledge on many of the students' reading abilities and levels during their short amount of time in the classrooms, the educators also considered students abilities when grouping them. The educators used resources such as NEWSELA to provide differentiated texts to students on the same topic. With this tool, they could provide the same article at various reading levels. Additionally, educators used small groups to provide scaffolded instruction on top of what was provided in the whole group. One educator mentioned, "I worked with one small group and provided additional explicit instruction on the literacy strategy to make sure they understood and grasped the new content."

Similar to their use of small groups, many educators utilized partner work as a strategy to provide support to students. As mentioned earlier, oftentimes, partner work was used to provide opportunities for students to share their ideas with a peer before sharing with the whole group. Others planned partner work to share reading responsibility and facilitate discussions over various texts. For example, an educator noted, "Students will work in pairs and read three different excerpts that look at the impact of anti- Semitic myths today."

Finally, educators used partner work to support struggling readers and enhance engagement and access to the text. As this educator stated, "Students worked with a partner or in a small group which I had hoped would help with engagement." While another said that partner-based pre-work allowed students "to learn information from their peers prior to being introduced to the new vocabulary."

Another consideration for the instructional design was the use of Universal Design for Learning principles. All three principles, including multiple means of representation, engagement, and expression, were considered throughout lessons. For example, when providing new information to the students, educators used a variety of modalities. As this educator noted, "I decided to use a multimodal approach to implement this lesson, I showed a video on sound energy, a word bank, and pictures to increases vocabulary and reading skills." When considering engagement, the educators tried to include ways to bring in student interest and draw on connections to their lives. Some educators gave students the option to respond in a variety of ways, including verbally or written.

The educators also planned for instructional supports that could be utilized by all students during the lessons. While a variety was used, there were a few that were frequently seen. One of the most common was the use of sentence starters, which were used for different purposes. For example, at times, they were used to help students when they were writing about the topics provided. This was evident in either open-ended response assignments such as providing students with a sentence starter as a topic sentence "In the film of Ancient Egypt, historians have learned a great deal about the building of the pyramids . . .," or embedded into graphic organizers such as "The article is referring to . . ." or "The article is discussing the idea that. . . ." To set students up for success during discussions, the educators would also provide students with sentence stem starter sheets. These could be more general, such as "I agree because. . . ., I disagree because . . .," or more specifically related to the content.

Another common instructional support used as a differentiated strategy across the lesson was the use of visual supports. Educators cited a variety of visual supports ranging from visual images to represent vocabulary terms to the use of short video clips to engage students and demonstrate concepts within the lesson. Similar to other educators, this educator indicated that "I used visuals to help the students see . . . how the body system worked." These various visual tools were often cited in relation to the focus learners identified needs. For example, one reflection talked about the focus learner's visual needs, and one way the educator was able to clarify the meaning of a passage was that they "drew out my understanding of some of the key terms such as barrier, and bigotry."

Accommodations

Aside from differentiated supports for groups of students, the educators utilized accommodations to help individual learners. Much of the evidence for specific accommodations for individual students was evident through the educators' plans to work directly with individual students on the content. As this educator noted, "I will be working with my focus learner while they complete their Frayer Model, prompting them as they work through the task. They will also have access to the Chromebooks if to look up synonyms or examples for the vocabulary word they choose."

When considering the individual needs, many educators knew that their students struggled with reading comprehension and that the complexity of the text would hinder their understanding of the content. Thus, they considered several strategies to help individual students. One frequent strategy that was planned was "chunking the text." "I believe that in breaking down and chunking direct instruction, it allows the group of target students to better grasp and engage in the material as the content is not overwhelming in volume," explained one of the educators.

Reflecting on Instruction

Educators were asked to engage in the reflection process in order to discuss various aspects of the lesson implementation, including student engagement, use of explicit instruction, implementation of literacy strategies, alignment with student needs, and student success in the lesson. Themes emerged relating to how educators determined if lessons were successful or not, both within the lesson and after the lesson. In addition, themes emerged regarding the levels of accountability that educators took related to the perceived success or perceived failure of lessons.

Within the lesson

Educators first showed evidence of evaluation of the lesson's success as they reflected on their own actions within the lesson and often indicated that they recognized an individual or group need that they had not anticipated and made specific shifts or changes in the moment to respond to that need. These shifts and changes were typically based on at least one form of informal evaluation of the lesson's success in which the educator engaged while teaching the lesson. Educators commonly cited reviewing student work, observation, class discussion, student engagement or lack of, and behavioral management needs as sources of data that caused them to initiate some sort of change. One educator indicated informal data were used to implement a change in the pacing of an instructional film:

> While watching the film, it was my goal to check in with the students every ten minutes, for understanding. However, after I had checked in with the class twice, I realized that the students were missing significant details. After the first twenty minutes, I would pause the movie every time something pertinent was stated and ask "what just happened?" to ensure the students understood what was going on in the film.

Another educator cited a shift in reading responsibility within the lesson, "I started to lose their attention; I decided that me reading the entire text would be more effective. . . . I would engage them by asking more questions to review the information I had read from the text."

After the lesson

Educators next showed evidence of evaluation of the lesson's success as they reflected on either formal or informal data after the lesson. Some educators' reflections included formal data that provided a clear measurement of student mastery of a learning goal. Two examples of educators using data to determine the success of their lessons are as follows: "80% related fiction to reality, 75% explained author's purpose, 40% utilized textual support," and "within five lessons my students ended up going from scoring 2/19 and 3/19 on short-answer assessments on the structure and composition of Illinois' legislative and executive branches of government to both scoring over 90% on that body of material." Each quote directly related to the lesson's learning objective and provided data from the assessment named on the lesson plan.

Other educators evaluated the success of their lessons based on various informal data sources. Examples of informal data that educators used included reviewing student work, analyzing class discussion, or teacher observation from the lesson. Educators named an assessment on the lesson plan that was submitted for the class. The content of the assessments often varied. Some focused more on the literacy aspect of the lesson, and others focused more on the content knowledge that was expected for students to learn. Assessments rarely linked the two pieces in order to evaluate student mastery, highlighting the complexity of providing instruction in an inclusive, content literacy course.

A majority of educators reflected specifically on the strengths, needs, and accomplishments of their target learners. Their reflections showed examples of an individualized student view and often made clear connections to the pre-lesson student description, as this educator noted, "Regarding my two focus special needs students, I found that they were really engaged in this activity. . . . The accommodations of giving them concrete, written directions, fewer memory pairs, and maintaining proximity to them helped keep them on track." In addition, the reflections on formal, informal, or individual students largely showed a clear connection to the learning goal and high levels of alignment.

While many of the educators used either formal or informal sources to evaluate the success of the lesson, others provided a reflection based on opinion. Some focused on the students' opinions of the lesson. For example, educators made comments such as, "[The students] expressed satisfaction with my performance," or "They clapped for me at the end and congratulated me on my first ever student teaching experience." Others focused on their own feelings of how the lesson went, as this educator indicated, "I was very satisfied with this science lesson and felt that the students gained a lot of knowledge."

Typically, where educator's reflections were lacking, their lesson plans also lacked clarity and detail. In general, as lesson plans were more explicit, reflections were as well. Educators who did not have that data and detail within their reflections most often cited student engagement as evidence as this educator did, "The students I observed seemed engaged with the reading and writing associated with the lesson." These reflections were absent of a clear connection to the learning goal.

Accountability for the lesson's success

Within the lesson reflection, educators often indicated that one or more components within the lesson did not go as they had hoped or planned. During this portion of reflections, varying levels of accountability were observed by educators. Some educators took responsibility, admitted fault, or discussed a missed opportunity. For example, "The next time I use a discussion web, I intend to introduce it, model its usage, and hold a practice argument before asking students to even think about filling one out." Another educator indicated an important lesson:

> I learned that I did not model enough and that I was so nervous I went kind of fast explaining the activities and that I was not ready to deal with the unexpected since I was so focused on what I needed to get through rather than being in the moment.

Finally, several educators took responsibility for the lesson upon their own preparation, as did this educator:

> What I learned about my literacy instruction from implementing this lesson is that with any lesson, the more comfortable you are with the lesson, the better you are equipped to teach. I felt like I should have gone over the lesson more before trying to teach it.

A smaller number of educators seemed to shift the focus of the error to unlucky situations, actions, or inactions of other adults or issues with student's abilities, moods, or schedules (common areas of concern for a first-year teacher). For example, one educator cited a behavioral situation, "Close to the end of the lesson, one student began making faces at another student sitting directly across from him, which prompted the other student to get upset and tell on the first student who was making the faces." Another educator indicated that the focus learner's motivation was a major problem in the lesson, "My focus learner, did not want to complete any work independently and did not try at all to think beyond what was already written." Finally, some educators struggled to manage the needs of all students in the inclusive setting:

> I noticed that many of the diverse learners were left in some way to fend for themselves and because of the pace they are left without understanding. . . . Although I wanted to get every student involved, I cannot because it takes away from instruction time.

These varied approaches to accountability for the lesson's success highlight the importance of lesson reflection and the personal and complex nature of a special educators' instruction within inclusive content classes.

Complexity of Planning Interdisciplinary Lessons

The educators demonstrated that planning for integrated lessons that include developing content through literacy is a complex process that requires a lot of skills and knowledge related to both subject areas (literacy and content). Some of the most complex areas of lesson planning that were evident for preservice educators included aligning standards, objectives, and assessments; integrating literacy into content areas; and meeting the individual needs of students in these inclusive classrooms.

Aligning standards, objectives, and assessments

The most difficult area for educators in terms of planning their lessons was demonstrating alignment between the standards, objectives, and assessments to one another and to the instructional sequence and activities. Across almost every preservice special educator, the alignment was either not evident or loosely aligned. There were a few common mistakes made across teachers. The language between standards and objectives were loosely aligned, such as one educator choose the core standard, "Compare the point of view of two or more authors . . .," yet the language in the written objective stated, "Identify figurative language in a text."

In addition, educators selected content standards; however, the language was rarely used in the lesson objectives to anchor the lesson. Oftentimes, the planned assessment did not accurately measure the skills identified in the objectives and standards. For example, an educator stated that the objectives for the lesson were to "compare and contrast. . . . illustrate . . ., and identify." However, the planned assessment simply stated, "Students will engage in an in-class discussion." Finally, educators would often select up to four to five core standards for each lesson; however, more than half were not evident in the objectives, assessments, or instructional activities planned.

Integrating literacy into content area

Though there was a selection of evidence-based practices that support literacy development and content area knowledge, many educators struggled to align the two sets of standards and instructional practices for a meaningful integrated lesson plan. For example, oftentimes, when referring to the literacy strategy they planned to use, educators mentioned that they would integrate the use of explicit strategy instruction; however, there were many misconceptions related to explicit instruction. Thus, oftentimes, they modeled how to complete a science experiment or the steps to an activity, and they called that explicit strategy instruction.

An example statement from one educator that was a similar reflection across many was, "I know I used explicit instruction because the students knew what to do to complete the task." Other times, at the beginning of their lesson plans, the educators would describe a specific literacy strategy they were planning to use, such as QAR (Question-Answer, Relationship) or SQ3R (Survey, Question, Read/Recite/Review); however, there was limited to no evidence of a direct integration within the lesson; as such, there were many statements like, "Students will complete a QAR," but no additional detail to show the connection between the content and the strategy.

Meeting the individual needs of students

As discussed earlier, many of the educators considered the needs of individual students who either had disabilities or reading difficulties, by planning various support tools. Though some seemed to be intentional, it also appeared that educators were selecting supports from a generic list and did not consider the individual needs of the students. Examples of individualized support for students included considering reading levels, for example, one educator in an eighth-grade classroom specifically stated, "The student reads at a 4th-grade level; therefore, they will be provided with a modified version of the text to provide them access to the content." While more generic supports simply stated, "The students will receive highlighters," or "I will check in with the student every 5 minutes," in these cases, it was unclear their reasoning for the decisions.

DISCUSSION

As we conducted the content analysis of lesson plans and reflections from the course, it was evident from our findings that our preservice special educators focused a great deal on how to teach new content using literacy strategies. Specifically, they utilized a variety of evidence-based practices, such as explicit instruction to model reading to learn content area material. Across most preservice special educators, there was evidence of using a variety of graphic organizers to assist students in understanding the information in the class, and they also considered the prior knowledge of students by asking many questions and engaging in short activities to build background knowledge primarily through vocabulary development.

Finally, through this experiential experience, it was clear that the preservice special educators were not only tapping into what they had learned about supporting students with disabilities, but they were also knowledgeable on how to use this information within content area classes (Amolloh, Wanjiru, & Lilian, 2018). This experiential experience increased the amount of time that our preservice special educators engaged directly with students with disabilities in a real-world setting, which assisted them in making connections between the information learned in their class and their ability to apply this learning with students with disabilities (Leko et al., 2015).

This experience also made it clear to all how complex it is for preservice special educators to consider and manage all aspects of instructing students with disabilities in inclusive content area classes. Not only did preservice special educators have to have knowledge of the subject area, but they also needed to make decisions on what literacy practices or strategies would work best for the materials used in class while taking into consideration the literacy needs of the students and the lesson focus the content area teacher emphasized.

Due to the complexity of teaching students with disabilities, these types of experiential experiences need to be integrated into all special education teacher education programs if we want our preservice special educators to successfully transition into teaching, particularly in inclusive classes. As teacher educators, we must identify opportunities for purposeful practice throughout the teacher education program to facilitate the development of their teaching skills and learn to negotiate their varied responsibilities (Sayeski et al., 2019).

IMPLICATIONS

Our review of preservice special educators' assignments relating to their experiential experiences leads us to a few implications for our special education teacher education program.

As teacher educators, we know that preservice special educators not only need to have multiple exposures to the content they are learning, but they also need to have opportunities to actively engage in using this knowledge as they work directly with students with disabilities (Brown, Roediger, & McDaniel, 2014). Therefore, it is key that they participate in structured field experiences, such as this experiential experience in a content area class, prior to student teaching, since it is important for their development as teachers.

As we know, this type of meaningful practice using experiential learning experiences in instructing students with disabilities can be incorporated in early coursework (Hughes & Braun, 2019; Sayeski et al., 2019). Thus, we suggest that teacher educators create structured experiences in each course in their program, as we are doing ourselves, that allow preservice special educators to not solely observe teachers and classrooms, but that these experiences provide opportunities to work directly with students to facilitate the development of their instructional skills from the very start of the teacher education program.

As teacher educators integrate these structured experiential experiences into all the courses, it allows the preservice special educator to apply the knowledge from their coursework through their engagement with students with disabilities in a variety of situations and settings, which allow them to enhance their teaching practices and prepare for the multiple roles and responsibilities that special educators experience. Although preservice special educators may struggle in some aspects of the experience, as our students did, these experiential experiences are a valuable component of the teacher education program.

Although experiential experiences can enhance a preservice special educators' instruction, it is important that these experiences are designed to provide them with ongoing feedback from peers, teachers, and faculty. This feedback on their instruction and interactions with students assists preservice special educators in their choice of instructional practices and strategies in real time. Typically, this type of performance feedback is built into the student teaching experience (Cornelius & Nagro, 2014); however, it is imperative that we also include this process in early field experiences which will allow preservice special educators to not only reflect on their own instruction, but it also provides avenues for them to receive feedback from multiple individuals.

However, unlike during student teaching, most of these early experiential experiences are linked to courses that may not have a university supervisor overseeing it. Therefore, it is key that faculty who are teaching the classes incorporate a systematic cycle of practice and feedback for their students, since we know that multiple opportunities to practice and receive feedback enhance preservice special educators' acquisition and implementation of instructional practices (Peeples et al., 2018; Sayeski et al., 2019). Thus, as teacher educators, we need to create robust teacher education programs that provide preservice special educators not only with a strong knowledge base (Aşikcan, Pilten, & Kuralbayeva, 2018) and opportunities to practice meeting the needs of students with disabilities (Rock et al., 2016), but that it also gives them chances to reflect on their instruction and hear from others about their progress.

LIMITATIONS

This investigation is not without a few limitations. The study focused on capturing preservice special educators' perspectives during an experiential experience, so the data were solely self-reported rather than direct observations or interviews. Furthermore, the sample consisted solely of all the preservice special educators from our university taking the course; therefore, a comparison group was not available to tease out the impact of the course itself.

To extend this research, future investigations should consider adding an observation and interview component and include a comparison group. Information obtained from these types of studies can provide valuable information to teacher educators as they design teacher education programs to better prepare preservice special educators to meet the literacy needs of students with disabilities in inclusive content area classes.

CONCLUSION

Findings in this study revealed the complexity of preparing interdisciplinary lessons for students with disabilities and the need for preservice special educators to be given multiple opportunities to engage in this type of experiences within inclusive content area classes. Implications for special education teacher preparation programs are discussed. Effective special educators make a difference in the literacy development and achievement of students with disabilities.

Specifically, in content area classes, special educators can enhance vocabulary and comprehension of subjects such as science and social studies for students with disabilities. Thus, it is critical that preservice special educators are provided with quality teacher education programs that are inclusive of the knowledge and skill needed to effectively embed literacy strategies into content area instruction to meet the unique needs of students with disabilities. Successful teacher education programs engage preservice special educators in developing not only their knowledge of the theories behind best literacy practices, but they also provide opportunities for them to practice and reflect on their teaching throughout the program.

REFERENCES

Alger, C. L. (2007). Engaging student teachers' hearts and minds in the struggle to address (il) literacy in content area classrooms. *Journal of Adolescent & Adult Literacy*, *50*, 620–630. doi: 10.1598/JAAL.50.8.1

Aşikcan, M., Pilten, G., & Kuralbayeva, A. (2018). Investigation of reflecting reading comprehension strategies on teaching environment among preservice classroom teachers. *International Electronic Journal of Elementary Education*, *10*(4), 397–405.

Amolloh, O. P., Wanjiru, K. G., & Lilian, G. K. (2018). Work-based learning, procedural knowledge, and teacher trainee preparedness towards teaching practice at the University of Nairobi, Kenya. *International Journal of Learning, Teaching and Educational Research*, *17*(3), 96–110.

Berg, J. L., & Wehby, J. (2013). Preteaching strategies to improve student learning in content area classes. *Intervention in School and Clinic*, *49*(1), 14–20. https://doi.org/10.1177/1053451213480029

Bohon, L. L., McKelvey, S., Rhodes, J. A., & Robnolt, V. J. (2017). Training for content teachers of English Language Learners: using experiential learning to improve instruction. *Teacher Development*, *21*(5), 609–634. doi: 10.1080/13664530.2016.1277256

Boyle, J. R., Forchelli, G. A., & Cariss, K. (2015). Notetaking interventions to assist students with disabilities in content area classes. *Preventing School Failure: Alternative Education for Children and Youth*, *59*(3), 186–195.

Brown, P. C., Roediger, H. L., & McDaniel, M. A. (2014). *Make it stick: The science of successful learning*. Boston, MA: Belknap Press.

Brownell, M. T., Sindelar, P. T., Kiely, M. T., & Danielson, L. C. (2010). Special education teacher quality and preparation: Exposing foundations, constructing a new model. *Exceptional Children, 76,* 357–377. https://doi.org/10.1177/0014402 91007600307

Castles, A., Rastle, K., & Nation, K. (2018). Ending the reading wars: Reading acquisition from novice to expert. *Psychological Science in the Public Interest, 19*(1), 5–51. https://doi.org/10.1177/1529100618772271

Ciampa, K. (2017). Building bridges between technology and content literacy in special education: Lessons learned from special educators' use of integrated technology and perceived benefits for students. *Literacy Research and Instruction, 56*(2), 85–113.doi: 10.1080/19388071.2017.1280863

Cornelius, K. E., & Nagro, S. A. (2014). Evaluating the evidence base of performance feedback in preservice special education teacher training. *Teacher Education and Special Education, 37,* 133–146. https://doi.org/10.1177/0888406414521837

DeGraff, T. L., Schmidt, C. M., & Waddell, J. H. (2015). Field-based teacher education in literacy: Preparing teachers in real classroom contexts. *Teaching Education, 26,* 366–382. https://doi.org/10.1080/10476210.2015.1034677

Fang, Z. (2014). Preparing content area teachers for disciplinary literacy instruction: The role of literacy teacher educators. *Journal of Adolescent & Adult Literacy, 57,* 444–448.doi: 10.1002/jaal.269

Fenty, N. S., & Brydon, M. (2017). Integrating literacy and the content curriculum to support diverse learners. *Learning Disabilities: A Contemporary Journal, 15,* 225–238.

Fisher, D., & Frey, N. (2015). Revisiting content area literacy instruction. *Principal Leadership, 15,* 54–57.

Helfrich S. R., & Bean, R. M. (2011). What matters: Preparing teachers of reading. *Reading Horizons, 50,* 241–262.

Hughes, M. T., & Braun, G., (2019). Practice makes perfect: Enhancing preservice special educators' literacy instruction through experiential learning experiences. *International Electronic Journal for Elementary Education, 12,* 93–101.

Kane, S. (2017). *Literacy and learning in the content areas*. New York: Taylor & Francis.

Kohlbacher, F. (2006). The use of qualitative content analysis in case study research. *Sozialforschung/Forum: Qualitative Social Research, 7*(1), 1–30. Retrieved from https://www.qualitative-research.net/index.php/fqs/article/view/75/153

Lacina, J., & Block, C. C. (2011). What matters most in distinguished literacy teacher education programs? *Journal of Literacy Research, 43,* 319–351. https://doi.org/10.1177/1086296X11422033

Leko, M. M., Brownell, M. T., Sindelar, P. T., & Kiely, M. T. (2015). Envisioning the future of special education personnel preparation in a standards-based era. *Exceptional Children, 82,* 25–43. https://doi.org/10.1177/0014402915598782

Mandinach, E. B. (2012). A perfect time for data use: Using data-driven decision making to inform practice. *Educational Psychologist, 47*(2), 71–85.doi: 10.1080/00461520.2012.667064

Mayring, P. (2014). *Qualitative content analysis: Theoretical foundation, basic procedures and software solution*. Retrieved from Open Access Repository, Klagenfurt. http://nbn-resolving.de/urn:nbn:de:0168-ssoar-395173

Ness, M. K. (2016). Reading comprehension strategies in secondary content area classrooms: Teacher use of and attitudes towards reading comprehension instruction. *Reading Horizons: A Journal of Literacy and Language Arts, 49*, 58–84. doi: 10.1080/02568543.2010.531076

Parker-Katz, M., Hughes, M. T., & Lee, G. (2017). Preparing educators to teach literacy: Knowledge, dilemmas, and practices. In M. T. Hughes & E. Talbott (Eds.), *The Wiley Handbook of Diversity in Special Education* (pp. 467–492). Hoboken, NJ: Wiley-Blackwell.

Peeples, K. N., Hirsch, S. E., Gardner, S. J., Keeley, R. G., Sherrow, B. L., McKenzie, J. M., Randall, K. N., Romig, J. E., & Kennedy, M. J. (2018). Using multimedia instruction and performance feedback to improve preservice teachers' vocabulary instruction. *Teacher Education and Special Education, 42*(3), 227–245. https://doi.org/10.1177/0888406418801913

Poch, A. L., & Lembke, E. S. (2018). Promoting content knowledge of secondary students with learning disabilities through comprehension strategies. *Intervention in School and Clinic, 54*, 75–82. https://doi.org/10.1177/1053451218765238

Roberts, C. A., Tandy, J., Kim, S., & Meyer, N. (2019). Using content area literacy strategies during shared reading to increase comprehension of high school students with moderate intellectual disability on adapted science text. *Education and Training in Autism and Developmental Disabilities, 54*, 147–160.

Rock, M. L., Spooner, F., Nagro, S., Vasquez, E., Dunn, C., Leko, M., . . ., & Jones, J. L. (2016). 21st century change drivers: Considerations for constructing transformative models of special education teacher development. *Teacher Education and Special Education, 39*, 98–120. doi:10.1177/0888406416640634

Sayeski, K. L., Hamilton-Jones, B., Cutler, G., Earle, G. A., & Husney, L. (2019). The role of practice and feedback for developing teacher candidate's opportunities to respond expertise. *Teacher Education and Special Education, 42*(1), 18–35. doi: 10.1177/0888406417735876

Scruggs, T. E., Mastropieri, M. A., & Okolo, C. M. (2008). Science and social studies for students with disabilities. *Focus on Exceptional Children, 41*, 1–24. doi: 10.17161/fec.v41i2.6835

Shepherd, K. G., Fowler, S., McCormick, J., Wilson, C. L., & Morgan, D. (2016). The search for role clarity: Challenges and implications for special education teacher preparation. *Teacher Education and Special Education, 39*, 83–97. https://doi.org/10.1177/0888406416637904

Spear-Swerling, L. (2009). A literacy tutoring experience for prospective special educators and struggling second graders. *Journal of Learning Disabilities, 42*, 431–443. https://doi.org/10.1177/0022219409338738

Wozencroft, A. J., Pate, J. R., & Griffiths, H. K. (2015). Experiential learning and its impact on students' attitudes toward youth with disabilities. *Journal of Experiential Education, 38*(2), 129–143. https://doi.org/10.1177/1053825914524363

Chapter 5

What Do *They* Want to Know: Exploring What Preservice Teachers Want and Expect from Their Preparation Coursework

Rory P. Tannebaum

Teacher educators expect a great deal from their preservice teachers (PSTs). Beyond learning foundational methods for engaging students and managing classrooms, PSTs are also expected to incorporate into their pedagogical decision-making critical issues grounded in matters of race (Banks, 1993; Ladson-Billings, 1998), socioeconomic status and class (Kozol, 1991), sex and gender (Crocco, 2001), religion (McClain & Neilsen, 1997), and sexual orientation (Mayo, 2013).

This is in addition to understanding issues of accountability (Burroughs, Groce, Webeck, 2005), accommodations for students with special needs (Espin et al., 2001), the integration of new and consistently evolving technology (Berson et al., 2000), and amassing a large enough content knowledge to effectively teach one of the several content areas (if not more than one). Mastering any one of these components to "good" instruction could take years, yet those in teacher education often expect PSTs to gain a deep understanding of each of these components and place them within the larger context of effective teaching prior to entering into the classroom as novice educators.

What is perhaps most intriguing about this is that traditional PSTs must complete a great deal of general education requirements simply to graduate and participate in a range of extracurricular activities just to become marketable. In addition to all of this, these individuals must somehow maintain a social life during this critical time in their lives in which they are making new friends, learning about themselves, and living away from their families for the first time in their lives. In other words, the expectation for having the traditional PST master the frequently idealistic objectives put forth within scholarly journals and academic conferences may actually be too much for students to *truly* grasp within such a limited amount of time.

And though this certainly does not apply to every PST, many traditional college students have neither the time nor the motivation to truly delve into the issues that are at the very foundation of the work consistently being produced by academics within teacher education. Rather, the focus of the traditional PST is on learning engaging ways to teach content and practical ways for managing a classroom of students (certainly both of which are valuable skills to gain within a teacher preparation program). And though these two aims are not learned within a vacuum, PSTs often see them as the more "practical" knowledge to gain in a teacher education program.

This is not to say that the stated aims and objectives are not worthy (or even necessary) for PSTs to understand as they seek to become truly powerful and effective educators. Rather, these aims—as a collective outcome—are *essential* to providing K–12 students with the most effective and equity-based education as well as pushing the field forward into new and progressive areas of study. And, to the credit of those within academia, new and progressive research is being published and presented at an incredible pace.

Despite the critical nature of this research and the inarguably essential knowledge that it provides to scholars and teachers alike, one component in teacher education that is less explored is that of the perspectives of the traditional PST and what they want to know and learn before they enter into the classroom as novice educators (Clark & Byrnes, 2015). In this sense, the typical eighteen- to twenty-two-year-old aspiring teachers may differ in what they consider to be essential from the conversations and research occurring within higher education. If this is the case, it may be of interests for teacher education to re-evaluate both what it teaches to aspiring educators and how it is taught within teacher preparation programs. Given this aim, the following research questions were decided upon by the researcher and explored through a multiphased empirical study.

Research Questions

1. What knowledge and skills do PSTs value in their teacher preparation coursework?

   a. To what extent does this differ between PSTs within early childhood education (pre-K–2), elementary education (2–6), and secondary education (6–12)?

2. To what extent do PSTs enrolled in a Social Justice and Schooling course at a liberal arts college in the Northeast prioritize learning about principles of social justice in their teacher preparation coursework?

The purpose of the present empirical study was to attempt to answer these questions using a rigorous empirical approach seeking to understand the perspectives of thirty-eight PSTs.

THEORETICAL FRAMEWORK

This study is grounded in broad and critical ideas about the purposes of education as written about and discussed within academia for the past century. Such themes include—though certainly are not limited to—the aims of a democratic education, the goals of critical theory within the field of education, and the objective of developing PSTs into reflective, reform-oriented educators capable of overturning the status quo and effectively engaging their students through meaningful pedagogy. The work of select authors within these areas sought to guide the research being conducted and will be briefly described within this section.

At the foundation of the current study were various broad and overarching theories about the connections between society and schools. Prominent scholars and their associated works guiding these theories included—though certainly were not limited to—Gutmann (1999), Parker (2003), and Dewey (1916). Though these works certainly provide varying perspectives, their underlying themes of using the American school system to develop students into capable and participatory citizens served as a strong foundation for this research and the context in which the study occurred.

Like most scholarship within the field of education, the researcher of the study operated under the assumption that schools are meant to prepare students to become active and informed citizens. Schools, therefore, are meant to provide students with equal opportunities for growth and achievement both throughout and after graduation (Dewey, 1916; Gutmann, 1999).

More specific to the principles of creating effective citizens was the topic of critical theories within the field of education. This study was situated within broad ideas and scholarship of several prominent authors including —though not limited to—Ladson-Billings (1998), Banks (1993), and Delpit (2006). Broadly speaking, the notion that the school should be a place for teachers and students to work together to collectively overturn the status quo and fight against injustices and inequities was used as a lens in which to view the purposes of education. Because the course in which the study was situated emphasized topics of social justice and diversity, critical theories pertaining to equality and equity played a key role in the foundation of the study.

Both the broad aims of education and those that emphasize critical aims within the field were paired with underlying principles regarding what types of educators the field of teacher education seeks to create. In other words, the theoretical ideals underlying the broad aims of education were connected to the practical elements of what teachers who achieve these aims do within the K–12 classroom. Key authors and their underlying ideas helped to guide the research and provide a foundation when considering the extent to which the aims of the teacher education align with the aims of PSTs.

Though Darling-Hammond and Bransford (2007), Cochran-Smith (2005), Zeichner (2003) do differ in their approaches and aims, their underlying objectives of creating progressive, reflexive, and reform-oriented educators served as a guiding principle to the present study.

Collectively, the themes of what those within teacher education want students to know in terms of the purposes of education as well as the current practices occurring in the traditional teacher education program laid the foundation for exploring what PSTs want to know within their coursework. The aim, for that matter, was to use key theories within recent scholarship in teacher education to learn about the extent to which teacher educators have similar aims to PSTs.

LITERATURE REVIEW

Despite the seemingly important perspective of PSTs, a thorough literature review led to only one recent empirical study exploring what PSTs want to learn from their preparation programs. That study—conducted by Clark and Byrnes (2015)—found that millennial PSTs "saw themselves as accepting of differences, hesitant to learn about assessment, very impressed with their teaching abilities, but not highly skilled in their ability to provide critique and feedback" (p. 379).

Among other aims, Clark and Byrnes sought to explore how the PSTs who fall under the umbrella of the "millennials" term differ from novice educators of different generations. Ultimately, the authors found that the participants had differing capacities, interests, and goals than non-millennial PSTs. Not only were the participants more interested in the diverse backgrounds of their students and ways to adjust the curriculum accordingly, but they also found that their participants saw less value in teacher education than academia may assume.

This is not to say, however, that additional literature does not exist, detailing what PSTs want to learn from their coursework. For instance, there appears to be a significant amount of research detailing PSTs' understandings and perspectives of various topics in education that are deemed "critical" by educational scholars and theorists. Castro (2010), as an example, attempted to synthesize the research on what PSTs think about culturally diverse classrooms and the implications for millennial PSTs, reflecting a similar study conducted by Gomez (1993). In Castro's synthesis, it was discovered that PSTs' views toward diversity have begun to shift over the past two decades, but that several issues still exist in terms of how they think about issues of multicultural education.

Likewise, Garmon (2004) had studied how to change PSTs' beliefs about diversity in their own classroom (ultimately exploring six factors that led to positive multicultural development). More specifically, Ríos and Montecinos (1999) conducted a similar study with ethnically diverse PSTs, and Ross and Smith (1992) sought to understand how PSTs perceived and understood classroom diversity.

Additionally, there exists a great deal of literature exploring how preservice teachers think about their content - regardless of the grade level in which they intend on teaching. For instance, McGowen and Davis (2001) explored what elementary PSTs want to know in terms of mathematical content knowledge for the elementary classroom, offering multiple strategies for improving how PSTs learn about content that they want to "get right" when teaching. Similarly, Wilson, Cooney, and Stinson (2005) studied what nine high school teachers view as "good" mathematics teaching and how it develops. Mellado (1997) explored how PSTs think about the nature of science.

And Ross (1987) conducted a study not about social studies content but about what PSTs think about the social studies. Goldman and Grimbeek (2016) looked specifically at what PSTs want to know about puberty and sexuality education. The finding of this study reflected that of the previous studies in that it found the PSTs felt ill-prepared to teach this area and hoped for guidance on how to effectively teach it. Likewise, Şad and Göktaş (2014) assessed the perspectives of PSTs on using mobile phones and laptops as teaching tools within the K–12 classroom. More specific to practice, Zepeda and Ponticell (1998) sought to explore what PSTs want to know through their field experiences by studying 114 PSTs and their views on how they are supervised.

All of the previously listed literature—albeit extremely important in understanding how to best fix misconceptions—differ from the current study in that it does not focus on what PSTs want to know; rather, it asks what they know about what teacher educators want them to know. The difference in this research is the focus on perspective. Little research focuses specifically on the voice of PSTs and their general interests in learning and growth as PSTs. The current body of literature that exists focuses more heavily on inservice teachers or is content-specific and seeks to explore what PSTs want to know about specific content areas. This study attempts to take a step back and look at the perspectives of PSTs in a broader sense.

METHODS

This study was primarily grounded in qualitative methods of inquiry as a means to provide participants with an abstract space to vocalize their views on their teacher education program (Merriam, 1998; Stake, 1995; Yin, 2009). However, an activity producing a set of basic statistics was used in addition to the qualitative component as a means to verify findings from the qualitative methods employed. It would, however, be a mistake to categorize the present research as a mixed-methods study, as the statistics portion was neither used to guide the data nor used to provide definitive answers. The following section seeks to describe the methods used to answer the research questions guiding the study.

Participants

Participants were selected through convenience sampling (Merriam, 1998). Students in two sections of a course titled "Social Justice and Schooling" in the spring of 2017 were asked to volunteer to participate in the study. Of the forty-nine students who were asked to participate, forty-two agreed. The data of thirty-eight participants were included within the final data analysis of the study. The data of the four students who were not included in the final data involved one student who did not submit the required data and three students who did not intend on teaching after graduating. Each of the final thirty-eight participants was between the ages of eighteen and twenty-two and planned on working within the field of education upon graduation. Of the thirty-eight participants, eight intended on teaching within early childhood education, twenty-seven wanted to teach elementary-aged children, and three wanted to work at the secondary level.

Context

This study took place at a moderately sized, private, liberal arts Catholic school in the Northeastern region of the United States. The institution in which the study took place has an emphasis on Augustinian values which—among other focal points—seeks to emphasize the need for social justice, equitable treatment of all citizens, and reform-oriented action (aligning with many of the broad principles of a democratic education). The college—both within and outside of the teacher education department—seeks to blend components of social justice and experiential learning to assist in the development of action-oriented graduates who aim for change in society regardless of their major or postgraduate intentions.

The course in which the study took place, specifically, was a freshman-oriented course titled "Social Justice and Schooling," which explores how schools and society often reproduce social norms. Further, the course is meant to expose aspiring educators about ways in which schools and society function together to maintain the status quo and, in many ways, provide different forms of school based on students' race, socioeconomic status, sex, gender, religion, location, or one of any other number of traits. Finally, the course is meant to teach students to be advocates for social justice and social change.

Data Collection and Sources

Data for the present study were collected in two phases. The first phase involved students participating in a "ranking activity" in which they ranked nine topics in education based on their own interest. The second phase involved students responding to five open-ended questions. Both phases occurred in class and were completed on a voluntary basis. The ultimate goal—as will be described—was to synthesize the data from the two phases as a way to both increase the reliability and validity of the data (Miles & Huberman, 1994).

Phase I: Ranking activity

At the beginning of the study, participants were provided with a list of nine topics covered within their teacher preparation coursework (listed within the appendix of this chapter). Participants were asked to rank the topics based on interest and then send them back to the researcher who averaged out the rankings both across all thirty-eight participants and based on career ambitions. More specifically, "points" were assigned based on the rankings ranging from 9 to 1. For instance, if a student placed "engaging methods" at the top of their list, that topic then received "9 points." Whereas if the student put "technology" at the bottom of their list, that topic then received "1 point." The results of this activity can be viewed in table 5.1.

It should be noted that the topics presented to students are often not mutually exclusive and it could rightfully be argued that there exists overlap between several of the topics. However, the topics were isolated from one based on the required coursework of the participants (e.g., technology and methods were separated to represent a single course on effective pedagogy as well as another course specifically on using technology in the classroom). The findings presented will attempt to synthesize the rankings and find the overlap from this phase. In other words, the topics were isolated prior to the study being conducted, but the data collected from this phase were later synthesized for various themes and consistencies.

Table 5.1. Results from Phase I ("Ranking Activity")

All Participants (n = 38)		Early Childhood PSTs (n = 8)		Elementary PSTs (n = 27)		Secondary PSTs (n = 3)	
Points	Topic	Points	Topic	Points	Topic	Points	Topic
274 −0.16%	Methods	60 −0.16%	Methods	194 −0.14%	Methods	23 −0.17%	Content
225 −0.13%	Diversity	54 −0.15%	Child and Adolescent Development	167 −0.13%	Management	20 −0.15%	Methods
221 −0.13%	Content	43 −0.12%	Content	164 −0.13%	Diversity	19 −0.14%	Diversity
217 −0.13%	Management	42 −0.12%	Diversity	155 −0.13%	Content	18 −0.13%	Child and Adolescent Development
200 −0.17%	Child and Adolescent Development	41 −0.11%	Professionalism	137 −0.11%	Special Needs	15 −0.11%	Professionalism
185 −0.11%	Professionalism	39 −0.11%	Management	129 −0.11%	Professionalism	14 −0.10%	ELLs
184 −0.11%	Special Needs	37 −0.10%	Special needs	128 −0.11%	Child and Adolescent Development	10 −0.07%	Management
104 −0.06%	ELLs	25 −0.07%	Technology	71 .06%	ELLS	10 −0.07%	Special Needs
102 −0.06%	Technology	19 −0.05%	ELLS	70 −0.06%	Technology	6 −0.04%	Technology
Total points 1712		360		1215		135	

Notes: Engaging Methods for Teaching = "Methods," Issues of diversity, including race, class, gender, sex, socioeconomic status, and religion = "Diversity," Content Knowledge (science, social studies, math, etc.)—"Content," Classroom Management = "Management," Professionalism (resumes, faculty and staff meetings, working with colleagues, etc.) = "Professionalism," Incorporating Technology into the Classroom = "Technology," Working with Students who have special needs (e.g., modern and severe disabilities) = "Special Needs," Child and Adolescent Development (i.e., how students grow and think) = "Child and Adolescent Development," Effectively working with and teaching English language learners (ELLs) = "ELLs."

Phase II: Open-ended responses. Three weeks after phase I of the study, the researcher sent participants a document with five open-ended response questions regarding what they wanted and expected to learn within their teacher preparation coursework (these questions can be found within appendix A). These responses were paired with each participants' data from phase I of data collection and organized based on the question. This allowed the researcher to see themes based on both individual students and each specific question asked within phase II. The goal for this approach was to verify the statements collected and to provide multiple forms of data exploring multiple complex and abstract issues (Patton, 2002).

Data Analysis

The aim throughout data analysis was to effectively synthesize the data collected from phase I and phase II and, in doing so, expose themes that were well supported and consistently present within the data. To do this, the two sets of data were gradually explored and merged together using an open-coding form of analysis (Glaser, 1978). Ultimately, the data were organized in a way where the data could be viewed using a number of lenses including—though not limited to—the participants' majors, their ultimate goals after graduating, and across all thirty-eight participants, regardless of their ambitions. This was done by first placing the open-ended responses from phase II next to each individual students' data from phase I to provide a broad picture of each student's interests and expectations (and to increase validity and reliability) and to paint a broad picture of all the thirty-eight participants.

In other words, in an Excel Spreadsheet, each individual student had an assigned "row" showing how they ranked the nine topics from phase I as well as their responses to each open-ended question. Once this had been constructed, the researcher then explored the data looking for findings and color-coordinating the spreadsheet as various themes appeared to emerge. After this had been completed, the researcher then organized the students based on their ultimate career goals in an attempt to see if the findings differed based on the participants' interests in teaching at the early childhood, elementary, or secondary level. Ultimately, the aim throughout data analysis was to synthesize the data throughout various lenses and to discover consistent and evidence-supported themes that answered the aforementioned research questions.

Limitations

A primary limitation of the current study involved the idea that PSTs do not know what they should want to know until they have been exposed to such ideas. It is, understandably, difficult for PSTs to understand the knowledge and skills they would like to develop prior to spending time in the K–12 classroom or completing their coursework and being able to reflect on the gaps they have in their understanding of the field.

Likewise, the context in which the research took place could serve as a limitation to the current study. Because the study exclusively took place within a course titled "Social Justice and Schooling," it is easy to imagine how participants were impacted by both the content of the material and the purpose of the course. Participants, for that matter, may have responded differently in a class not grounded in issues of diversity and social justice.

Similarly, a third and final limitation to the study involved the participants enrolled in the course in which the study took place. Unfortunately, only three participants sought to teach at the secondary level and, therefore, the findings from their responses are less valid than those of the early childhood or elementary education majors. Though the three participants provided strong data that aligned heavily with those of the other PSTs, more secondary education majors would have helped to validate the findings specifically from this demographic.

FINDINGS

Several critical findings emerged throughout the data collection and analysis phases of the study. The five critical findings to the current research, however, were as follows: (1) PSTs want to learn engaging methods of teaching; (2) PSTs want to learn to "manage" and "control" a class; (3) diversity is important, depending on the type of data; (4) PSTs believe teaching is—to some extent—a "natural ability"; and (5) technology is not prioritized by PSTs. This section seeks to explore these findings and provide supporting evidence. Following this section, the discussion portion of the chapter will synthesize the findings and explore their meaning within the broad context of teacher preparation.

Finding I: PSTs Want to Learn Engaging Methods

Regardless of the source being used or the aims of the participants, it became clear early in the data collection and analysis portion of the study that the participants were most interested in learning about effective methods of teaching. Within the "ranking activity"—the first phase of the research— "engaging methods" earned 274 points (0.16 percent) across the thirty-eight participants' responses, while "issues of diversity" came in a distant second, earning 225 points (0.13 percent).

This sizable gap represents a clear interest of PSTs for learning how to teach students with engaging methods. More specifically—and as demonstrated in table 5.1—the participants majoring in early childhood education and elementary education ranked "methods" well ahead of the other topics, while the participants majoring in secondary education placed in just below their interest in learning about content.

Phase II of the study reflected similar interests. Across each of the four questions asked to the participants regarding what they wanted or expected to learn, countless comments were made regarding how to effectively teach using effective methods. The majority of these comments revolved around the idea of "engaging students," "getting students involved," "learning how to teach the content," or some other variation on those ideas. Again, regardless of participants' postgraduation ambitions, almost all of the thirty-eight participants made some mention of methods during phase II's data set.

It became clear throughout the data collection and analysis phases that participants—all PSTs—were interested in learning about how to teach students in an effective manner. Even while situated within the context of a course that is grounded in the theoretical side of education, the participants consistently noted their expectations and interests in learning about pedagogy that engages students.

Finding II: PSTs Want to Learn to "Manage" and "Control" a Class

Similar to finding I, PSTs have a clear interest in learning how to "manage" or "control" a class of K–12 students. Regardless of the data source being used or the grade level the participants intend on teaching, there was a consistent theme expressed from the participants about wanting and expecting to learn how to prevent behavioral issues. This finding aligned heavily with the practical emphasis seen in finding I where students—in a sense—viewed the theoretical and the practical components of their program as being somewhat separate and, when pressed, chose to focused on the latter of the two.

The open-ended responses made this clear in terms of the types of skills and knowledge the participants were interested in learning. Participants were asked in two separate questions both what they expected to learn from their teacher education program (broadly speaking) and what specific skills they wanted to learn. Within their short answer responses to these two questions, the thirty-eight participants mentioned some form of classroom "management" or "control" twenty-six times. Thirteen of these comments came from their expectations of what they thought they would learn, while the other thirteen came from the specific skills they wanted to learn. It should be noted that these mentions—all twenty-six of them—came from twenty separate participants (53 percent of the sampling).

This is noteworthy as over half of the participants mentioned their interest in learning how to manage their classroom without being prompted to do so.

Despite being able to write about literally any topic that they wanted to learn about, the responses were flooded with comments about "dealing with students," "classroom management," "managing a classroom," "hav[ing] good control," and "run[ning] a classroom." This was easily the most consistent theme within the qualitative responses and it largely reflected the ranking activity in which the participants also placed a great deal of weight on the value of learning about classroom management (as seen in table 5.1).

Finding III: Diversity in One Form of Data

An interesting finding within the data stemmed from the two different data sources. While the "ranking activity" demonstrated an interest of the participants in learning how to work with students from diverse backgrounds (reflecting the findings of Clark and Byrnes), the same could not be said about the open-ended response questions. Instead of focusing on students with diverse backgrounds, the open-ended responses rarely saw mentions of this topic. Rather, the open-ended responses focused heavily on the participants' interests in learning content knowledge and practical ways to teach.

This is clearer from the fact that all thirty-eight participants placed little—if any—emphasis on learning how to teach ELLs. Despite the emphasis on diversity in phase I of the research, the participants ranked this topic as their second-to-last topic of interest as a collective group. Despite having to take a class on social justice as well as one specifically on how to effectively teach ELLs, the participants of the study consistently ranked this topic as one that they neither had much interest in learning (this despite the fact that the majority of students in neighboring districts come from diverse backgrounds and speak a variety of languages).

Perhaps not incidentally, the three main references to students' diversity came from three participants of the study who were of nonwhite backgrounds (of the four who participated in the study). The three participants who made these comments—two of whom were African American and one who was of Hispanic descent—were the only three in the study to note that students of various backgrounds within their qualitative answers in phase II and that they need to be cognizant of this fact.

Finding IV: Teaching Is—To Some Extent—A "Natural Ability"

For better or worse, most of the participants of the study claimed that their ability to be an effective teacher was not contingent on them completing a teacher preparation program but, rather, simply having a natural talent. Within phase II of the research—the qualitative questionnaires—thirty-five of the thirty-eight participants answered the open-ended question of whether teaching is a "natural ability" and, if so, to what extent is this true. Of those thirty-five students, twenty-nine (0.83 percent) suggested that there is a component to teaching that some people are born with, while only six (0.17%) made a clear emphasis on the idea that effective pedagogy could be learned within teacher education and with experiences in K–12 classrooms.

This is not to say that they did not see value in their program, but that much of what they were learning was seen as seconded to an innate talent that they either have or do not have. Such a finding could mean that many PSTs see their experiences in a teacher preparation program as a way to get endorsed and licensed as opposed to a way to become an effective educator. In this sense, teacher preparation is seen more as a gateway to the classroom as opposed to a means to grow as an educator. It should be noted, however, that this is not the first study to come to this finding.

Clark and Byrnes (2015) similarly noted that "millennial preservice teachers in our study did not place a high value on teacher educators" (p. 392) and that oftentimes there appears a disconnect between the development of "good" teachers and teacher education (Walsh, Glaser, & Dunne-Wilcox, 2006). Such a finding being reaffirmed within this study, again, is not to say that there is no value in teacher education or the research conducted within the field. Rather, it is to say that, as Clark and Byrnes (2015) suggest, the field needs to become better at being more connected to PSTs and their own lives, styles of learning, and interests within the field.

Finding V: Technology Is Not Prioritized by PSTs

Despite the current emphasis on using technology in the K–12 classroom and the proliferation of both tangible technology and social media, the thirty-eight participants in this study placed little to no emphasis on learning how to use technology for their teaching (Berson et al., 2000; Şad & Göktaş, 2014). While it could be argued that technology falls under the umbrella of "engaging methods," there existed little evidence in either the qualitative or quantitative data to suggest that the participants wanted to learn about how to use technology within their pedagogy.

For instance, in three of the four categories within phase I of the research (all participants, early childhood education majors, elementary education majors, and secondary education majors), three of the four groups ranked technology as the topic they are least interested in and the fourth placed it as the second-to-last topic. In all four groups, the points assigned totaled to less than 0.06 percent of the possible points.

This was similarly seen within phase II of the study in which there was not a single reference across all thirty-eight participants about learning how to effectively incorporate and manipulate technology within the K–12 classroom. And, collectively, all thirty-eight participants only assigned 102 points out of a possible 1,712 points (0.06%), thus further showing a collective disinterest in learning about technology in the classroom—despite knowing an entire course of their program of study was dedicated to this topic.

It is reasonable to believe that the participants of the study—who all fell under the umbrella term of "millennials"—felt that they already understood how to use technology more so than their instructors. Given the current stigma in society about younger generations understanding technology and its application more than the previous generation, it is logical for the participants to believe that PSTs do not place much confidence in their instructors to teach them how to use technology.

DISCUSSION

The five findings of the present study collectively paint a picture of PSTs who are both interested in a range of topics and who differ in their priorities of what they want and expect to learn throughout their programs of study. What the findings of the study suggest is that PSTs are often interested in learning about the topics that they either saw their own teachers struggle with or that they saw their own teachers implement in class—reflecting Lortie's (1975) "apprenticeship of observation" theory. For instance, the lack of interest in learning how to use technology is a possible reflective of a generation of PSTs how did not see their own teachers effectively use technology.

And the participants' interest in learning classroom management is possibly grounded in years of watching their own teachers struggle to maintain a positive classroom setting. Though these ideas are speculative in nature, enough research exists discussing how educators teach the way they were taught and it is relatively logical to assume that those same educators want to learn how to teach in that way (Cox, 2014; Goodlad, 1982; McMillan, 1985; Owens, 2013).

This is also somewhat evident in the amount of attention the participants paid to ELLs. Perhaps due to their own experiences in K–12 education and the attention they saw dedicated to students learning English, the participants ranked learning how to teach ELLs in phase I quite low and made no mentions of them in pShase II—despite their being over 150 open-ended responses submitted in total. This, too, however could stem from the participants of the study predominantly attending private schools in relatively homogenous districts wherein they were not exposed to students from a variety of backgrounds.

Similarly, each group of participants—early childhood, elementary, and secondary majors—emphasized both how to teach K–12 students and the importance of learning the content they would need to know to be a competent educator. Such a finding reflects the notion that many PSTs are interested in the practical nature of their program. In other words, what they will need to know on the surface in order to be effective at teaching at the K–12 level. This is not to say that the participants were not interested in the abstract and theoretical knowledge underlying their curriculums, but that they were less interested in it at this point of their programs.

As the data and finding III suggest, however, issues of diversity and social justice are important to students. Despite only being consistent in one form of data (phase I), participants *did* show an interest in learning about social justice, diverse classroom, and ethical and reform-oriented pedagogy. The data representing this interest, however, were simply overshadowed by the interests the participants showed toward issues of management, content knowledge, and engaging forms of pedagogy.

CONCLUSION

Teacher education and the academics who make up the field consistently present and publish research that is cutting edge and intended to improve the experience of educators at all levels. However, this research can often appear disconnected from the views and interests of PSTs; whose voices are often removed from the conversation about what aspiring educators should know and be able to do by the time they graduate and enter into the classroom as novice teachers. In order to better serve PSTs, the field needs to conduct more research specifically on what PSTs know and want to learn from their teacher education programs. Doing so, ideally, will help connect what goes on within academia with the growth of new teachers who evolve with each generation.

It should be noted, however, that those in academia should not be expected to adjust their means and aims based on what a traditional college student may want to study, but it is difficult to envision the field progressing without taking into consideration what is valued by the PSTs who are seeking to become effective educators. Because of this, those in teacher education should seek to collaborate more with the PSTs they are educating and listening to their own expectations and interests prior to designing coursework and program models. Building such relationships and adjusting practice accordingly will help provide the traditional PST with a more cohesive and relatable experience and, ultimately, a more effective and open-minded K–12 educator.

Appendix A: Phase I—Ranking Activity

Social Justice and Schooling
Spring 2017

The following list is in absolutely no particular order. What I would like for you to do is "rearrange" the following topics into a new order that best represents which one you think is the most important to the least important. In other words, if you think learning "classroom management" is the most important thing to learn while in college, move that topic to the top of the list. Once you have completed this activity, please save this document as a Microsoft Word file and email it to the researcher.

Engaging Methods for Teaching
Issues of Diversity, Including Race, Class, Gender, Sex, Socioeconomic
    Status, Religion
Content Knowledge (Science, Social Studies, Math, etc.)
Classroom Management
Professionalism (Resumes, Faculty and Staff Meetings, Working with Col-
    leagues, etc.)
Incorporating Technology into the Classroom
Working with Students who have Special Needs (e.g., Modern and Severe
    Disabilities)
Child and Adolescent Development (i.e., How Students Grow and Think)
Effectively Working with and Teaching ELLs.

If I have forgotten any topic that you think is missing from this list, can you please write it in this space right here?

REFERENCES

Banks, J. A. (1993). Chapter 1: Multicultural education: Historical development, dimensions, and practice. *Review of Research in Education, 19*(1), 3–49. https://doi.org/10.3102/0091732X019001003

Berson, M., Diem, R., Hicks, D., Mason, C., Lee, J., & Dralle, T. (2000). Guidelines for using technology to prepare social studies teachers. *Contemporary Issues in Technology and Teacher Education, 1*(1), 107–116.

Burroughs, S., Groce, E., & Webeck, M. L. (2005). Social studies education in the age of testing and accountability. *Educational Measurement: Issues and Practice, 24*(3), 13–20. doi: 10.1111/j.1745-3992.2005.00015.x

Castro, A. J. (2010). Themes in the research on preservice teachers' views of cultural diversity implications for researching millennial preservice teachers. *Educational Researcher, 39*(3), 198–210. doi: 10.3102/0013189X10363819

Clark, S. K., & Byrnes, D. (2015). What millennial preservice teachers want to learn in their training. *Journal of Early Childhood Teacher Education, 36*, 379–395. https://doi.org/10.1080/10901027.2015.1100148

Cochran-Smith, M. (2005). The new teacher education: For better or for worse? *Educational Researcher, 34*(7), 3–17. https://doi.org/10.3102/0013189X034007003

Cox, S. E. (2014). Perceptions and influences behind teaching practices: Do teachers teach as they were taught? Doctoral Dissertation, Brigham Young University.

Crocco, M. S. (2001). The missing discourse about gender and sexuality in the social studies. *Theory into Practice, 40*(1), 65–71. doi: 10.1207/s15430421tip4001_10

Darling-Hammond, L., & Bransford, J. (2007). *Preparing teachers for a changing world: What teachers should learn and be able to do.* San Francisco, CA: Jossey-Bass.

Delpit, L. D. (2006). *Other people's children: Cultural conflict in the classroom.* New York: The New Press.

Dewey, J. (1916). *Democracy and education.* New York: MacMillan.

Espin, C. A., Busch, T. W., Shin, J., & Kruschiwtz, R. (2001). Curriculum-based measurement in the content areas: Validity of vocabulary-matching as an indicator of performance in social studies. *Learning Disabilities Research and Practice, 16*(3), 142–151. doi: 10.1177/1534508413489724

Garmon, M. A. (2004). Changing preservice teachers' attitudes/beliefs about diversity: What are the critical factors? *Journal of Teacher Education, 55*(3), 201–213. https://doi.org/10.1177/0022487104263080

Glaser, B. G. (1978). *Theoretical sensitivity: Advances in the methodology of grounded theory* (Vol. 2). Mill Valley, CA: Sociology Press.

Goldman, J. D., & Grimbeek, P. (2016). What do preservice teachers want to learn about puberty and sexuality education? An Australian perspective. *Pastoral Care in Education, 34*(4), 189–201.

Gomez, M. L. (1993). Prospective teachers' perspectives on teaching diverse children: A review with implications for teacher education and practice. *The Journal of Negro Education, 62*(4), 459–474.

Goodlad, J. I. (1982). Let's get on with the reconstruction. *Phi Delta Kappan, 64*(1), 19–20.

Gutmann, A. (1999). *Democratic education.* Princeton, NJ: Princeton University Press.

Kozol, J. (1991). *Save inequalities.* New York: Basic Books.

Ladson-Billings, G. (1998). Just what is critical race theory and what's it doing in a nice field like education? *International Journal of Qualitative Studies in Education, 11*(1), 7–24.doi: 10.1080/095183998236863

Lortie, D. (1975). *Schoolteacher: A sociological analysis.* Chicago, IL: University of Chicago Press.

Mayo Jr, J. B. (2013). Expanding the meaning of social education: What the social studies can learn from gay straight alliances. *Theory & Research in Social Education, 41*(3), 352–381. https://doi.org/10.1080/00933104.2013.815489

McClain, J. E., & Nielsen, L. E. (1997). Religion in the elementary classroom— a laboratory approach. In *Meeting the standards: social studies readings for K-6 educators* (p. 102). National Council for the Social Studies.

McGowen, M. A., & Davis, G. E. (2001). What mathematical knowledge do pre-service elementary teachers value and remember? Proceedings of the 23rd Meeting of the North American Chapter of the International Conference on Psychology of Mathematics Education, Snowbird, Utah.

McMillan, C. (1985). *Do teachers teach as they are taught to teach?* Retrieved from http://www.americanreadingforum.org/Yearbooks/85_yearbook/pdf/27_McMillan.pdf

Mellado, V. (1997). Preservice teachers 'classroom practice and their conceptions of the nature of science. *Science & Education, 6*(4), 331–354. doi: 10.1023/A:1008 674102380

Merriam, S. (1998). Qualitative research and case study applications in education. San Francisco, CA: Jossey-Bass Publishing.

Miles, M. B., & Huberman, A. M. (1994). *Qualitative data analysis: An expanded sourcebook.* Thousand Oaks, CA: Sage Publications.

Owens, S. (2013). We teach how we've been taught: Expeditionary learning unshackling sustainability education in US public schools. *Journal of Sustainability Education, 5.* Retrieved from http://www.susted.com/wordpress/content/2013/06/

Parker, W. (2003). *Teaching democracy: Unity and diversity in public life.* New York: Teachers College Press.

Patton, M. Q. (Ed.). (2002). *Qualitative research & evaluation methods.* Thousand Oaks, CA: Sage Publications.

Ríos, F., & Montecinos, C. (1999). Advocating social justice and cultural affirmation: Ethnically diverse preservice teachers' perspectives on multicultural education. *Equity & Excellence, 32*(3), 66–76. https://doi.org/10.1080/1066568990320308

Ross, D. D., & Smith, W. (1992). Understanding preservice teachers' perspectives on diversity. *Journal of Teacher Education, 43*(2), 94–103. https://doi.org/10.1177/0022487192043002003

Ross, E. W. (1987). Teacher perspective development: A study of preservice social studies teachers. *Theory & Research in Social Education, 15*(4), 225–243. https://doi.org/10.1080/00933104.1987.10505547

Şad, S. N., & Göktaş, Ö. (2014). Preservice teachers' perceptions about using mobile phones and laptops in education as mobile learning tools. *British Journal of Educational Technology, 45*(4), 606–618. doi: 10.1111/bjet.12064

Stake, R. E. (1995). *The art of case study research.* Thousand Oaks, CA: Sage.

Walsh, K., Glaser, D., & Dunne-Wilcox, D. (2006). *What elementary teachers don't know about reading and what teacher preparation programs aren't teaching.* Washington, DC: National Council for Teacher Quality.

Wilson, P. S., Cooney, T. J., & Stinson, D. W. (2005). What constitutes good mathematics teaching and how it develops: Nine high school teachers' perspectives. *Journal of Mathematics Teacher Education, 8*(2), 83–111. doi: 10.1007/s10857-005-4796-7

Yin, R. K. (2009). *Case study research: Design and methods* (4th Ed.). Thousand Oaks, CA: Sage Publishing.

Zeichner, K. M. (2003). The adequacies and inadequacies of three current strategies to recruit, prepare, and retain the best teachers for all students. *Teachers College Record, 105*(3), 490–519.

Zepeda, S. J., & Ponticell, J. A. (1998). At cross-purposes: what do teachers need, want, and get from supervision? *Journal of Curriculum and Supervision, 14*(1), 68–87.

Chapter 6

Examining Coping Strategies of Preservice Teachers Completing Different Routes to Certification

Amanda A. Olsen and Roberta J. Scholes

According to the Teacher Follow-Up Survey developed by the National Center for Education Statistics, in the 2012–2013 school year, 8 percent of public school teachers have left the field, with 53 percent indicating that working conditions were better in their current position (Goldring, Taie, & Riddles, 2014). Research completed by the National Commission on Teaching and America's Future (NCTAF, 2012) has supported this finding by reporting that over 30 percent of the newly certified teachers leave the field within five years and over 300,000 veteran teachers leave the field yearly for retirement.

More recently, Redding and Henry (2018), found that approximately 4.6 percent teachers leave the field throughout the school year, amounting to 25 percent of the yearly turnover when accounting for within-year turnover. This "revolving door" of teachers has even been estimated to cost school districts in the United States over US$7.2 billion each year (NCTAF, 2012). It should be noted that large teacher turnover also affects veteran teachers who must devote additional time to provide continued support for newcomers. This added responsibility results in less time for professional development activities and class preparations (Kopkowski, 2008; Sass, Seal, & Martin, 2011).

A main influencer of teacher turnover rates is related to the high levels of stress experienced in the teaching profession (Herman, Hickmon-Rosa, & Reinke, 2017; Kyriacou, 2011). According to Sass, Seal, and Martin (2011), teachers experience many sources of stress resulting from poor student behavior, lack of social support from superiors and colleagues, workload stress, and job dissatisfaction. Furthermore, school districts are demanding that teachers are held more accountable (Clotfelter et al., 2004).

Not only are teachers held accountable for their students' performance on state tests, they are also responsible for their students' nutritional needs, social well-being, and emotional welfare (Lambert & McCarthy, 2006; Richards, 2012). With such a high number of stressors present in the teaching profession, numerous newly certified and veteran teachers are rapidly choosing to leave the field because they are not satisfied with their current job (Kopkowski, 2008; Olsen & Huang, 2019). Many of these individuals did not develop the appropriate coping skills to thrive in their environment (Howard & Johnson, 2004).

Teachers who choose to remain in the teaching profession are forced to develop coping strategies to deal with the increasing number of stressors present in the field (Paquette & Rieg, 2016). According to Lazarus (1966; 1981), coping is a process that requires an individual's effort in thought and action to manage demands the individual has appraised as overwhelming or stressful. This process is highly contextual, meaning it must change over time and across different environments to be effective (Folkman & Lazarus, 1985). How an individual appraises a stressful event can mediate that individual's response in that specific situation (Stoeber & Rennert, 2007).

Since the coping process is an individual's appraisal of a distressing event, it is not surprising that the coping process has a unique relationship with stress (Lazarus, 1966; 1981). Research conducted by Moritz et al. (2016) suggested that there are two different ways an individual can choose to cope with their stress. Adaptive coping strategies typically involve the individual taking some sort of action to decrease the stressor (Sirois & Kitner, 2015). Examples include actively attempting to avoid or prevent the stressor, seeking emotional support to cope with the stressor, or pursuing information to combat the stressor (Carver, Scheier, & Weintraub, 1989).

In contrast, maladaptive coping strategies focus on an individual's attempt to regain control during a stressful event, typically by avoiding rather than solving the problem (Lazarus & Folkman, 1984). Maladaptive coping strategies typically involve behavioral disengagement or giving up, mentally attempting to escape from the stressor through distractions, or denying that the stressor even exists (Carver, Scheier, & Weintraub, 1989).

How an individual applies adaptive and maladaptive coping strategies within their life has been linked to individual well-being (Lazarus & Folkman, 1984). Individuals who use adaptive coping methods tend to be more psychologically healthy (Duangdao & Roesch, 2008; Moskowitz et al., 2009; Woloshyn & Savage, 2018), with individuals who use more maladaptive coping methods typically facing more negative outcomes such as anxiety and depression (Moskowitz et al., 2009; Roesch et al., 2005). These dynamically different outcomes demonstrate the importance of learning and implementing adaptive coping strategies.

Studies have shown that the development and use of adaptive coping strategies is instrumental in decreasing teacher stress and reducing attrition within the education field (Chang, 2013; Faulk, Gloria, & Steinhard, 2012). For example, teachers reported a greater sense of personal accomplishment when they engaged in adaptive coping methods (Mitchell & Hastings, 2001). In addition, others were found to display happier emotions and partake in more positive coping strategies such as reframing situations (Fredrickson & Joiner, 2002; Moskowitz et al., 1996; Ntoumanis & Biddle, 1998). These results were especially true when teachers believed that they could adapt to be in control of a stressful situation and could meet the demands of the classroom (Taylor et al., 2016).

However, not all teachers develop adaptive coping strategies. Some teachers who are unable to manage the many demands of the classroom develop maladaptive coping strategies (Faulk, Gloria, & Steinhard, 2012). This could have negative consequences because teachers who have a tendency to utilize maladaptive coping strategies were likely to burnout more quickly (Hastings & Brown, 2002). Negative emotions were also linked to an increase in maladaptive coping strategies such as behavioral disengagement (Ntoumanis & Biddle, 1998). When teachers do not believe that they can control their professional environment, they are more likely to fall victim to these maladaptive coping strategies and experience negative outcomes (Taylor et al., 2016).

It should be noted that while current studies have only examined the coping strategies used by certified teachers, it is equally important to understand the coping strategies implemented by preservice teachers (Clunies-Ross, Little, & Kienhuis, 2008). This is because if preservice teachers are already using maladaptive coping strategies before they enter the field, it is possible that they will be more likely to burnout once they become certified educators (Hasting & Brown, 2002). In addition to analyzing preservice teachers, certification route could also contribute to whether preservice teachers develop adaptive or maladaptive coping strategies.

Therefore, the purpose of this study is to determine whether preservice teachers taking different routes to certification engage in more adaptive or maladaptive coping styles, specifically comparing the traditional teacher certification route against two nontraditional certification routes. Hopefully by understanding the coping strategies of preservice teachers taking different routes to certification, changes to encourage the development of adaptive coping strategies in teacher education programs can be implemented to help avoid preventable teacher attrition.

For this study, the researchers predicted that the undergraduate students would display more maladaptive coping strategies compared to the two graduate student groups due to possible confounding variables such as age, level of maturity, and lack of life experiences. This could be problematic because if undergraduate preservice teachers are already using maladaptive coping strategies during their certification program, it is logical to believe that these individuals will be at a higher risk to burnout once they enter the field.

METHOD AND DESIGN

The research design for this study was a three-group, cross-sectional survey design, using a general linear model, one-way fixed-effect multivariate analysis of variance (MANOVA). To test the assumptions of a MANOVA, skewness and visual inspections of histograms were used to test for normality and Box's M was conducted to test for homogeneity of variance. To investigate group differences, the Games–Howell *post-hoc* was applied since there was a doubt that the population variances were equal (Field, 2018).

The effect sizes were measured with partial eta squared (η^2). The independent variable was group, specifically undergraduates, and the two unique graduate certification routes. The dependent variables were nine scales of the Cope Instrument (Carver, Scheier, & Weintraub, 1989). The results were considered significant at the $p < 0.05$ level.

Participants

The participants in this study were three different samples of preservice teachers, which were operationally defined by the researchers as those who have not been an instructor of record in the classroom. These different samples included students enrolled in the Fellows Program, the SMAR^{2}T Program, and a sophomore undergraduate education class. The Fellows Program participants comprised graduate students who completed their undergraduate degree and finished their student teaching but had never been an instructor of record.

The SMAR^{2}T Program participants were enrolled in an accelerated master's program, where the students were working toward certification for grades six to twelve in mathematics or science. Students from the SMAR^{2}T Program had never been student-taught or been an instructor of record in the classroom. Finally, the undergraduate education class comprised sophomore students who have never been student-taught or been an instructor of record. It should also be noted that not all undergraduate students would graduate from the teacher education program and pursue a career in teaching. For further explanation of the differences between the three groups of participants, see table 6.1.

A total of 201 people were recruited to participate in this study. About 20 percent of the participants identified as males and 80 percent identified as females. A majority of the participants identified as white (93 percent), with

Table 6.1. Demographic Information about the Sample Populations

Demographic Information	Undergraduates	SMAR²T Program	Fellows Program
Age	Sophomores in College	1–5 Years Removed from College	Recent College Graduates
Degree Pursuing	Bachelor's Degree	Master's Degree	Master's Degree
Teaching Experience	Field Experience (16 hours)	Field Experience (16 hours)	Multiple Field Experiences, Including Student Teaching
Unsupervised Teaching in the Classroom	None	None	Minimal through Student Teaching

the remaining participants identifying as either African American, Latinx, Asian, or Other (7 percent). Finally, the ages of the participants were varied, ranging from age eighteen to age thirty-seven, although a majority identified as age twenty-three or younger (90 percent).

All participants were enrolled in the teacher education program at a large research-intensive Midwestern university in the United States. The teacher education program at this university offers a variety of standards-based programs that lead to both initial and advanced teacher certification. All participants were striving to become certified or had been certified in a variety of areas, including early childhood, elementary, middle school, and secondary education. Participants volunteered at the request of the researchers and were not compensated monetarily.

Materials

The survey used in this study was the Cope Instrument, developed by Carver, Scheier and Weintraub (1989). The original, sixty-item, self-report questionnaire had fourteen different scales that were classified into two categories, adaptive and maladaptive. This instrument was originally validated through multiple pilot studies using college undergraduate students.

In the original instrument, the adaptive coping scales included: the Active Coping Scale ($\alpha = 0.62$), which asked questions like, "I concentrate my efforts on doing something about it"; the Planning Scale ($\alpha = 0.80$), which asked questions like, "I make a plan of action"; the Suppression of Competing Activities Scale ($\alpha = 0.68$), which asked questions like, "I keep myself from getting distracted by other thoughts or activities"; the Restraint Coping Scale ($\alpha = 0.72$), which asked questions like, "I restrain myself from doing anything too quickly"; the Seeking Social Support for Instrumental Reasons

Scale ($\alpha = 0.75$), which asked questions like, "I try to get advice from some-one about what to do"; the Seeking Social Support for Emotional Reasons Scale ($\alpha = 0.85$), which asked questions like, "I discuss my feelings with someone"; the Turning to Religion Scale ($\alpha = 0.92$), which asked questions like, "I put my trust in God"; the Positive Reinterpretation and Growth Scale ($\alpha = 0.68$), which asked questions like, "I try to grow as a person as a result of the experience"; and finally the Acceptance Scale ($\alpha = 0.65$), which asked questions like, "I get used to the idea that it happened" (Carver, Scheier, & Weintraub, 1989).

In addition to the adaptive cope scales, there were also five maladaptive cope scales. These scales included: the Focusing On and Venting of Emotions Scale ($\alpha = 0.77$), which asked questions like, "I get upset and let my emotions out"; the Behavioral Disengagement or Helplessness Scale ($\alpha = 0.63$), which asked questions like, "I admit to myself that I can't deal with it, and quit try-ing"; the Mental Disengagement Scale ($\alpha = 0.45$), which asked questions like, "I turn to work or other substitute activities to take my mind off things"; the Denial Scale ($\alpha = 0.71$), which asked the individual questions like, "I refuse to believe that it has happened"; and the Alcohol-Drug Disengagement Scale, which asked questions like, "I use drugs or alcohol to make myself feel bet-ter" (Carver, Scheier, & Weintraub, 1989). Due to only one question being asked on the Alcohol-Drug Disengagement Scale, alpha was not reported in the original scale.

For this study, the Cope Instrument was modified. The researchers decided not to include the Acceptance ($r_s = 0.07$) and Focus On and Venting of Emo-tions ($r_s = 0.16$) Scales. The Acceptance Scale was excluded because there was no strong inverse correlation relationship with the Denial Scale. The weakness of this correlation demonstrated that there might have been a con-ceptual flaw within the design of the instrument (Carver, Scheier, & Wein-traub, 1989). The Denial Scale ($\alpha = 0.71$) was used instead of the Acceptance Scale ($\alpha = 0.65$), due to its higher alpha level. The Focus On and Venting of Emotions Scale ($\alpha = 0.77$) was also not included because Carver, Scheier, and Weintraub found this scale of a "questionable value" (Carver, Scheier, & Weintraub, 1989, p. 273).

This is because the Focus On and Venting of Emotions Scale was inversely correlated with the Denial Scale, Behavioral Disengagement Scale, Mental Disengagement Scale, and the Alcohol-Drug Disengagement Scale. This inverse correlation was odd because Focus On and Venting of Emotions should have been related to the other maladaptive coping strategies. Due to these issues, the Acceptance Scale and Focus On and Venting of Emotions Scale were excluded from this study.

The researchers also decided to exclude the Mental Disengagement Scale ($\alpha = 0.60$), the Active Coping Scale ($\alpha = 0.52$), and the Restraint Coping

Scale ($\alpha = 0.58$). These three scales were excluded due to their subpar alpha levels (Cronbach, 1951). In addition, the researchers also developed three additional questions for the Alcohol-Drug Disengagement Scale to increase scale validity. The question format for this survey was a four-point Likert scale where: $1 =$ I don't do this at all, $2 =$ I do this a little bit, $3 =$ I do this a moderate amount, and $4 =$ I do this frequently.

Procedure

This study was completed using Qualtrics, an online survey software program. First, participants were given a link to a consent form, which defined the parameters of the study and stated that the participants could voluntarily withdraw at any point. After the subjects agreed and consented to participate, they were automatically directed to the survey. Before beginning the survey, participants were asked to think about what they typically do when faced with a stressful event. The participants were given a two-week window to complete the approximately thirty-minute survey.

After the data collection phase ended, the researchers compiled and analyzed the data. This study was approved by the IRB and was determined to be exempt. The return rate for the Cope Instrument was good, with a 100 percent response rate from the SMAR²T Program participants, an 85 percent response rate from the undergraduates, and a 77 percent response rate from the Fellows Program participants.

RESULTS

The analysis of data and findings are discussed in the sections that follow. The Reliability of the Cope Scale and the results of the Cope Scale are discussed.

Analysis of Reliability for the Cope Scale

Table 6.2 reports the reliability for Cope Scale Instrument (Carver, Scheier, & Weintraub, 1989) modified by the researchers. After analyzing Cronbach's alpha, the scales ranged from mediocre ($\alpha \geq 0.62$) to excellent ($\alpha > 0.90$) alpha levels (Cronbach, 1951). The Planning Scale consisted of four items ($\alpha = 0.83$), the Suppression of Competing Activities Scale consisted of four items ($\alpha = 0.62$), the Seeking Social Support—Instrumental consisted of four items ($\alpha = 0.79$), the Seeking Social Support—Emotional Scale consisted of six items ($\alpha = 0.92$), the Positive Reinterpretation and Growth Scale consisted of four items ($\alpha = 0.81$), the Turning to Religion Scale consisted of four items ($\alpha = 0.96$), the Denial Scale consisted of four items ($\alpha = 0.84$), the

Table 6.2.   Reliability for the Modified Cope Scale

Cope Scales	Cronbach's Alpha	Number of Items
Planning Scale	0.83	4
Suppression of Competing Activities Scale	0.62	4
Seeking Social Support—Instrumental Scale	0.79	4
Seeking Social Support—Emotional Scale	0.92	6
Positive Reinterpretation and Growth Scale	0.81	4
Turning to Religion Scale	0.96	4
Denial Scale	0.84	4
Behavioral Disengagement Scale	0.69	4
Alcohol-Drug Disengagement Scale	0.94	4

Behavioral Disengagement Scale consisted of four items ($\alpha = 0.69$), and the Alcohol-Drug Disengagement Scale consisted of four items ($\alpha = 0.94$). Due to the Active Cope Scale's ($\alpha = 0.52$), the Mental Disengagement Scale's ($\alpha = 0.60$), and the Restraint Coping Scale's ($\alpha = 0.58$) poor reliability coefficients, they were cut from the analysis. The researchers used a cutoff of $\alpha = 0.60$ for their scales because that is what Carver, Scheier, and Weintraub (1989) used in their original study.

Analysis of Results for the Cope Scale

A general linear model, MANOVA, was conducted on three different preservice certification groups (undergraduates, SMAR^{2}T Program, and Fellows Program) by nine coping strategy factors (Carver, Scheier, & Weintraub, 1989). Preliminary analyses included testing for normality, homogeneity of variance-covariance matrices, and the presence of outliers.

The data were distributed normally, evidenced by visual inspections of the histograms for each of the dependent variables as well as skewness within the reasonable limits for the analysis ($< +/- 1$). Outliers were inspected overall and by group using univariate (inspecting z scores $> +/- 3$ standard deviations) and multivariate (using Mahalanobis distance) procedures. As a result, six observations were removed or less than 5 percent of the dataset. Participants with missing data were also excluded in the final analysis. Box's M tested homoscedasticity, and although this p-value was significant ($p = 0.02$), this test is highly sensitive. Due to the removal of outliers, the researchers were not worried about this significant finding (Field, 2018).

The results from the MANOVA revealed significant differences among the nine different cope scales on the dependent variables, Wilk's $\lambda = 0.841$, $F(18,358) = 1.80$, $p = 0.024$, multivariate $\eta^2 = 0.08$. An analysis of variance (ANOVA), using Welch's t-test to correct for unequal group sizes, was conducted on each dependent variable as a follow-up test to the MANOVA.

The results from the one-way ANOVA found multiple scales to be statistically significant, including: the Planning Scale $F(2,187) = 3.22$, $p = 0.042$, where 7 percent of the variance in coping strategy was attributed to certification route ($\eta^2 = 0.07$); the Denial Scale, $F(2,187) = 7.05$, $p < 0.001$, where 4 percent of the variance in coping strategy was attributed to certification route ($\eta^2 = 0.04$); the Behavioral Disengagement Scale, $F(2,187) = 7.32$, $p < 0.001$, where 5 percent of the variance in coping strategy was attributed to certification route ($\eta^2 = 0.05$); and the Alcohol-Drug Disengagement Scale, $F(2,187) = 6.67$, $p = 0.002$, where 2 percent of the variance in coping strategy was attributed to certification route ($\eta^2 = 0.02$). According to Cohen (1988), an effect size of 0.2 is small, 0.5 is medium, and 0.8 is large.

To further explore the differences among means, the Games-Howell *post-hoc* was used. According to Field (2018), the Games-Howell *post-hoc* is optimal when there is doubt that the population variances are equal due to unequal group sizes. For the Planning Scale, undergraduate students were significantly less likely to plan compared to the Fellows Program participants, $p = 0.022$, and the SMAR^{2}T Program participants, $p = 0.003$.

Similarly, for the Denial Scale, the undergraduate students were significantly more likely to be in denial compared to the SMAR^{2}T Program participants,

Table 6.3. Comparison of Means for the Cope Scale

	Undergraduates n = 98	SMAR²T n = 22	Fellows n = 81	F (η²)	df
Planning	3.07$_a$ (0.64)	3.52$_{ab}$ (0.47)	3.34$_b$ (0.49)	3.22* (0.07)	2,187
Suppression of Competing Activities	2.53 (0.53)	2.61 (0.66)	2.54 (0.52)	.206	2,201
Seeking Social Support—Instrumental	3.08 (0.64)	3.19 (0.54)	3.21 (0.60)	1.08	2,201
Seeking Social Support—Emotional	2.93 (0.75)	2.86 (0.69)	3.16 (0.69)	2.85	2,198
Positive Reinterpretation and Growth	3.08 (0.59)	3.10 (0.56)	3.21 (0.60)	1.12	2,198
Turning to Religion	2.60 (1.11)	2.26 (1.10)	2.41 (1.05)	1.15	2,200
Denial	1.59$_a$ (0.65)	1.17$_b$ (0.31)	1.45$_a$ (0.59)	7.05** (0.04)	2,187
Behavioral Disengagement	1.64$_a$ (0.58)	1.27$_b$ (0.27)	1.42$_b$ (0.46)	7.31** (0.05)	2,187
Alcohol-Drug Disengagement	1.48$_a$ (0.70)	1.17$_b$ (0.40)	1.42$_{ab}$ (0.59)	6.67** (0.02)	2,187

Notes: * = $p < 0.05$, ** = $p < 0.001$. Standard deviations appear in parentheses below means. Means with differing subscripts within rows are significantly different at the $p < 0.05$. Likert scale where: 1 = I don't do this at all, 2 = I do this a little bit, 3 = I do this a moderate amount, and 4 = I do this frequently.

$p = 0.001$, and the SMAR²T Program participants were more likely to be in denial compared to the Fellows Program participants, $p = 0.025$. For the Behavioral Disengagement Scale, the undergraduate students were more likely to be behaviorally disengaged compared to the SMAR²T Program participants, $p < 0.001$. Finally, for the Alcohol-Drug Disengagement Scale, the undergraduate students were significantly more likely to cope using alcohol or drugs compared to the SMAR²T Program participants, $p = 0.039$.

DISCUSSION

Due to the large amounts of stress certified teachers experience in the field, turnover in the profession is very high (Ryan et al., 2017). To cope with high levels of stress, it has been established that adaptive coping strategies need to be developed for teacher retention to increase (Chang, 2013; Faulk, Gloria, & Steinhard, 2012; Fredrickson & Joiner, 2002; Moskowitz et al., 1996; Ntoumanis & Biddle, 1998; Taylor et al., 2016). When individuals do not have the skills necessary to adapt to stressful situations, they often turn toward maladaptive coping strategies, which have been linked to increased teacher burnout (Faulk, Gloria, & Steinhard, 2012; Hastings & Brown, 2002; Ntoumanis & Biddle, 1998; Taylor et al., 2016).

This study increases the understanding of how preservice teachers cope, particularly because three different routes to certification were investigated. Analyzing different routes to certification is important because many institutions throughout the United States house multiple academic programs that deviate from the traditional certification route (Shuls & Trivitt, 2015). Although this study only compared the traditional teacher certification route (sophomore undergraduate students) against two nontraditional certification routes (SMAR²T Program Participants and the Fellows Program Participants), the results have demonstrated that not all preservice teachers are similar or are equipped with the necessary skills to cope with stressors.

This is especially true for the sophomore undergraduate students who scored significantly lower on adaptive coping scales, such as the Planning Scale, and scored significantly higher on maladaptive coping scales, such as the Denial Scale, the Behavioral Disengagement Scale, and the Alcohol-Drug Disengagement Scale, compared to participants who followed a nontraditional certification route.

Although this study was not experimental, the researchers did analyze participant age, gender, and ethnicity by the Cope Scale (Carver, Scheier, & Weintraub, 1989) and did not find any statistically significant differences. These results appear to support that age, gender, and ethnicity do not influence whether individuals were more likely to use adaptive or maladaptive coping strategies. These findings were surprising as multiple studies have found that as people age, their coping strategies typically become more adaptive and mature (Snyder, Barry, & Valentino, 2015; Wingo, Baldessarini, & Windle, 2015).

There are many reasons for these findings, including cognitive development and increased experience dealing with dynamic life situations (Hertel et al., 2015). Due to these previous studies, the researchers expected to find a significant difference between age and the Cope Scale (Carver, Scheier, & Weintraub, 1989). However, since no statistically significant difference was found, it is possible that certification route could account for some of these differences.

In addition, the Planning Scale was found to be less utilized by the sophomore undergraduate students compared to the SMAR²T Program and the Fellows Program participants. According to Carver, Scheier, and Weintraub (1989), in order to score high on the Planning Scale, the individual must be able to create action strategies and think critically about how to handle the stressor. Although age was not statistically significant, it could be argued that, as students develop and mature throughout their college experience, they become more able to take initiative or plan when confronted with something unfavorable (Boburka et al., 2014).

This could explain why sophomore students were less likely to score high on the Planning Scale compared to the SMAR²T Program and Fellows Program Participants, who were on average three to four years older. Research completed by Martin et al. (2003), found that secondary-aged students with behavioral problems who were given opportunities to take initiative or be in control of their own self-direct pursuits were better able to plan and complete their academic goals.

Azevedo and Cromley (2004) found similar results with undergraduate students who were given opportunities to self-regulate or plan their own learning. These findings suggest that students completing a traditional certification route should have more opportunities to take initiative or plan within their educational curriculum to further the development of their adaptive coping abilities when confronted with stressors (Azevedo & Cromley, 2004; Boburka et al., 2014; Martin et al., 2003).

Furthermore, to increase the adaptive coping skills of students seeking traditional certification routes, decreasing the use of maladaptive coping skills should be addressed. This is because sophomore undergraduate students were more likely to score high on the Denial Scale, the Behavioral Disengagement Scale, and the Alcohol-Drug Disengagement Scale, compared to the graduate students. It is not surprising that the sophomore undergraduates scored statistically significantly higher on the Alcohol-Drug Disengagement Scale compared to the other groups, because sophomore college students are arguably in an environment where alcohol and/or drugs are easy to obtain and frequency used (Levin et al., 2012). However, teacher education programs should be both aware of and addressing the negative impact drugs and alcohol can have on their students (Hingson, Zha, & Smyth, 2017).

Additionally, it is not surprising that sophomore undergraduate students scored high on both the Behavioral Disengagement Scale and the Denial Scale due to their similar factor loadings during the development of the original Cope Scale (Carver, Scheier, & Weintraub, 1989). Specifically, Czyz et al. (2013) found that stressed college students exhibited high levels of disengagement and maladaptive behavior. However, Wyatt and Oswalt (2013), found that the stressors graduate students and undergraduate students face are different, with undergraduates feeling more negative emotions due to academic performance.

Wyatt and Oswalt (2013) also found that graduate students were more likely to seek mental healthcare facilities. This research demonstrates that undergraduate students are possibly less equipped to handle maladaptive stressors compared to their graduate counterparts, which again suggests that the traditional certification route for individuals wanting to become teachers should be modified (Ickes et al., 2015).

LIMITATIONS

There were multiple limitations that could have influenced or changed the outcomes from this study. First, this study used intact special groups (Fellows Program and SMAR²T Program), which were composed of mostly white females. Due to the researchers' interest in these intact special groups, random assignment could not be used. This threat to validity could have influenced the study's ability to be replicated and possibly its ability to be generalized, especially for people who do not identify as white. However, it should be noted that this sample is representative of individuals who pursue teaching, since a majority of teachers are white and female (Loewus, 2017).

To account for the homogeneity of variance violations, specifically because group sizes were unequal, Welch's t-test was used to provide more conservative outcomes. Finally, there was questionable reliability scores for three of the nine scales due to their Cronbach's alpha being below 0.80 (Cronbach, 1951). However, these scales were not eliminated because these alpha levels were similar to what Carver, Scheier, and Weintraub (1989) found in their original study. In future studies, the researchers could increase the number of items in each scale and increase the sample size of the participants to strengthen alpha levels.

CONCLUSION

Numerous studies have demonstrated that certified teachers in education are more likely to burnout when they utilize maladaptive coping strategies compared to teachers who use adaptive coping strategies. This constant turnover of teachers has negatively affected student achievement, district budgets, and veteran teacher responsibilities (Lambert & McCarthy, 2006; NCTAF, 2012; Richards, 2012, Sass, Seal, & Martin, 2011). In order for teacher burnout to decrease, it is important to understand how preservice teachers are coping before they begin their first year as a certified teacher in the classroom.

The results of this study have demonstrated that traditional sophomore undergraduate students are less likely to adaptively cope and are more likely to maladaptively cope compared to the nontraditional Fellows Program and SMAR²T Program. It is possible that once these sophomore preservice teachers enter the field, they will quickly burnout unless preventative solutions are incorporated into preservice teacher education programs to develop students' coping skills. By increasing the adaptive coping strategies utilized by preservice teachers, burnout in the field could decrease, which could save school districts money and decrease unnecessary stress placed on veteran teachers (NCTAF, 2012; Sass, Seal, & Martin, 2011; Woloshyn & Savage, 2018).

REFERENCES

Azevedo, R., & Cromley, J. (2004). Does training on self-regulated learning facilitate students' learning with hypermedia? *Journal of Educational Psychology*, *96*(3), 523–535. https://dx.doi.org/10.1037/0022-0663.96.3.523

Boburka, R., Wesp, R., Eshun, S., & Drago, A. (2014). An assessment of the effectiveness of a classroom activity designed to teach the value of lifelong learning. *Studies in Continuing Education*, *36*(1), 54–66. https://doi.org/10.1080/01580 37X.2013.783473

Carver, C., Scheier, M., & Weintraub, J. (1989). Assessing coping strategies: A theoretically based approach. *Journal of Personality and Social Psychology*, *56*(2), 267–283. https://dx.doi.org/10.1037/0022-3514.56.2.267

Chang, M. (2013). Toward a theoretical model to understand teacher emotions and teacher burnout in the context of student misbehavior: Appraisal, regulation and coping. *Motivation Emotion*, *37*, 799–817. https://doi.org/10.1007/s11031-012-9335-0

Clotfelter, C. T., Ladd, H. F., Vigdor, J. L., & Diaz, R. A. (2004). Do school accountability systems make it more difficult for low-performing schools to attract and retain high-quality teachers? *Journal of Policy Analysis and Management*, *23*(2), 251–271. https://doi.org/10.1002/pam.20003

Clunies-Ross, P., Little, E., & Kienhuis, M. (2008). Self-reported and actual use of proactive and reactive classroom management strategies and their relationship with teacher stress and student behavior. *Educational Psychology*, *28*(6), 693–710. https://doi.org/10.1080/01443410802206700

Cohen, J. (1988). *Statistical power analysis for the behavioral sciences* (2nd Ed.). Hillsdale, NJ: Erlbaum.

Cronbach, L. J. (1951). Coefficient alpha and the internal structure of tests. *Psychometrika, 16*(3), 297–334. https://doi.org/10.1007/BF02310555

Czyz, E. W., Horwitz, A. G., Eisenberg, D., Kramer, A., & King, C. A. (2013). Self-reported barriers to professional help seeking among college students at elevated risk for suicide. *Journal of American College Health*, *61*(7), 398–406. https://dx.doi.org/10.1080%2F07448481.2013.820731

Duangdao, K. M., & Roesch, S. C. (2008). Coping with diabetes in adulthood: A meta-analysis. *Journal of Behavioral Medicine*, *31*(4), 291–300. https://doi.org/10.1007/s10865-008-9155-6

Faulk, K. E., Gloria, C. T., & Steinhardt, M. A. (2012). Coping profiles characterize individual flourishing, languishing and depression. *Anxiety, Stress & Coping*, *26*(4), 378–390. https://doi.org/10.1080/10615806.2012.708736

Field, A. P. (2018). *Discovering statistics using IBM SPSS Statistics*. Los Angeles, CA: Sage.

Folkman, S., & Lazarus, R. S. (1985). If it changes it must be a process: Study of emotion and coping during three stages of a college examination. *Journal of Personality and Social Psychology 48*(1), 150–70. https://psycnet.apa.org/doi/10.1037/0022-3514.48.1.150

Fredrickson, B. L., & Joiner, T. (2002). Positive emotions trigger upward spirals toward emotional well-being. *Psychological Science*, *13*(2), 172–175. https://doi.org/10.1111/1467-9280.00431

Goldring, R., Taie, S., & Riddles, M. (2014). Teacher attrition and mobility: Results from the 2012–13 teacher follow-up survey (NCES 2014-077). Washington, DC: National Center for Education Statistics.

Hastings, R. P., & Brown, T. (2002). Coping strategies and the impact of challenging behaviors on special educators' burnout. *Mental Retardation*, *40*(2), 148–156. https://doi.org/10.1352/0047-6765(2002)040%3C0148:CSATIO%3E2.0.CO;2

Herman, K. C., Hickmon-Rosa, J., & Reinke, W. M. (2017). Empirically derived profiles of teacher stress, burnout, self-efficacy, and coping and associated student outcomes. *Journal of Positive Behavior Interventions*, *20*(2), 90–100.

Hertel, G., Rauschenbach, C., Thielgen, M., & Krumm, S. (2015). Are older workers more active copers? Longitudinal effects of age-contingent coping on strain at work. *Journal of Organizational Behavior*, *36*(4), 514–537. https://doi.org/10.1002/job.1995

Hingson, R., Zha, W., & Smyth, D. (2017). Magnitude and trends in heavy episodic drinking, alcohol-impaired driving, and alcohol related mortality and overdose hospitalizations among emerging adults of college ages 18–24 in the United States, 1998–2014. *Journal of Studies on Alcohol and Drugs*, *78*(4), 540–548. https://doi.org/10.15288/jsad.2017.78.540

Howard, S. & Johnson, B. (2004). Resilient teachers: Resisting stress and burnout. *Social Psychology of Education*, *7*(4), 399–420. https://doi.org/10.1007/s11218-004-0975-0

Ickes, M. J., Brown, J., Reeves, B., & Zephyr, P. M. D. (2015). Differences between undergraduate and graduate students in stress and coping strategies. *Californian Journal of Health Promotion*, *13*(1), 13–25.

Kopkowski, C. (2008, April). Why they leave. Retrieved from National Education Association website: http://www.nea.org/home/12630.htm

Kyriacou, C. (2011). Teacher stress: Directions for future research. *Educational Review*, *53*(1), 27–35. https://doi.org/10.1080/00131910120033628

Lambert, R., & McCarthy, C. (Eds.) (2006). *Research on Stress and Coping Series: Understanding teacher stress in an age of accountability*. Greenwich, CT: Information Age Publishing.

Lazarus, R. S. (1966). *Psychological stress and the coping process*. New York: McGraw-Hill.

Lazarus, R. S. (1981). The stress and coping paradigm. In C. Eisdorfer, D. Cohen, A. Kleinman, & P. Maxim (Eds.), *Models for Clinical Psychopathology* (pp. 177–214). New York: Spectrum.

Lazarus, R. S., & Folkman, S. (1984). *Stress, appraisal, and coping*. New York: Springer.

Levin, M. E., Lillis, J., Seeley, J., Hayes, S. C., Pistorello, J., & Biglan, A. (2012). Exploring the relationship between experimental avoidance, alcohol use disorders, and alcohol-related problems among first-year college students. *Journal of American College Health*, *60*(6), 443–448. https://doi.org/10.1080/07448481.2012.673522

Loewus, L. (2017). The nation's teaching force is still mostly white and female. *Education Week*. Retrieved from https://www.edweek.org/ew/articles/2017/08/15/the-nations-teaching-force-is-still-mostly.html

Martin, J., Mithaug, D., Cox, P., Peterson, L., Van Dycke, J., & Cash, M. (2003). Increasing self-determination: Teaching students to plan, work, evaluate, and adjust. *Council for Exceptional Children*, *69*(4), 431–447.

Mitchell, G., & Hastings, R. P. (2001). Coping, burnout, and emotion in staff working in community services for people with challenging behaviors. *American Journal of Mental Retardation*, *106*(5), 448–459. https://doi.org/10.1352/0895-8017(2001)106%3C0448:CBAEIS%3E2.0.CO;2

Moritz, S., Jahns, A., Schroder, J., Berger, T., Lincoln, T., Klein, J., & Goritz, A. (2016). More adaptive versus less maladaptive coping: What is more predict of symptom severity? Development of a new scale to investigate coping profiles across different psychopathological symptoms. *Journal of Affective Disorders*, *191*, 300–307. https://doi.org/10.1016/j.jad.2015.11.027

Moskowitz, J. T., Folkman, S., Collette, L., & Vittinghoff, E. (1996). Coping and mood during AIDS-related caregiving and bereavement. *Annals of Behavioral Medicine*, *18*(1), 49–57. https://doi.org/10.1007/BF02903939

Moskowitz, J. T., Hult, J. R., Bussolari, C., & Acree, M. (2009). What works in coping with HIV? A meta-analysis with implications for coping with serious illness. *Psychological Bulletin*, *135*(1), 121–141. https://doi.org/10.1037/a0014210

National Commission on Teaching and America's Future (NCTAF). (2012). *The high cost of teacher turnover.* Washington, DC: NCTAF.

Ntoumanis, N., & Biddle, S. J. H. (1998). The relationship of coping and its perceived effectiveness to positive and negative affect in sport. *Personality and Individual Differences, 24*(6), 773–788. https://doi.org/10.1016/S0191-8869(97)00240-7

Olsen, A. A., & Huang, F. L. (2019). Teacher job satisfaction by principal support and teacher cooperation: Results from the Schools and Staffing Survey. *Education Policy Analysis Archives, 27*(11), 1–27. http://dx.doi.org/10.14507/epaa.27.4174

Paquette, K. R., & Rieg, S. A. (2016). Stressors and coping strategies through the lens of early childhood/special education pre-service teachers. *Teaching and Teacher Education, 57,* 51–58. https://doi.org/10.1016/j.tate.2016.03.009

Redding, C., & Henry, G. T. (2018). New evidence on the frequency of teacher turnover: Accounting for within-year turnover. *Educational Researcher, 47*(9), 577–593.https://doi.org/10.3102%2F0013189X18814450

Richards, J. (2012). Teacher stress and coping strategies: A national snapshot. *The Educational Forum, 76,* 299–316. https://doi.org/10.1080/00131725.2012.682837

Roesch, S. C., Adams, L., Hines, A., Palmores, A., Vyas, P., Tran, C., . . ., Vaughn, A. A. (2005). Coping with prostate cancer: A meta-analytic review. *Journal of Behavioral Medicine, 28*(3), 281–293. https://doi.org/10.1007/s10865-005-4664-z

Ryan, S. V., von der Embse, N. P., Pendergast, L. L., Saeki, E., Segool, N., & Schwing, S. (2017). Leaving the teaching profession: The role of teacher stress and educational accountability policies on turnover intent. *Teaching and Teacher Education, 66,* 1–11. https://doi.org/10.1016/j.tate.2017.03.016

Sass, D., Seal, A., & Martin, N. (2011). Predicting teacher retention using stress and support variables. *Journal of Educational Administration, 49*(2), 200–215. http://dx.doi.org/10.1108/09578231111116734

Shuls, J. V., & Trivitt, J. R. (2015). Teacher effectiveness: An analysis of licensure screens. *Educational Policy, 29*(4), 645–675. https://doi.org/10.1177%2F089590 4813510777

Sirois, F., & Kitner, R. (2015). Less adaptive or more maladaptive? A meta-analytic investigation of procrastination and coping. *European Journal of Personality, 29,* 433–444. https://doi.org/10.1002/per.1985

Snyder, K., Barry, M., & Valentino, R. (2015). Cognitive impact of social stress and coping strategy throughout development. *Psychopharmacology, 232*(1), 185–195. https://dx.doi.org/10.1007%2Fs00213-014-3654-7

Stoeber, J., & Rennert, D. (2007). Perfectionism in school teachers: Relations with stress appraisals, coping styles, and burnout. *Anxiety, Stress, & Coping, 21*(1), 37–53. https://doi.org/10.1080/10615800701742461

Taylor, C., Harrison, J., Haimovitz, K., Oberle, E., Thomson, K., Schonert-Reichl, K., & Roeser, R. (2016). Examining ways that a mindfulness-based intervention reduces stress in public school teachers: A mixed-methods study. *Mindfulness, 7*(1), 115–129. https://doi.org/10.1007/s12671-015-0425-4

Wingo, A., Baldessarini, R., & Windle, M. (2015). Coping styles: Longitudinal development from ages 17 to 33 and associations with psychiatric disorders. *Psychiatry Research, 225*(3), 299–304. https://doi.org/10.1016/j.psychres.2014.12.021

Woloshyn, V., & Savage, M. (2018). Increasing teacher candidates' mental health literacy and stress coping skills through an elective mental health and wellness course. *International Journal of Inclusive Education, 24*(9), 921–935. https://doi.org/10.1080/13603116.2018.1497097

Wyatt, T., & Oswalt, S. (2013). Comparing mental health issues among undergraduate and graduate students. *American Journal of Health Education, 44*(2), 96–107. https://doi.org/10.1080/19325037.2013.764248

Preparing Teachers for Literacy Instruction Across and Within the Disciplines: The What and the How

Chyllis E. Scott, Diane M. Miller,
Erin K. Washburn, and Erin M. McTigue

As schools are becoming more culturally, linguistically, and technologically diverse, teachers need to be prepared to effectively facilitate students' learning using literacy-oriented instruction across all grade levels and within all disciplines (e.g., mathematics, science). Further, with the adoption and implementation of the Common Core State Standards (National Governors Association Center for Best Practices, & Council of Chief State School Officers, 2010), the need for knowledgeable and skilled teachers of discipline-specific (Shanahan & Shanahan, 2008; 2012) and multimodal literacies (Hicks, 2006; 2018) in middle and high school is as important as ever.

To date, much research has been conducted to highlight preservice teachers' (PSTs') beliefs (Bean, 1997; Fang, 1996) and knowledge (Mishra & Koehler, 2006; Risko et al., 2008; Shulman, 1986) about teaching literacy in discipline-specific classrooms (e.g., math, science, and social studies). Additionally, researchers have conducted studies on the impact of teacher preparation on PSTs and their use of discipline-specific literacy strategies in the context of fieldwork, practicum, and student teaching (Bean, 1997; Daisey, 2012; Feret & Smith, 2010; Lenski & Thieman, 2013; Warren-Kring & Rutledge, 2011).

However, few researchers, to our knowledge, have synthesized this body of research as a whole. Though previous research has examined preservice and inservice teacher attitudes and beliefs (e.g., Colwell, 2016; Daisey, 2009; Hall, 2005), knowledge, (e.g., Bean, 1997; Dowdy & Campbell, 2008), and resistance to literacy instruction (e.g., Bean, 1997; O'Brien & Stewart, 1990), upon completion of larger synthesis of research (Miller, Scott, & McTigue, 2018; Scott, McTigue, Miller, & Washburn, 2018), it was noted that limited research focuses on the *what* (e.g., discipline-specific instruction) and the *how* (e.g., application) of PSTs' preparation for the classroom.

While Hikida et al. (2019) more recently reviewed how PSTs are prepared to teach reading processes, their work does not specifically focus on content area and disciplinary literacy instruction. Therefore, the purpose of this work is to share findings from this research synthesis that examined the content and instructional approaches used to prepare PSTs to teach discipline-specific literacy.

Constructs of Literacy

Researchers (e.g., Darling-Hammond & Youngs, 2002; Fisher & Ivey, 2005) continually assert that PSTs need appropriate training to teach literacy in general and in content-specific classes. Thus, teacher preparation for literacy instruction must do more than address PSTs' beliefs about literacy practices. Teacher preparation must also provide opportunities for future teachers to deepen their knowledge about literacy and literacy practices and fieldwork experiences for authentic application of such practices. For this study, we focused on both content-area literacy (Vacca & Vacca, 2005) and disciplinary literacy (Shanahan & Shanahan, 2008), as PSTs need to understand how literacy processes generally function *across* subject-specific classrooms—content-area literacy—and more specifically operate *within* subject-specific classrooms—disciplinary literacy.

METHODS

Part of a larger study (Scott et al., 2018), the following research question was constructed to guide this synthesis: according to systematically reviewed research on PSTs and literacy instruction across and within the disciplines, how is literacy instruction taught and incorporated into teacher preparation courses?

Context of the Larger Study

To contextualize the specific purpose of this research synthesis, we will first provide a brief overview of the large-scale systematic literature review that was initially conducted and thus prompted the research question for the present study. Similar to other large-scale literature reviews and systematic literature reviews, the preceding study employed the methodological process of a systematic review (e.g., Hannes, Claes, & Belgian Campbell Group, 2007; Risko et al., 2008; Scott et al., 2018; Torgerson, 2007) to investigate and synthesize findings for nearly five decades of research focused on literacy across the disciplines and preservice and inservice teachers.

We opted to conduct a systematic review rather than a meta-analysis in order to include empirical research using diverse methodologies (e.g., quantitative, qualitative, and mixed methods). The systematic review method is a four-step process in which studies are identified, screened according to predetermined inclusionary criteria, evaluated for quality, and synthesized to draw conclusions (Miller et al., 2018; Scott et al., 2018; Torgerson, Porthouse, & Brooks, 2005).

To conduct the search for the larger study, we used a variety of online databases that index educational research (i.e., Educational Resources Information Center, ProQuest Education Journals, PsycINFO, and ComDisDome). Three intersecting terms were used to guide the search: *content area(s)*, *literacy instruction/strategies*, and *preservice* or *inservice teachers*.

The ultimate purpose of the search was broad—eligible studies were then methodically assessed for relevance and quality by using a set of screening and coding criteria. Studies were screened using the following criteria: (1) peer-reviewed and published in English, (2) published between the years of 1969 and 2017, (3) conducted in the United States, and (4) posed research questions that were aimed at the empirical examination of literacy instruction for preservice and/or inservice teachers (Scott, 2013; Scott et al., 2018).

Notably, the second criterion was established due to Harold Herber's 1970 publication, *Teaching Reading in Content Areas*, the first published research-based resource that provided literacy strategies for teaching reading in the content areas. Therefore, according to the inclusionary criteria, a study could be excluded for multiple reasons (e.g., not peer-reviewed, or published before 1969 or after 2018).

Using these criteria, abstract-level screening was applied to 3,413 articles, and 714 articles were screened at the full-text level. After screening, 151 articles that met all criteria during the full-text screening were reviewed for quality using the Methodological Quality Questionnaire (MQQ; see table 7.1). Ultimately, fifty-three studies scored well enough on the MQQ to be the subject of the larger review. Modeled after the systematic review guidelines established by Torgerson (2007) and adapted by Risko et al. (2008), studies were then evaluated for methodological quality.

The purpose for assessing the methodological quality of studies was to include research in the synthesis that was consistent with research norms for quality research (Risko et al., 2008; Torgerson, Porthouse, & Brooks, 2005). The MQQ's seven indicators were used to analyze the studies' quality and effectiveness, which included: (1) theory and theory alignment, (2) link to findings, (3) methods, (4) reliability, (5) validity, (6) description of participants and sample, and (7) consistency of findings/conclusions with data

Table 7.1. Methodological Quality Questionnaire

Standard	Quality Criteria
Standard 1: Provides clear argument that links theory and research and demonstrates coherent chain of reasoning. Explicates theoretical and previous research in a way that builds the formulation of the question(s).	**1.1** Explicates theory and/or previous research in a way that builds the formulation of the posed question(s)/purpose(s)/objective(s) that can be investigated empirically. **1.2** Explicitly links findings to previous theory and research or argument for study.
Standard 2: Applies rigorous, systematic, and objective methodology to obtain reliable and valid knowledge relevant to educational activities and programs.	**2.1** Ensures that methods are presented in sufficient detail and clarity to clearly visualize procedures (e.g., another person could actually collect the same data). Data collection should be described so that readers can replicate the procedures in a quantitative study or follow the trail of data analysis in a qualitative study. For a quantitative study, researcher(s) should report some of the following: number of observations, interviews, or documents analyzed; if interviews and observations are taped and/or transcribed; duration of observations; diversity of material analyzed; and degree of investigator's/s' involvement in data collection and analysis. **2.2** Provides evidence of *reliability*. Was this evidence provided for the data collected (e.g., describe coefficients, test-retest, Cronbach's alpha)? Did researcher(s) provide information about instrument development and study populations (e.g., content-area writing strategies)? For qualitative studies, were characteristics of reliability, credibility, and/or trustworthiness addressed and reported? **2.3** Provides evidence of *validity*. Was this evidence provided for the data collected (e.g., does the instrumentation measure what it is designed to measure and accurately perform the intended function)? Is there information about instrument development and adaptations for specialized populations (e.g., content-area writing strategies)? For qualitative studies, were characteristics of reliability, credibility, and/or trustworthiness addressed and reported? **2.4** Describes participants. Was the sample well characterized (e.g., the age/grade and the type of content area)?
Standard 3: Presents finding(s) and makes claims that are appropriate to and supported by the methods that have been employed.	**3.1** Findings and conclusions are legitimate or consistent with data collected.

Note: Adapted from Scott (2013); See also Acosta & Garza (2011); Scott et al. (2018). (under review); Risko et al. (2008).

(Acosta & Garza, 2011; Miller et al., 2018, Risko et al., 2008; Scott, 2013; Scott et al., 2018).

Description of the Present Study

As per the previously detailed search and review process, fifty-three studies met all screening criteria and scored favorably on the MQQ, and twenty-nine of those studies specifically addressed PSTs. Thus, we extracted those to conduct the current study. To identify the research addressing the preparation of PSTs, we included differing program configurations, such as those combined with undergraduate degrees, five-year programs, and programs embedded in master's degrees. Of the twenty-nine studies, twenty-five (86.2 percent) included undergraduate-level PSTs, two (6.9 percent) involved five-year post-baccalaureate students, and two (6.9 percent) focused on graduate students in a master's program.

Three of the articles encompassed courses for both preservice and inservice teachers. Additionally, the twenty-nine studies examined varying instructional settings for the PSTs. The predominate setting, represented in 79.3 percent ($n = 23$) of the studies, was within the realm of content-area literacy and/or disciplinary literacy methods courses. Remaining instructional experiences included method courses in language arts ($n = 1$), mathematics and reading ($n = 1$), physics ($n = 1$), science and reading ($n = 1$), and social studies ($n = 2$).

In the twenty-nine studies, researchers used a variety of data sources: class and student artifacts (e.g., course projects, discussion logs, learning logs, observations, reflection papers), pre- and post-inventories/surveys, focus groups, and interviews. These studies also used the following methodologies: 75.9 percent ($n = 22$) qualitative, 13.8 percent ($n = 4$) quantitative, and 10.3 percent ($n = 3$) mixed-methods (Scott et al., 2018). Although the qualitative studies 75.9 percent ($n = 22$) were a little less clear in their description of specific methodologies, the majority (58.6 percent, $n = 17$) used constant comparison and inductive open-coding pattern analyses, whereas 17.2 percent ($n = 5$) of the included studies used themes and discourse analyses.

To answer this particular research question, which highlights *what* instruction the PSTs were receiving in these courses, we conducted an additional review of the inclusionary studies. During the re-reading, we concentrated on the *what* of the courses. We closely evaluated the content and approaches taught in each of the courses detailed in the studies. For this secondary analysis, we organized the studies chronologically to better illustrate what research has been conducted, when changes in research occur, and what trends are revealed over time.

The secondary analysis also allowed us to examine *how* PSTs are prepared for literacy instruction. The key features of table 7.2 were the two application columns: Application I and Application II.

Table 7.2. Article Application I and Application II

Study (in Chronological Order)	Application I	Application II
O'Brien D. G., & Stewart, R. A. (1990). Preservice teachers' perspectives on why every teacher is not a teacher of reading: A qualitative analysis.	• Constructed a text-based, thirty-minute lesson • Lessons were constructed using a framework for integrating pre-, during-, and post-reading activities/strategies	NA
Konopak, B. C., Readence, J. F., & Wilson, E. K. (1994). Preservice and inservice secondary teachers' orientation toward content-area reading.	• Developed three sets of lesson plans on syllabication, vocabulary, and comprehension	NA
Reinke, K., Mokhtari, K., & Willner, E. (1997). Preservice teachers' perceptions of the integration of mathematics, reading, and, writing.	• Extensive discussion and reflection about issues pertaining to curriculum integration	• Tutored an elementary school-age student in mathematics, reading, or integrated math and reading
Bean, T. W. (1997). Preservice teachers' selection and use of content-area literacy strategies.	• Microteaching • Content-area literacy strategies (i.e., graphic organizer, anticipation guide, word map, KWL [Know, Want to learn, Learned], Jigsaw, etc.)	• Microteaching during five-day-per-week practicum and during student teaching
Nourie, B. L., & Lenski, S. D. (1998). The (in)effectiveness of content area literacy instruction for secondary preservice teachers.	NA	NA
Donahue, D. M. (2000). Experimenting with texts: New science teachers' experience and practice as readers and teachers of reading.	• Read their selected text and wrote, responded, and shared their journal with their course partner and the instructor	NA
Donahue, D. (2003). Reading across the great divide: English and math teachers' apprentice one another as readers and disciplinary insiders.	• Read a discipline text and weekly reflection • Exchanged logs with partners and responded "in writing with comments and questions" • Used and applied "fix-up" strategies	NA

Lesley, M. (2004). Looking for critical literacy with post-baccalaureate content-area literacy students.	• Course discourse: activities and discussions. • Writers' workshop • Socratic method (discussions)	NA
Lesley, M. Watson, P., & Elliot, S. (2007). "School" reading and multiple texts: Examining the metacognitive development of secondary-level preservice teachers.	• Course discourse: thematic unit, think-aloud activity, in-class journal writing, peer-editing	
Sheridan-Thomas, H. K. (2007). Making sense of multiple literacies: Exploring pre-service content-area teachers' understanding and applications.	• Course discourse: multiple literacy projects • Online discussions • Multi-unit project, self-assessment • Reflect on specific applications	• Engaged in thirty-five hours of fieldwork in middle or high school. • Assisted with group work or individual students in classes. • Tutored students during study halls and after-school programs. • Talked with one or more students about their out-of-school literacies. • Reflected on specific applications.
Dowdy, J. K., & Campbell, D. (2008). The dance of diversity: White male teachers and arts based instruction for classrooms.	• Readings • Discussions • Workshops focusing on reading and writing • Recorded interdisciplinary connections to include in mini-lessons for grammar, vocabulary, discussion prompts, writing, and art • literature circle discussions • worked in small groups to create a written dramatization of a scene from the novel	• Taught arts-based lesson plans during their student teaching placement (secondary level) • 1 Ten-lesson plan presentation • Field experience • Dramatization/lessons were later presented to group of elementary students • Lessons were shared/taught with the elementary/middle school students following the dramatization of the novel
Wilburne, J. M., & Napoli, M. (2008). Connecting mathematics and literature: An analysis of pre-service elementary school teachers' changing beliefs and knowledge.	NA	
Daisey, P. (2009). The reading experiences and beliefs of secondary pre-service teachers.	• Practiced and modeled with peers • Tasks, roles, debriefed • Took field notes of experience	NA
Olson, M. R., & Truxaw, M. P. (2009). Preservice science and mathematics teachers and discursive metaknowledge of text.	NA	• Participated in practicum. • Conducted think-alouds with school-age students

(Continued)

Table 7.2. (Continued)

Study (in Chronological Order)	Application I	Application II
Nokes, J. D. (2010). Preparing novice history teachers to meet students' literacy needs.	• Reading • Journaling with course peers/partner	• Required to spend approximately thirty-five to forty classroom observation hours • Helped students • Evaluated student work • Taught lessons • Wrote a series of reflective papers on their observations and experiences in the classroom
Feret, A. J., & Smith, J. J. (2010). Literacy and art: Collage for pre-service teacher.	• Observed a class • Developed lesson plan	• With the supervising teacher's approval, constructed and implemented three consecutive lessons to address the problematic area • lesson format was focused on one literacy skill (listening, reading, speaking, writing)
Warren-Kring, B. Z., & Rutledge, V. C. (2011). Adolescents' comprehension and content area education students' perceptions: Benefits from one-on-one tutoring.	• Course preparations • Readings • Observations	• Twenty hours of field placement • After four weeks of assessment and reading instruction in the course, students began tutoring (one-on-one) with a secondary student at two local schools.
Alvermann, D. Rezak, A. T., Mallozzi, C. A., Boatright, M. D., & Jackson, D. E. (2011b). Reflective practice in an online literacy courses: Lesson learned from attempts to fuse reading and science instruction.	• Online training • Video training • Lesson/video samples	• Four intervention lesson plans debriefing and feedback from mentor(s)
Alvermann, D., Friese, E, Beckmann, S., & Rezak, A. (2011a). Content area reading pedagogy and domain knowledge: A Bourdieusian analysis.	• Online feedback • Online discussions about modules • Lesson plans • Online mentoring relationship	• Prospective teacher: developed lesson plans and completed online module activities • Practicing teacher: implemented lesson plans and reflections

Daisey, P. (2012). The promise of secondary content-area literacy field experiences.	• Presented a three-minute tradebook project to their classmates • Biography presentations • Presented a fifteen-minute snapshot of the lesson to the class, noted benchmark, described students, showed reading material, shared their prepared pre-, during-, and after-reading activities
	• Thirty practicum hours in secondary class in their subject area • Presented three-minute tradebook project • Presented three-minute biography project. At the end of the semester, presented forty-five- to fifty-minute pre-, during-, and after-reading lesson • Received cooperating verbal feedback
Pytash, K. E. (2012). Engaging preservice teachers in disciplinary literacy learning through writing.	• Contacted professionals • Formed small groups based on their content area and shared the knowledge gained from contacting their professionals in their respective fields • Used information and their background knowledge to create a list of genres valued in their discipline
Barry, A. L. (2012). "I was skeptical at first": Content literacy in the art museum.	• Chose a work of art and explained how they could use it to teach a concept • Brainstormed, collaborated, read, researched, wrote, and problem-solved
van Zee, E. H., Jansen, H., Winograd, K., Crowl, M., & Devitt, A. (2012). Integrating physics and literacy learning in a physics course for prospective elementary and middle-school teachers.	• Applied skills, activities, and knowledge to activities in class	• Taught one of the topics explored in class • Gained experience teaching science with a small group of the children
Park, J. Y. (2013). All the ways of reading literature: Preservice English teachers' perspectives on disciplinary literacy.	• Completed project • Reflected on what they saw as the work of their discipline, how to approach discipline-specific texts (e.g., peer-reviewed science journals, literary criticism, proofs, primary documents), and what reading practices were demanded by the discipline

(Continued)

Table 7.2. (Continued)

Study (in Chronological Order)	Application I	Application II
Pytash, K. E. (2013). Secondary preservice teachers'' development of teaching scientific writing.	• Conducted an in-depth study on a genre that is important in science • To use knowledge to write an original piece of writing	• Ninety-hour practicum
Lenski, S. J., & Thieman, G. Y. (2013). What work samples reveal about secondary pre-service social studies teachers' use of literacy strategies.	• Instructional planning • Investigated and described the instructional context, including school and classroom data such as class size; gender; racial, ethnic, and linguistic diversity; poverty level; and student exceptionalities	• Completed a work sample, including classroom context, unit rationale, detailed lesson plans, sample instructional materials, attention to literacy, lesson reflections, and pre- and post-assessment data • Student teaching I work samples include unit of study lasting two to three weeks • Student teaching II work samples include four-to-five-week unit of study
Rodriguez, T. L. (2015). A content area reading course re-imagined: A situated case study of disciplinary literacies pedagogy in secondary English teacher education.	• Personal literacy history essay • Five digital book club lesson plans and reflections • Three-week interdisciplinary unit plan created with peers in social studies and science education • Observational field notes of three digital book club meetings	• Field experience • Lesson plans • Digital book club
Colwell, J. (2016). Examining preservice teachers' beliefs about disciplinary literacy in history through a blog project.	• Small-group discussion • Analyzed and reflected on sample lessons, unit plans, and textbook excerpts	• Sixty field-based hours, through this course. • Blog project (incorporate computer-mediated communication) lasted 12 weeks during a fall semester
Saine, P., & West, J. A. (2017). Content area teacher candidates' self-efficacy beliefs of teaching writing online.	• Class discussions • Projected their laptops onto white board in classroom and walked through their thinking as they read the student's draft and explained their reasoning	• Teacher candidates and high school students virtually interacted using the platform Edmodo (http://edmodo.com) • Gave feedback to high school students' multigenre papers

Application I studies described instructions that occurred within the context of the course, including the content, strategies, and activities the PSTs learned in the course and/or how they applied the content for their *own* learning (e.g., writing lesson plans, conducting course discussions with their peers, writing reflective logs, or teaching mini-presentations in the context of their college course with their peers). *Application II* studies extended the learning to experiences and opportunities in the practicum, student-teaching assignment, or fieldwork experience, such as microteaching, designing and teaching lesson plans, or tutoring K–12 students. These two applications are both relevant in the preparation of teachers and are critical components of this research synthesis.

RESULTS

Of the twenty-nine studies, twenty-seven (93.1 percent) were identified as either Application I (34.5 percent, $n = 10$) or as Application II (58.6 percent, $n = 17$). However, two studies did not meet either of the application classifications and instead addressed PSTs' attitudes toward reading in content classrooms and reading in general. Nourie and Lenski (1998) conducted their study with PSTs enrolled in a state-required content literacy course, but they focused on the pre- and post-results from two surveys (i.e., Mikelecky Behavioral Reading Attitude Measure, A Scale to Measure Attitudes toward Reading in Content Classrooms by Vaughn, 1977).

Additionally, Daisey (2009) further explored beliefs and attitudes and discovered that content-area courses help PSTs become more open to the view that reading can be enjoyable, rather than negative. PSTs were immersed into "reading opportunities" and were encouraged to "expand, rethink, experience, value, and ultimately model reading" (Daisey, 2009, p. 170). Initially, PSTs may view reading negatively, but content-area literacy classes can make a positive impact on personal as well as future teaching literacies. However, since the details pertaining to course assignments and course pedagogy were not clearly provided, these articles are not included in either of the application categories.

Research and PST Preparation: Application I

The ten studies categorized as Application I focused on secondary PSTs in content-area literacy courses and their beliefs and preparation for integrating literacy strategies and literacy instruction into content instruction, as evidenced by course readings, discussions, lesson planning, projects, and/or presentations conducted in the course or lessons taught to their peers.

Researchers explored PSTs' beliefs, attitudes, and theoretical orientations toward content-area literacy (Konopak, Readence, & Wilson, 1994; O'Brien & Stewart, 1990), experience as readers and teachers of reading (Donahue, 2000), literacy apprenticeship and disciplinary boundaries (Donahue, 2003), application of critical literacies and metacognitive development (Lesley, 2004; Lesley, Watson, & Elliot, 2007), and disciplinary literacy perspective (Park, 2013) through writing and scientific writing (Pytash, 2012; 2013), art (Barry, 2012), and physics (van Zee et al., 2012).

O'Brien and Stewart (1990), two researchers who have spent years evaluating PSTs' content-area literacy beliefs and attitudes, aimed to "interpret and catalogue preservice teachers' perspective on content reading instruction" (p. 104). The authors wanted to know if the participating secondary PSTs were resistant to teaching reading in the context of content-specific classes. For the study, the secondary PSTs participated in a variety of course activities, such as readings, small-group and whole-class discussions, various reading strategies, and administering assessments and microteaching experiences in their undergraduate course. O'Brien and Stewart (1990) concluded that "preservice teachers hold misconceptions about content reading common among their practicing peers" (p. 101). Although the PSTs gained knowledge and experiences in literacy pedagogy, their misconceptions persisted.

Other studies also investigated PSTs' attitudes, beliefs, and practices with literacy (e.g., reading and writing) instruction, particularly within content-area/disciplinary literacy instruction. Konopak and colleagues (1994) explored secondary PSTs' and inservice teachers' theoretical orientations about "content area reading and instruction" (p. 221). The PSTs were enrolled in either one of the two sections of a required content-area methods reading course and completed surveys, belief statements, and a series of three lesson plans on "decoding, vocabulary, and instruction" (Konopak et al., 1994, p. 222).

The researchers found that PSTs' orientations were varied about reading development, and differences were found between the PSTs and inservice teachers. PSTs favored an interactive approach, while inservice teachers favored reader-based instruction. These findings support the suggestion that theoretical orientations of reading processes of teachers impact their instructional decision-making processes.

The two previous studies (Konopak et al., 1994; O'Brien & Stewart, 1990) focused on more general beliefs and theoretical orientations, whereas Donahue's (2000) case study captured PSTs' personal reading experiences particularly as new science teachers. Through reading various texts, journaling, and in-depth discussions and feedback with peers in the course, the PSTs were positioned as students and experienced the learning firsthand. Upon course completion, the

PSTs exhibited growth toward valuing reading overall, yet they did not "value the type of typically required in science classrooms and textbooks, or the limited reason for that reading, to recall information" (Donahue, 2000, p. 738).

Similarly, Donahue (2003) worked specifically with English language arts (ELA) and mathematics PSTs. He researched the course's main assignment, a reading apprenticeship portfolio designed for teachers to reflect on their learning as readers, apply meaning to their content, practice literacy strategies, and read across disciplines. Ultimately, Donahue's (2003) exploratory study was to help "teacher educators think about how to engage all new teachers in discussions about one of their most important responsibilities: ensuring that all students read well . . . [and] spur teacher educators' reflections about how best to spark the metacognitive conversations" (p. 28). The participating PSTs gained knowledge about themselves as learners, putting literacy strategies into practice and promoting metacognition.

Furthermore, PSTs' reading development supports the application of critical literacies (Lesley, 2004). In her study, PSTs enacted critical literacies into their teaching, which teach "students to give voice to oppressive experiences within oppressive social systems" (Lesley, 2004, p. 323). Through asking critical questions, exploring diverse perspectives, and facilitating discussions, participants viewed literacy as a tool for advocacy. Later, Lesley, Watson, & Elliot (2007) examined PSTs' metacognition to develop as teachers and improve their own reading skills.

The goal was for the PSTs to use and implement a variety of theme-related "print and non-print text[s]" (Lesley, Watson, & Elliot, 2007, p. 153) in the course rather than the typical course text. Through journaling, reader-response writing, and course discourse, the PSTs applied their knowledge to their thematic units but made minimal text-to-text and text-to-world connections related to the instruction of the class. In general, content-area literacy courses are important for critical reading (Lesley, Watson, & Elliot, 2007; Tovani, 2004) and self-monitoring through the reading process; however, PSTs continue to limit their practice and application.

While the earlier research was grounded primarily in content-area literacy, more recent research has transitioned to exploring disciplinary literacy. Content-area literacy refers to the instructional method of incorporating research-based, literacy strategies into the teaching and practices *across* the contents (Vacca & Vacca, 2005); in contrast, disciplinary literacy refers to the use of reading, writing, speaking, and listening to learn *within* the context of a specific content area or discipline (Shanahan & Shanahan, 2008). The 2008 publication from Shanahan and Shanahan opened up vibrant discussions and, though not immediate, increased the attention researchers paid to disciplinary literacy.

For instance, Pytash (2012) explored writing as a method to develop students' knowledge and literacy practices unique to teaching in their disciplines, affirming the need that "secondary [PSTs] learn to teach the demands of their content area in addition to particular aspects of their discipline that involve literacy" (p. 527). Pytash (2012) concluded that for PSTs to incorporate disciplinary literacy instruction successfully they need opportunities to engage in reading and writing themselves; this increased practice in disciplinary literacy promotes pedagogical and metacognitive knowledge. Studies such as this affirm the chronological nature of our synthesis, which illustrates that the content-area literacy research has shifted to include disciplinary literacy foci.

In another study connecting literacy within the context of disciplinary instruction, Barry (2012) situated PSTs within a specific discipline-based setting (i.e., art museum) where the students chose a work of art and described how they could use the work to teach a content-specific concept. The PSTs used both literacy knowledge and disciplinary knowledge to construct lessons based on their chosen works and museum experiences. Barry (2012) coded the data (using *In-Vivo* Coding and Verbatim Coding) by analyzing post-experience reflections and semester evaluations, and through her action research established the value of this experience.

The two most recent Application I studies (Park, 2013; Pytash, 2013) continue to concentrate on disciplinary literacy. Park (2013) examined how ELA PSTs understand disciplinary reading, while Pytash (2013) looked at how science PSTs teach writing. In their adolescent literacy course, PSTs in Park's (2013) study used a variety of literacy frameworks and readings to complete a project "in which they reflect on what they see as the work of their disciplines, how they approach discipline-specific texts, . . . and what reading practices are demanded by the discipline" (p. 366). Although the PSTs directly referenced some text-to-self and minimal text-to-world connections and seemed to value purposeful reading practice (Tovani, 2004), they made no text-to-text connections during class readings.

In the final study, Pytash (2013) situated her PSTs into a variety of science-related writing experiences. The PSTs conducted repeated close readings of different genres and studied writing strategies (i.e., Generating Interactions between Schemata and Texts, concept maps) to include in their final unit of study. According to Pytash (2013), "the purpose of the unit of study assignment was for [PSTs] to conduct an in-depth study on a genre they thought was important in science" (p. 800).

Responses to an open-ended question questionnaire, projects, reflections, and interviews showed that the PSTs needed opportunities to be reflective about the types of genres found in science, while accompanied with "the requirements for writing these genres" (Pytash, 2013, p. 802). The participants shared that the units were valuable and relevant for future use; in addition, they expressed enjoyment for the process and appreciation for the levels of engagement and creativity involved in the project.

The ten Application I studies reviewed in this section support the need for PSTs to (1) have literacy preparation, (2) take the minimum required content-area/disciplinary/adolescent literacy course, and (3) have instruction and training in literacy instruction across the disciplines. Still, secondary PSTs enter, and sometimes exit, content-area literacy courses with misconceptions about literacy, how it should be taught across the grade levels, and how it is connected to discipline-specific instruction.

Research and PST Preparation: Application II

The seventeen Application II studies explore literacy instructions implemented in the authentic secondary classroom environment, primarily focusing on secondary PSTs in content-area literacy and adolescent literacy courses that incorporate microteaching, tutoring, or fieldwork (e.g., practicum, student teaching, or internship). The researchers in these studies explored PSTs' beliefs and perceptions along with their domain and metaknowledge. The majority of the studies were intentional about how PSTs applied content-area/disciplinary literacy into their instructions, which include strategy selection, lesson development, understanding the needs of school-age students, and connecting literacy instruction to and for the disciplinary instruction.

Specifically, the following contexts for application were included: tutoring (Reinke, Mokhtari, & Willner, 1997; Warren-Kring & Rutledge, 2011), microteaching and practicum experience (Bean, 1997), fieldwork and tutoring (Sheridan-Thomas, 2007), lesson-planning development and implementation (Alvermann et al., 2011b; Dowdy & Campbell, 2008; Feret & Smith, 2010; Wilburne & Napoli, 2008), field/practicum experiences/student teaching (Feret & Smith, 2010; Nokes, 2010; Olson & Truxaw, 2009; Rodriguez, 2015; Wilburne & Napoli, 2008), a digital book club (Rodriguez, 2015), and online tutoring and instruction (Colwell, 2016; Saine & West, 2017).

In the first study, Reinke, Mokhtari, and Willner (1997) reported that PSTs have minimal knowledge about literacy-rich interdisciplinary teaching and learning in relationship to mathematics instruction. Therefore, the researchers explored the perceptions of 123 elementary education PSTs. Results from surveys indicated positive changes in PSTs' perceptions, both of the integration of teaching mathematics, writing, and reading in the classroom and of improving reading skills for a better understanding of mathematics.

Additionally, the authors created a tutoring component that provided the PSTs opportunities to integrate instruction and work with school-aged students (Reinke et al., 1997). The PSTs reported that instruction of mathematics and language arts can easily be combined when writing is used in mathematics instruction, and it is a helpful combination for learning problem-solving skills.

Bean (1997) conducted research that sought to understand PSTs' selection of appropriate literacy practices. In phase one of the study, twenty-seven PSTs in a content-area reading course participated in course assignments, including readings, textbook evaluation, microteaching, and the primary opportunity comprised of a five-day practicum. Bean (1997) found that the PSTs' strategy choices in the microteaching course-based assignment reflected much variety, whereas the choices made within the field experience setting reflected the "dominant influence" (p. 161) of the cooperating teachers' more traditional, teacher-centered approaches.

Bean claimed that PSTs regularly gravitated to less collaborative, more traditional strategies, though the selected strategies were not always the most suitable choice for their instruction and discipline (1997). In phase two of the study, Bean (1997) conducted follow-up interviews with the participants and concluded that a follow-up study would provide a better understanding of the PSTs' selection and use of content literacy instruction.

A decade after Bean's work, Sheridan-Thomas (2007) conducted relevant action research in her content-area literacy graduate course. She sought to find out what PSTs in a content-area course know, learn, and apply from her course steeped in multiple literacies. The PSTs completed a variety of course assignments (written, online discussion forums, reflective learning logs, and a paper on multiple literacies); in addition, the students were required to engage in fieldwork in local secondary schools.

Sheridan-Thomas (2007) reported that the PSTs made direct connection from "their own interactions when they were adolescents" (p. 132). The PSTs made these connections more easily than the PSTs described by Bean (1997) ten years prior, reflecting the increasing shift to the use of literacy strategies across content areas.

Next, Dowdy and Campbell (2008) investigated teachers' beliefs in the context of arts-based instruction. Unlike Sheridan-Thomas's (2007) course-based action research, Dowdy and Campbell (2008) followed up with prior PSTs who had previously "completed the Reading and Writing in Adolescence and Adulthood course" (p. 3) and interviewed the participants, who were presently teachers of record or students in a field-placement course. The authors found that integrating literacy practices into arts-based instruction provided PSTs with a stronger foundation to retain and comprehend content information, and they concluded that content-area classes should incorporate multiple perspectives, strategies, and resources in the support of a broader, more well-rounded construct of knowledge (Dowdy & Campbell, 2008).

Like the earlier study, Wilburne and Napoli (2008) limited their research to one content area. They examined eight elementary PSTs' beliefs about using literature in another discipline: mathematics. The PSTs, both ELA and mathematics, designed and implemented lesson plans incorporating young adult literature to make literacy and mathematics connections. Beyond lesson plans, the PSTs engaged in literature circles, reader response activities, interdisciplinary text-set units, and "twelve weeks of urban field experiences" (Wilburne & Napoli, 2008, p. 3). Using qualitative analyses, the authors thematically coded the data, and they concluded that the PSTs had significant shifts "in their beliefs, interest, and identification of benefits of teaching mathematics through literature and making connections across the curriculum" (Wilburne & Napoli, 2008, p. 1).

Olson and Truxaw (2009) began their study with the assumption that PSTs continue to struggle to see literacy's central role in learning, specifically mathematics and science. The researchers worked with twenty-four secondary PSTs during the practicum required by their semester-long methods course. Using traditional and online literacy practices, PSTs conducted think-aloud protocols with secondary school-aged students "to develop metaknowledge about school science and mathematics discursive practices" (Olson & Truxaw, 2009, pp. 425–426). Additionally, the PSTs worked with their peers to practice in a structured setting prior to implementing their lessons.

At the completion of the course, the authors (Olson & Truxaw, 2009) analyzed the PSTs' papers, notes, and memos that were recorded over the semester and, using inductive coding, acknowledged three discursive metaknowledge types: "(1) how textual authority shapes readings, (2) how literacy practices are dialogic, [and] (3) how literacy practices are contextual" (p. 426); furthermore they "contend that literacy practices surrounding content understanding in science and mathematics are familiar to [PSTs] as to be largely implicit" (p. 430). The researchers found that "[PSTs] developed discursive metaknowledge of the centrality of literacy to learning content" (Olson & Truxaw, 2009, p. 422).

Focusing on yet another discipline, Nokes (2010) conducted action research with the PSTs in his social studies methods courses. Nokes used explicit instruction to teach the PSTs how to select appropriate texts and instructional strategies, modeled effective literacy instruction with the reading assignments, and encouraged students to apply their new knowledge from the course into their concurrent field experiences.

An analysis of the PSTs' reading reflections, midterm and final examinations, practicum literacy papers, and course evaluations revealed that 113 of the 119 PSTs exhibited "a good or very good understanding of literacy-related instructional strategies on all of their reading reflections, with 36 candidates showing a very good understanding" (Nokes, 2010, p. 505). Notably, Nokes (2010) acknowledged that findings from this study have led to direct changes in the course, such as shifting from content-area reading to content-area literacy, integrating traditional and new literacies, and providing additional field-based opportunities for the PSTs to apply strategies learned from the course.

Echoing the arts-based focus of Dowdy and Campbell (2008), Feret and Smith (2010) worked with elementary and secondary art education PSTs enrolled in a content-area reading course taught in conjunction with student teaching. The PSTs observed an art class and, with the teacher's permission, "constructed and implemented three consecutive lessons to address the problematic area" (Feret & Smith, 2010, p. 41). For the lessons, the PSTs selected the particular format (class period, mini-lesson, whole class, or small group) and one "literacy skill (listening, reading, speaking, writing), as the method of instruction was a requirement" (Feret & Smith, 2010, p. 41).

Results indicated that the PSTs gained new knowledge and pedagogical practice for both themselves and their students. The observations afforded them opportunities to develop their skills as teachers and become more purposeful about their instructional techniques and instructional practices. The PSTs also gained a new understanding of the value of integrating literacy into content-specific classes (i.e., art). Feret and Smith (2010) concluded, "Literacy skills are integral elements of the elementary and secondary art classroom that impact artistic development on many levels" (p. 50).

While much of the research focused on PSTs' beliefs was coupled with application-based opportunities and experiences for PSTs themselves, Warren-Kring and Rutledge (2011) focused on transference of content-area literacy. They evaluated forty-eight PSTs' effectiveness of tutoring to observe changes in their attitudes over time, but they also examined the effects upon the school-aged students being tutored. For one semester, the PSTs applied the content-area literacy instructional strategies learned in class as they tutored adolescent students, allowing the authors to measure the students' reading comprehension scores in treatment and comparison groups.

The authors addressed two issues of concern: the call to align education courses with reading achievement, and the attitudes of teachers toward implementing literacy strategies into their content-area instruction. The study reported both comprehension improvement in the tutees and improvement in attitude and comfort level toward content-area literacy strategies for the PSTs.

Rather than focusing on the interactions between PSTs and their students, Alvermann et al.s (2011b) researched "11 pairs of prospective and mentor [science] teachers" to gain more insight into the PSTs' attempts to combine reading and science instruction (Alvermann et al., 2011b, p. 28). In a case study concentrated on one of those pairs, the PST was enrolled in an online content-area literacy course, through which the authors "documented the prospective science teacher's struggle to make sense of an online content literacy course that attempted to strengthen her capabilities to combine skills-based instruction (reading) with concept-based instruction (science)" (Alvermann et al., 2011b, p. 28). The PST completed nine modules related to the semester-long course's content, each of which included clinical practice, research-based and practitioner-oriented readings, strategy application instructions, and interactive (e.g., Internet) resources; additionally, she completed four intervention lesson plans, for which she received feedback from the instructor and her mentor.

In a related study, Alvermann et al. (2011a) turned their attention from science to gain a better understanding of reading and mathematics instruction through the experiences of two pairs of preservice and practicing teachers. With the mentorship of the practicing teachers, the PSTs developed and implemented lesson plans and wrote reflections. In one of the interviews, the researchers (Alvermann et al., 2011a) found that "there was some indication that [participant] understood the value in integrating reading strategies and domain knowledge, especially if it helped struggling readers to achieve in mathematics" (p. 16). However, the team concluded:

> Despite its good intentions, the online multilevel mentoring approach proved unable to alter some firmly entrenched beliefs about the way things are and the complex relationships that sustain the status quo of a field by privileging certain practices over others. (Alvermann et al., 2011a, p. 21)

In the Application I section, we reviewed Daisey's 2009 study in which she evaluated PSTs' content-area literacy beliefs but had insufficient information about the course and their learned application. Whereas, Daisey's 2012 study explored how PSTs learned and applied course content knowledge in a required field experience. The PSTs implemented lessons on pre-, during-, and after-reading strategies with secondary school-aged students in a mathematics class. Daisey (2012) reported that enthusiasm toward the integration of tradebooks and reading strategies into mathematics classes increased for the school-aged students, cooperating teachers, and the PSTs.

In another disciplinary literacy study, van Zee et al. (2012) closely examined listening, speaking, writing, reading, creating, and critiquing in science contexts. The researchers used class activities, assignments, and survey data to gain a better understanding of how the aspiring teachers' development of science concepts was enhanced by the integration of literacy practices.

The course, designed in "collaboration by faculty in the College of Science and the College of Education" and supported by the National Science Foundation, was developed to "prepare teachers to enhance literacy learning as they teach science" (van Zee et al., 2012, p. 670) and incorporated a variety of assignments and activities to enhance learning, such as interpreting physics learning experiences, using content-area literacy strategies (e.g., concept maps, KWL), small- and whole-group discussions, role-playing, creating websites, close readings, and reflective writing.

Most importantly, the course concluded with a field trip to a K–12 school/classroom where the PSTs taught a small science lesson. The authors noted, "For many, this [was] their first teaching experience. Our hope is that they begin forming an identity as teachers who enjoy science and who engage their students in exploring natural phenomena" (van Zee et al., 2012, p. 676).

Lenski and Thieman (2013) contributed to this discussion of implementation and questioned whether PSTs' preparation would differ in the twenty-first century. They explored the extent to which social studies PSTs would use literacy strategies in their student teaching by reviewing the PSTs' school context data, lesson plans, and reflections. According to Lenski and Thieman (2013), the PSTs incorporated literacy strategies into their instruction, as they "appropriated literacy strategies to fit their social studies lesson plans" (pp. 69–70) and regularly used "higher-level literacy strategies" (p. 70).

The findings also prompted the researchers to consider how courses and field placements could better support and scaffold students for teaching in diverse classrooms that include, for example, "poverty, diversity, and/or [English language learners] ELLs. Since one of the goals of [their] program is to prepare [PSTs] for high-poverty schools, we need to think about ways that students can stay in the same placement for two consecutive terms" (Lenski & Thieman, 2013, p. 77).

Rodriguez (2015), also concerned with the twenty-first-century direction of teacher preparation, reimagined how to better support and prepare her PSTs to teach reading within their content instruction. Rodriguez (2015) implemented the disciplinary literacy pedagogy (DLP), which "involved collaboration between experts in literacy and in the disciplines" (p. 165), and worked with colleagues in other disciplines (i.e., science and social studies) to redesign the course and PSTs' experiences.

Part of a larger study, this case study focused on one ELA PST. As part of the field experience, the PST participated in a digital book club which he tutored "in an after-school literacy program," developed lesson plans and an interdisciplinary unit, and wrote reflections (Rodriguez, 2015, p. 166). The researcher concluded that the combination of DLP and field experiences enhanced the learning experiences for the tutor and the tutee, thus warranting further research.

Building upon Rodriguez's (2015) research, the final two studies in this section use technology integration as a platform to inform and prepare their PSTs. First, Colwell (2016) explored PSTs' beliefs regarding disciplinary literacy through a blogging project assigned in a social studies methods course. According to Colwell (2016), the incorporation of "computer-mediated communication" into teacher preparation courses can "provide socially meaningful experiences and a sharing of knowledge" (Groenke, 2008; Rhodes & Robnolt, 2009; p. 36).

Aiming to "scaffold students' responses to engage, or further engage, their partners in disciplinary literacy" (Colwell, 2016, p. 39), twenty-eight PSTs participated in a twelve-week blog project with middle-school students from a history class. Constant comparison analysis of the blog entries revealed three emergent themes: positive beliefs about disciplinary literacy, impact of practice, and "influence of continued blog writing on beliefs" (p. 41). The researcher concluded that the blogging activity positively influenced the PSTs to consider the connections, both direct and indirect, between literacy and social studies instruction.

In the final Application II study, Saine and West (2017) examined PSTs' self-efficacy beliefs about online writing and teaching. The authors sought not only to help their thirty-six PSTs but also a group of secondary high school students. In a content-area literacy course, the PSTs used the virtual interaction of Edmodo (see http://edmodo.com) "to give feedback on the high school students' mulitgenre papers over a period of six weeks" (Saine & West, 2017, p. 71). Similar to other studies (such as Colwell, 2016; Daisey, 2009; O'Brien & Stewart, 1990; Warren-Kring & Rutledge, 2011), the PSTs were apprehensive about this assignment and teaching format; however, "The enactive mastery experiences candidates gained through this study contributed to their self-efficacy in the areas of giving feedback, working with students, and becoming tech-savvy teachers" (Saine & West, 2017, p. 73).

The research presented in the seventeen Application II studies offers a deeper understanding of what and how PSTs learn and use literacy and literacy instruction across and within the disciplines. As a cohesive unit, these studies lead to the following conclusions: (1) PSTs need applied and in-depth literacy preparation, (2) literacy instruction can be applied in content-area and disciplinary instruction, though they differ, and (3) appropriate course instruction and knowledge, as well as application with school-aged students, provides PSTs with the much-needed scaffolding for using literacy instruction across the disciplines in their future classrooms. Still, as previously mentioned, elementary and secondary PSTs need significant exposure and practice with literacy and literacy instruction.

DIRECTIONS FOR FUTURE RESEARCH AND IMPLICATIONS FOR TEACHER PREPARATION

Further preparation, support, and research are needed to prepare PSTs for teaching content-area and disciplinary literacy to culturally and linguistically diverse learners (Rodriguez, 2015). Moje and Speyer (2008) posited that a multi-literacy approach is necessary, and Watkins and Lindahl (2010) stated, "Teachers must target ELLs' needs, considering both language skills and skills contributing to content-area literacy" (p. 24). Targeted instruction helps teachers gain awareness about students' diverse needs (Watkins & Lindahl, 2010).

Though recent researchers have explored new literacies and twenty-first-century literacies (Colwell, 2016; Rodriguez, 2015; Saine & West, 2017), the parameters of our systematic search excluded studies that examined ELLs content-area literacies, specifically. Therefore, more research in this area is needed.

We encourage researchers and educators to continue deepening their knowledge and practice, especially in the actual application of teacher pedagogy. PSTs need exposure to instructional practices (Darling-Hammond & Youngs, 2002). Describing the Peter Effect, Applegate and Applegate (2004) stated that PSTs who are engaged in and enthusiastic about reading "are more likely to use instructional activates such as literature circles and discussions, which promote engagement" (p. 555).

Therefore, teacher educators need to provide PSTs with ample opportunities to apply and hone their teaching skills, as PSTs who value literacy instruction and integration in their own education programs are more likely to use literacy strategies and sources in their own classrooms. Further, because transference of learned course content to future classroom teaching does not always occur reliably (Bean, 1997), teacher educators also need to be forward-thinking about current and twenty-first-century students and classrooms when designing course content and fieldwork experiences classes (Alvermann et al., 2011a; Feret & Smith, 2010; Nokes, 2010; Rodriguez, 2015; Sheridan-Thomas, 2007; Warren-Kring & Rutledge, 2011).

It is also important to consider PSTs' development in concert with course content and fieldwork because PSTs are mostly likely to be at different stages of development in their preparation programs (Hall, 2005). Moreover, the research reviewed for this study demonstrates that careful integration of authentic practice (Barry, 2012; Bean, 1997; Colwell, 2016, Nokes, 2010; Park, 2013; Pytash, 2013; Rodriguez, 2015) for PSTs' own learning and future classroom application is critical for preparing the next generation of teachers.

CONCLUSION

Teacher preparation is the logical venue for proactively addressing teachers' resistance to teaching content-area literacy and disciplinary literacy strategies. Therefore, researchers (e.g., Darling-Hammond & Youngs, 2002; Fisher & Ivey, 2005) reaffirm that PSTs need appropriate preparation and practice to teach literacy skills and strategies, as evidenced by both Application I and Application II studies. PSTs need effective instruction in their college courses—courses that make them think, reflect, and apply.

Unlike the limited application of professional development trainings for inservice teachers, the more sustained nature of teacher preparation courses can prepare PSTs to diversify their instruction and preparation for their technologically, culturally, and linguistically diverse future student populations. Since evidence-based research demonstrates that teacher preparation, teacher knowledge, and instructional effectiveness of literacy strategies and instruction across and within the disciplines are highly influential in adolescent learners' literacy achievement (Risko et al., 2008), teachers should be prepared to effectively facilitate students' needs to reach higher levels of literacy in all disciplines and all grade levels.

Unlike the pendulous nature of many educational debates (e.g., phonics and whole language), the shift pertaining to content-area literacy and disciplinary literacy has followed a more logical and progressive pathway. As researchers and teacher educators, we must be aware of educational needs, trends, and even reform; for that reason, the chronological organization of the studies reviewed in this study highlights the influence of researchers who helped to advance our thinking along the pathway from content-area literacy (Vacca & Vacca, 1989; 2005) to disciplinary literacy (Shanahan & Shanahan, 2008; 2012).

The next step on this pathway is emerging as a hybrid of approaches that integrates literacy instruction both across and within content-area instruction and continues to immerse PSTs in the practice and application (Pytash, 2012) of literacy instruction. Recently, researchers have begun to recognize that the separation of content-area literacy and disciplinary literacy into distinct categories presents a "false dichotomy" (Brozo et al., 2013, p. 354) and a misleading "bifurcation" (Dunkerly-Bean & Bean, 2016, p. 448) of content-area curricular approaches (Scott & Miller, 2016). Thus, we presented the reviewed studies as they progressed along this pathway, revealing the trends of the *what* and *how* of teacher preparation in this area.

REFERENCES

References marked with an asterisk indicate studies included in this review

Acosta, S., & Garza, T. (2011). The podcasting playbook: A typology of evidence-based pedagogy for pre-K classrooms with English language learners. *Research in the Schools, 18*(2), 40–57.

Applegate, A. J., & Applegate, M. D. (2004). The Peter Effect: Reading habits and attitudes of preservice teachers. *The Reading Teacher, 57*(6), 554–563.

*Alvermann, D. E., Friese, E., Beckmann, S., & Rezak, A. T. (2011a). Content area reading pedagogy and domain knowledge: A Bourdieusian analysis. *The Australian Association for Research in Education, 38*, 203–220. doi:10.1007/s13384-011-0024-x

*Alvermann, D. E., Rezak, A. T., Mallozzi, C. A., Boatright, D. D., & Jackson, D. F. (2011b). Reflective practice in an online literacy courses: Lesson learned from attempts to fuse reading and science instruction. *Teachers College Record, 113*(1), 27–56.

*Barry, A. L. (2012). "I was skeptical at first": Content literacy in the art museum. *Journal of Adolescent & Adult Literacy, 55*(7), 597–607. doi:10.1002/JAAL00071

*Bean, T. W. (1997). Preservice teachers' selection and use of content literacy strategies. *The Journal of Educational Research, 90*, 154–163. doi:10.1080/00220671.1997.10543771

Brozo, W. G., Moorman, G., Meyer, C., & Stewart, T. (2013). Content area reading and disciplinary literacy: A case for the radical center. *Journal of Adolescent & Adult Literacy, 56*(5), 353–357. doi:10.1002/JAAL.153

*Colwell, J. (2016). Examining preservice teachers' beliefs about disciplinary literacy in history through a blog project. *Action in Teacher Education, 38*(1), 34–48. doi:10.1080/01626620.2015.1118414

*Daisey, P. (2009). The reading experiences and beliefs of secondary pre-service teachers. *Reading Horizons, 49*(2), 167–190.

*Daisey, P. (2012). The promise of secondary content-area literacy field experiences. *Literacy Research and Instruction, 51*, 214–232.

Darling-Hammond, L., & Youngs, P. (2002). Defining "highly qualified teachers": What does "scientifically-based research" actually tells us? *Educational Researcher, 31*(9), 13–25. doi:10.3102/0013189X031009013

*Donahue, D. M. (2000). Experimenting with texts: New science teachers' experience and practice as readers and teachers of reading. *Journal of Adolescent & Adult Literacy, 43*, 728–739.

*Donahue, D. (2003). Reading across the great divide: English and math teachers apprentice one another as readers and disciplinary insiders. *Journal of Adolescent & Adult Literacy, 47*, 24–37.

*Dowdy, J. K., & Campbell, D. (2008). The dance of diversity: White male teachers and arts based instruction for classrooms. *The High School Journal, 91*(4), 1–11.

Dunkerly-Bean, J., & Bean, T. (2016). Missing the *Savoir* for the *Connaissance:* Disciplinary and content area literacy as regimes of truth. *Journal of Literacy Research, 48*(4), 448–475.

Fang, Z. (1996). A review of research on teacher beliefs and practices. *Educational Research, 38*(1), 47–65, doi:10.1080/0013188960380104

*Feret, A. J., & Smith, J. J. (2010). Literacy and art: Collage for pre-service teachers. *Insight: A Journal of Scholarly Teaching, 5*, 37–53.

Fisher, D., & Ivey, G. (2005). Literacy and language as learning in content-area classes: A departure from "Every Teacher a Teacher of Reading." *Action in Teacher Education, 27*(2), 3–11. doi:10.1080/01626620.2005.10463378

Groenke, S. L. (2008). Missed opportunities in cyberspace: Preparing preservice teachers to facilitate critical talk about literature through computer-mediated communication. *Journal of Adolescent & Adult Literacy, 52*(3), 224–233. doi:10.1598/JAAL.52.3.5

Hall, L. A. (2005). Teachers and content-area reading: Attitudes, beliefs, and change. *Teacher and Teacher Education, 21*, 403–414. doi:10.1016/j.tate.2005.01.009

Hannes, K., Claes, L., & Belgian Campbell Group. (2007). Learn to read and write systematic reviews: The Belgian Campbell Group. *Research on Social Work Practice, 17*, 748–753. doi:10.1177/1049731507303106

Herber, H. L. (1970). *Teaching reading in content areas.* Englewood Cliffs, NJ: Prentice Hall.

Hicks, T. (2006). Expanding the conversation: A commentary toward revision of Swenson, Rozema, Young, McGrail, and Whitin. *Contemporary Issues in Technology and Teacher Education, 6*(1), 46–55.

Hicks, T. (2018). The next decade of digital writing. *Voices from the Middle, 25*(4), 9–14.

Hikida, M, Chamberlain, K., Tily, S., Daly-Lesch, A., Warner, J. R., & Schallert, D. L. (2019). Reviewing how preservice teachers are prepared to teach reading processes: What the literature suggests and overlooks. *Journal of Literacy Research, 51*(2), 177–195. doi:10.1177/108629X19833297

*Konopak, B. C., Readence, J. F., & Wilson, E. K. (1994). Preservice and inservice secondary teachers' orientation toward content-area reading. *The Journal of Educational Research, 87*, 220–227. doi:10.1080/00220671.1994.9941246

*Lenski, S. J., & Thieman, G. Y. (2013). What work samples reveal about secondary pre-service social studies teachers' use of literacy strategies. *Teacher Education Quarterly, 40*(1), 63–79.

*Lesley, M. (2004). Looking for critical literacy with post baccalaureate content-area literacy students. *Journal of Adolescent & Adult Literacy, 48*, 320–334. doi:10.1598/JAAL.48.4.5

*Lesley, M., Watson, P., & Elliot, S. (2007). "School" reading and multiple texts: Examining the metacognitive development of secondary-level preservice teachers. *Journal of Adolescent & Adult Literacy 51*, 150–162. doi:10.1598/JAAL.51.2.6

Miller, D. M., Scott, C. E., & McTigue, E. M. (2018). Writing in the secondary-level disciplines: A systematic review of context, cognition, and content. *Educational Psychology Review, 30*(1), 83–120. http://dx.doi.org/10.1007/s10648-016-9393-z

Mishra, P., & Koehler, M. J. (2006). Technological pedagogical content knowledge: A framework for teacher knowledge. *Teachers College Record, 108*(6), 1017–1054.

Moje, E. B., & Speyer, J. (2008). The reality of challenging texts in high school science and social studies: How teachers can mediate comprehension. In K. A. Hinchman & H. K. Sheridan-Thomas (Eds.), *Best practices in adolescent literacy instruction* (pp. 185–210). New York: Guilford Press.

National Governors Association Center for Best Practices, & Council of Chief State School Officers. (2010). *Common core state standards* (English language arts & literacy in history/social studies, science, and technical subjects). Washington, DC: National Governors Association Center for Best Practice & Council of Chief State Officers.

*Nokes, J. D. (2010). Preparing novice history teachers to meet students' literacy needs. *Reading Psychology, 31*, 493–523.

*Nourie, B. L., & Lenski, S. D. (1998). The (in)effectiveness of content-area literacy instruction for secondary preservice teacher. *The Clearing House: A Journal of Educational Strategies, Issues, and Ideas, 71*, 372–374. doi:10.1080/0009865980 9599595

*O'Brien D. G., & Stewart, R. A. (1990). Preservice teachers' perspectives on why every teacher is not a teacher of reading: A qualitative analysis. *Journal of Reading Behavior, 22*, 101–129. doi:10.1080/10862969009547699

*Olson, M. R., & Truxaw, M. P. (2009). Preservice science and mathematics teachers and discursive metaknowledge of text. *Journal of Adolescent & Adult Literacy, 52*(5), 422–431.

*Park, J. Y. (2013). All the ways of reading literature: Preservice English teachers' perspectives on disciplinary literacy. *English Education, 45*(4), 361–384.

*Pytash, K. E. (2012). Engaging preservice teachers in disciplinary literacy learning through writing. *Journal of Adolescent & Adult Literacy, 55*, 527–538. doi:10.1002/JAAL.00062

*Pytash, K. E. (2013). Secondary preservice teachers' development of teaching scientific writing. *Journal of Science Teacher Education, 24*, 793–810. doi:101007/s10972-013-9338-z

*Reinke, K., Mokhtari, K., & Willner, E. (1997). Preservice teachers' perceptions of the integration of mathematics, reading, and, writing. *Teacher Education and Practice, 13*(2), 61–69.

Rhodes, J., & Robnolt, V. (2009). Digital literacies in the classroom. In L. Christenbury, R. Bomer, & P. Smagorinsky (Eds.), *Handbook of adolescent literacy research* (pp. 153–169). New York, NY: Guilford.

Risko, V. J., Roller, C. M., Cummins, C., Bean, R. M., Collins Block, C. Anders, P. L., & Flood, J. (2008). A critical analysis of research on reading teacher education. *Reading Research Quarterly, 43*, 252–288. doi:10.1598.RRQ.43.3.3

*Rodriguez, T. L. (2015). A content area reading course re-imagined: A situated case study of disciplinary literacies pedagogy in secondary English teacher education. *Literacy Research and Instruction, 54*(2), 163–184. doi:10.1080/19388071.2014.997943

*Saine, P., & West, J. A. (2017). Content area teacher candidates' self-efficacy beliefs on teaching writing online. *Journal of Digital Learning in Teacher Education, 33*(2), 69–77. doi:10.1080/21532974.2017.1280433

Scott, C. E. (2013). Every teacher a teacher of reading?: A systematic literature review of content-area literacy (Unpublished doctoral dissertation). College Station: Texas A&M University.

Scott, C. E., & Miller, D. M. (2016). Content-area reading and writing: A brief historical perspective to inform research, policy, and teacher preparation. *Association of Literacy Educators and Researchers Yearbook, 38*, 199–217.

Scott, C. E., McTigue, E. M., Miller, D. M., & Washburn, E. K. (2018). The what, when, and how of preservice teachers and literacy across the disciplines: A systematic literature review of nearly 50 years of research. *Teaching and Teacher Education, 73*, 1–13. https://doi.org/10.1016/j.tate.2018.03.010

Shanahan, T., & Shanahan, C. (2008). Teaching disciplinary literacy to adolescents: Rethinking content-area literacy. *Harvard Educational Review, 78*(1), 40–59.

Shanahan, T., & Shanahan, C. (2012). What is disciplinary literacy and why does it matter? *Topics in Language Disorders, 32*(1), 7–18. doi:10.1097/TLD.0b013e318244557a

*Sheridan-Thomas, H. K. (2007). Making sense of multiple literacies: Exploring pre-service content-area teachers' understanding and applications. *Reading Research and Instruction, 46*, 121–150. doi:10.1080/19388070709558464

Shulman, L. S. (1986). Those who understand: Knowledge growth in teaching. *Educational Researcher, 15*(2), 4–14.

Torgerson, C. J. (2007). The quality of systematic reviews of effectiveness in literacy learning in English: A "tertiary" review. *Journal of Research in Reading, 30*, 287–315.

Torgerson, C., Porthouse, J., & Brooks, G. (2005). A systematic review of controlled trials evaluating interventions in adult literacy and numeracy. *Journal of Research in Reading, 28*, 87–107.

Tovani, C. (2004). *Do I really have to teach reading?: Content comprehension, grades 6–12*. Portland, ME: Stenhouse.

*Warren-Kring, B. Z., & Rutledge, V. C. (2011). Adolescents' comprehension and content area education students' perceptions: Benefits from one-on-one tutoring. *The Teacher Educator, 46*(3), 244–261.

Watkins, N. M., & Lindahl, K. M. (2010). Targeting content area literacy instruction to meet the needs of adolescent English Language Learners. *Middle School Journal, 4*(3), 23–33.

*Wilburne, J. M., & Napoli, M. (2008). Connecting mathematics and literature: An analysis of pre-service elementary school teachers' changing beliefs and knowledge. *IUMPST: The Journal, 2*, 1–15.

Vacca, R. T., & Vacca, J. A. (1989). *Content area reading* (3rd Ed.). New York: HarperCollins.

Vacca, R. T., & Vacca, J. A. (2005). *Content area reading: Literacy and learning across the curriculum* (8th Ed.). Boston: Allyn and Bacon.

*van Zee, E. H., Jansen, H., Winograd, K., Crowl, M., & Devitt, A. (2012). Integrating physics and literacy learning in a physics course for prospective elementary and middle school teachers. *Journal of Science Teacher Education, 24*(4), 665–691. doi:10.1007/s10972-

Vaughn, J. L. (1977). A scale to measure attitudes toward teaching reading in content classrooms. *Journal of Reading, 20*(7), 605–609.

Chapter 8

We Need *Better*, Not *More*: Results from a Study Examining the Impact of Duration and Quality of Field Experience on Teacher Preparation

Amanda L. Nolen and Karina R. Clemmons

The National Council for Accreditation of Teacher Education (NCATE) Blue Ribbon Panel on teacher preparation pointed to the demands on American schools to educate all students "including those from increasingly diverse economic, racial, linguistic, and academic backgrounds" (p. 1) and called these demands an unprecedented responsibility (2010). The panel stipulated that what was needed was not just revision but a complete transformation of the way in which teacher preparation is envisioned (NCATE, 2010). The NCATE report is one of several recent publications that advocates for the need to make field experiences the center of teacher education (American Association of Colleges for Teacher Education [AACTE], 2010; Ball & Forzani, 2009; Grossman & McDonald, 2008; Hollins, 2011; Solomon, 2009; U.S. Department of Education, 2011).

One strategy for teacher education reform proposed by many of these reports is what Darling-Hammond (2010) referred to as "a major overhaul of the relationships between universities and schools" (p. 42). A significant focus of the reform is the interplay between coursework and field experiences.

Darling-Hammond (2010) was critical of how traditional teacher education programs typically provide coursework prior to, and in isolation from, field experiences. As an alternative solution, the Blue Ribbon report supports a model which "fully integrates content, pedagogy, and professional coursework around a core of clinical experience" (NCATE, 2010, p. 9), depending on close collaboration between K–12 schools and teacher education programs. Darling-Hammond (2010) argued that highly effective programs are characterized by candidates spending lengthy amounts of time in the field throughout their program of study, with coursework interwoven with clinical work.

The idea that more *time* in the field is more *valuable* is a pervasive theme in current teacher education reform. Lengthy field experiences, particularly internships, are deemed as essential to prepare new teachers effectively, but little research exists to support this idea. The purpose of this study is to explore the value of field experience by examining the interchange between the *duration* of a particular experience and other aspects of the teachers' field experiences.

PERSPECTIVES AND THEORETICAL FRAMEWORK

The literature reviewed for this study reflects the perspectives on teacher self-efficacy and teacher preparation. As well, the literature reviewed focused on the duration of field experiences.

Teacher Self-Efficacy and Teacher Preparation Program Characteristics

Teacher self-efficacy, the sense of being capable of the tasks required for success, is recognized as being connected to teacher practice (Atiles, Jones, & Kim, 2012; Caprano, Caprano, & Helfeldt, 2010; Darling-Hammond, Chung, & Frelow, 2002; Lee et al., 2012). Teachers who feel well prepared to teach have higher teaching self-efficacy and sense of responsibility for student learning, and they plan to stay in teaching longer than new teachers who feel less well prepared by their programs or pathways to teaching (Darling-Hammond, Chung, & Frelow, 2002).

Research supports the idea that characteristics of teacher preparation programs and their corresponding field experiences affect teachers and their self-efficacy (Caprano, Caprano, & Helfeldt, 2010; Darling-Hammond, Chung, & Frelow, 2002; Lee et al., 2012). Caprano, Caprano, and Helfeldt (2010) found that teachers whose teacher education programs included a strong connection between coursework and field experiences, and whose field experiences reflected a strong university–school partnership felt more well prepared that those whose field experiences did not stress these components.

A study of beginning teachers in New York City found that teachers who complete a university-based teacher preparation program feel more well prepared to teach than teachers from alternate programs such as Teach for America or teachers who only complete licensure exams without any additional preparation for the classroom (Darling-Hammond, Chung, & Frelow, 2002). Darling-Hammond, Chung, and Frelow (2002) also found that several specific university-based teacher education programs produced graduates who felt more well prepared to teach. Though the characteristics of the programs that produced teachers who felt more prepared were not the focus of the study, a discussion noted possible characteristics of highly rated programs, such as the combination of study, reflection, and field experiences of approximately one year.

Research on field experiences in teacher preparation programs covers many broad topics such as reflection (Liakopoulou, 2012), school context (Mihaly et al., 2012), experience with diversity (Atiles, Jones, & Kim, 2012; Bergman, 2013), and literacy strategies (Otaiba et al., 2012; Sampson et al., 2013). Caprano, Caprano, and Helfeldt (2010) compared preservice teachers' perceptions of confidence based on their participation in different types of field experiences: traditional, professional development school model, and inquiry-based model. Their results suggested that the quality of field experiences have a more positive impact than simply the duration of time that teacher candidates spend in field experiences.

Duration of Field Experience

Field-based teacher preparation models, often referred to as clinically intensive, typically advocate placing teacher candidates in schools throughout the program rather than the traditional approach of starting with coursework on campus and culminating in school-based field experiences. Darling-Hammond (2010) argued that "the most powerful programs require students to spend extensive time in the field throughout the entire program, examining and applying the concepts and strategies they are simultaneously learning about in their courses" (p. 42). The AACTE advocates for a full year "residency" for candidates, stating that "extended clinical preparation has a significant impact on generating teachers who are effective in the classroom on day one" (2013, p. 16). However, year-long residencies are presently only found in 5 percent of programs (AACTE, 2013).

A feature that distinguishes clinically intensive teacher preparation models from traditional ones is the role of faculty. Zeichner (2010) argued that the role of tenure-track faculty in field supervision needs to become much more substantial rather than the dependence on clinical faculty. In the Boston Teacher Residency Project, course instructors, mentor teachers, and other field personnel work collaboratively toward the accomplishment of the competencies of the program, helping students "to make sense of the viewpoints held by the many teacher educators he or she encounters" (Solomon, 2009, p. 482).

Proponents of clinically intensive models have also addressed the structure of student learning. Ball and Forzani (2009) argued that the quality of learning in teacher preparation must be reconceived. They explained how effective teacher preparation requires extensive time in the field, providing multiple opportunities for observing, analyzing, practicing, and coaching, and measuring of performance against exemplars. Similarly, Lampert et al. (2013), Hollins (2011), and Solomon (2009) have all argued that learning to teach requires cycles of repeated planning and practice followed by reflection and feedback through which routines and conceptual knowledge are gradually built.

The importance of the field placement of teacher candidates in field experiences has also been the focus of scrutiny. Darling-Hammond (2010) argued that "the clinical side of teacher education has been fairly haphazard, depending on the idiosyncrasies of loosely selected placements with little guidance about what happens in them" (p. 40). Zeichner (2010) also criticized the process in which he claimed that administrative and logistical factors often take precedence over the pedagogical needs of the student teacher.

In summary, supporters of clinically intensive models advocate for programs that are centered around a vital shift in how universities and field sites work together in the process of preparing teacher candidates. They envision programs grounded in clinical experiences and culminating in year-long residencies. Unfortunately, these reports pose arguments based almost entirely on theory and rhetoric rather the findings of empirical research. There is little evidence of the outcome of longer field experiences related to candidate performance, program quality, or even pragmatically, the ability of programs to recruit and retain students.

The purpose of this study is not to challenge the value of field experiences but rather to explore *how much* is enough and what specific characteristics of field experiences produce well-prepared teachers. This study fills a critical gap in educational research related to duration and quality of teacher field experiences and informs the national debate on teacher preparation reform by examining the following research question: How does duration of field experience/internship, along with program characteristics, predicts early career teachers' sense of preparedness to teach?

METHODS AND MODES OF INQUIRY

Beginning in May 2010, all Arkansas early career teachers teaching a five-year period or less received a survey to reflect upon and evaluate their teacher preparation program curriculum, field experiences, and their own sense of preparedness for teaching upon graduating from the program. This study was located in Arkansas because the state significantly exceeds the national average on teacher retention and teacher quality (NCTQ, 2014) and provides an intrinsically valuable case for investigation for the benefit of the national discussion on quality teacher preparation.

DATA SOURCES AND ANALYSIS

As of May 2013, a total of 1,149 completed surveys were returned by Arkansas' early career teachers. Respondent characteristics resembled those in the Arkansas early career teacher workforce. Respondent characteristics resembled relatively closely those of all Arkansas beginning teachers: 75.7 percent were female; 51.5 percent were thirty-five years old or younger; 80 percent were white, 1.4 percent Hispanic, 6.2 percent African American, 0.3 percent Asian or Pacific Islander, and 10.9 percent were "other" or chose not to respond.

Approximately 63 percent of respondents had obtained licensure through a traditional undergraduate teacher education program through a university. Another 19.8 percent obtained licensure through preparation from a nontraditional Master's of Arts in Teaching (MAT) graduate program. Finally, 17.4 percent were prepared through an alternative route in the state (i.e., Teach for America or the Arkansas Department of Education). These percentages slightly underestimate the percentage of newly hired teachers from alternative programs and slightly overestimate the percentage from nontraditional programs.

The survey consisted of six sections devoted to teacher preparation program, field experiences, preparation for the classroom, mentoring and induction, future plans, and background information. The focus of this study examines the respondents' field experiences (e.g., duration and variety), program characteristics, and their sense of preparedness for teaching upon leaving their program. The survey contained questions targeted at predicting the teachers' sense of preparedness for their first years of teaching four areas: (1) promoting student learning, (2) teaching critical thinking and social development, (3) understanding learners, and (4) developing instructional leadership.

The teachers were asked how much time they spent student teaching as part of their preparation prior to becoming a classroom teacher. Over 25 percent of the respondents ($n = 275$) indicated that they spent between seven months and one year in their student teaching placement and almost 24 percent ($n = 258$) reported that they spent more than one year in the field. The remaining teachers reported receiving between four and six months of student teaching (19.9 percent, $n = 229$), between one and three months (10.1 percent, $n = 116$), and finally 15.4 percent ($n=177$) reported spending fewer than four weeks in their student teaching placement.

In addition to length of their student teaching experience, teachers were asked to respond to items about the characteristics of the teacher preparation program they attended. These characteristics included whether or not the program articulated a clear vision for teaching and learning, emphasized teaching in rural schools, emphasized teaching in high-poverty schools, and demonstrated coherence among courses as well as between courses and field-work. A summary of responses is presented in table 8.2.

Student teaching quality included a cluster of eight items, as shown in table 8.1. These items addressed the quality of the cooperating teacher, the degree to which a cooperating teacher's methods and philosophies corresponded with those of the program faculty, the amount of supervision and feedback provided to the student teacher, and the student teacher's access to a faculty advisor. Student teaching variety included a cluster of seven items, as shown in table 8.2. These items addressed whether the students' field experiences varied across settings and student abilities, including English language learners (ELLs). On each of the items, at least 44 percent reported that their student teaching experiences allowed them to teach different student abilities, different student socioeconomic groups, different student ethnic groups, and different grade levels.

Finally, the thirty preparedness items included on the survey are based on the work of Darling-Hammond, Chung, and Frelow (2002) and of Silvernail's (1998) four factors that best describe a teacher's sense of preparedness. The four factors addressed the teachers' sense of preparedness to (1) promote student learning, (2) teach critical thinking and social development, (3) understand learners, and (4) develop instructional leadership. An index was created by taking the mean of each respondent's responses across the thirty items, thus creating a composite score ranging from 1 to 4. Table 8.3 summarizes the wording of the items included in the index.

A multiple regression analysis was conducted to determine how well the length of field experiences/internship, the variety of field experiences/internship, quality of field experiences/internship experiences, and program characteristics predicted early career teachers' sense of preparedness to teach.

Table 8.1. Length of Student Teaching/Internship Experience of Arkansas Early Career Teachers

		Frequency	Percentage	Valid Percentage	Cumulative Percentage
	None	177	15.4	16.4	16.4
	Less than 4 weeks total	24	2.1	2.2	18.6
	1–3 months	116	10.1	10.7	29.3
	4–6 months	229	19.9	21.2	50.5
	7 months—1 year	277	24.0	25.4	75.9
	More than 1 year	258	22.6	23.9	100.0
	Total	1081	94.1	100.0	
Missing	System	68	5.9		
Total		1149	100.0		

Table 8.2. Teacher Preparation Program Characteristics and Student Teaching/Internship Placements of Arkansas Early Career Teachers

Program Characteristics	Disagree n	Disagree %	Somewhat Disagree n	Somewhat Disagree %	Somewhat Agree n	Somewhat Agree %	Agree n	Agree %
My program articulated a clear vision for teaching and learning.	24	2.2	44	4.0	228	20.9	797	72.9
My program placed a lot of emphasis on teaching in rural schools.	204	19.1	275	25.7	374	35.0	216	20.2
My program placed a lot of emphasis on teaching in high-poverty schools.	193	18.0	257	24.0	379	35.4	241	22.5
My program had a strong sense of coherence among courses.	54	5.0	103	9.5	359	33.1	567	52.4
My program had a strong sense of coherence between coursework and field experiences.	41	3.6	106	9.2	340	29.6	597	55.1

Student Teaching/Internship Experience	Yes n	Yes %	No n	No %
Vary by grade level	810	76.4	251	23.6
Vary by school level	489	46.4	566	53.6
Vary by school district	509	48.9	532	51.1
Vary by student race/ethnic composition	598	59.3	411	40.7
Vary by student socioeconomic status (SES)	584	52.9	521	47.1
Vary by number of ELL students	490	48.9	512	51.1
Vary by academic ability of students	563	56.2	438	43.8

Table 8.3. Early Career Teacher Preparedness Based on Silvermail's (1998) Thirty Dimensions of Teaching

	Mean	Std. Deviation	n
Teach subject matter concepts, knowledge, and skills in ways that enable students to learn	1.64	.719	1037
Understand how different students in your classroom are learning	1.78	.763	1034
Identify and address learning needs and/or difficulties of students	1.92	.782	1035
Set challenging and appropriate expectations of learning and performance for students	1.74	.713	1032
Develop curriculum that builds on students' experiences	1.78	.741	1033
Evaluate curriculum materials for their usefulness and appropriateness for your students	1.81	.787	1033
Identify and obtain materials and use community resources to create a multicultural curriculum	1.96	.842	1031
Relate classroom learning to the real world	1.53	.679	1032
Understand how students' social, emotional, physical, and cognitive development influences learning	1.66	.732	1028
Understand how students' family and cultural backgrounds may influence learning	1.65	.740	1033
Identify and address special learning needs and/or difficulties	1.93	.810	1033
Teach in ways that support new English language learners	2.34	.934	1026
Choose teaching strategies for different instructional purposes	1.68	.732	1020
Motivate individual students and classes of students to engage in the learning process	1.68	.735	1032
Develop a classroom environment that promotes social development and group responsibility	1.58	.718	1030
Develop students' questions and discussion skills	1.73	.757	1032
Engage students in cooperative group work as well as independent learning	1.63	.714	1032
Use questions to stimulate different kinds of student learning	1.65	.715	1025
Help students learn to think critically and solve problems	1.79	.674	1028
Encourage students to see, question, and interpret ideas from diverse perspectives	1.79	.736	1028
Plan instruction by using knowledge of learning subject matter, curriculum, and student development	1.62	.700	1030
Understand how factors in the students' environment outside of school may influence their life and learning	1.63	.735	1029
Work with parents and families to better understand students and support their learning	1.87	.790	1029
Use a variety of assessments to determine student progress	1.72	.771	1027
Evaluate and reflect on your practice to improve instruction	1.56	.691	1029

	Mean	Std. Deviation	n
Maintain an orderly, purposeful learning environment	1.58	.709	1027
Plan and solve problems with colleagues	1.59	.708	1027
Assume leadership responsibilities in your school	1.80	.769	1025
Teach classes that included a wide variety of student ability levels	1.72	.756	1029
Teach in high-poverty settings	1.92	.850	1025

Note: 1 = "Very prepared"; 2 = "Somewhat prepared"; 3 = "Somewhat unprepared"; and 4 = "Very unprepared."

Table 8.4. Model Summary Table for Predictors of Early Career Teachers' Preparedness

Model	R	R^2	Adjusted R^2	Std. Error of the Estimate	R^2 Change	F Change	df1	df2	Sig. F Change
1	.108*	.012	.010	.521	.012	5.91	1	967	.015
2	.516**	.266	.258	.451	.255	34.39	5	960	.000
3	.534***	.286	.267	.448	.019	1.87	7	954	.073

Note:
   *. Predictors: (Constant), length of student teaching/internship;
  **. Predictors: (Constant), length of student teaching/internship, program characteristics;
 ***. Predictors: (Constant), length of student teaching/internship, program characteristics, student teaching/internship variety.

RESULTS

The variable descriptions and frequencies can be found in tables 8.1–8.3. The linear combination of student teaching/internship length, variety, program characteristics, and the quality of the cooperating teacher/placement significantly predicted teacher preparedness, $F_{13,954} = 9.33, p < 0.0001$. The adjusted R^2 value was 0.35 (0.312 adjusted), indicating that approximately 35 percent of the variance in teachers' sense of preparedness was explained by these three predictors (table 8.4). However, the beta weights, presented in table 8.5, suggested that when all factors were considered, program characteristics and the quality of the cooperating teacher contribute to the preparedness of the teachers.

Length of Time in the Field as a Predictor of Teacher Preparedness

As seen in table 8.4, the first model examined the effect of length of time in the field during their teacher preparation program on the sense of preparedness of early career teachers. When considered alone, length of time

Table 8.5. Unstandardized and Standardized Coefficients for Regression Model Predicting Early Career Teacher Preparedness

Model		Unstandardized Coefficients		Standardized Coefficients		
		B	Std. Error	Beta	t	Sig.
1	(Constant)	1.961	.101		19.512	.000
	Length of time in the field — Roughly, how much time did you spend in a PreK–12 classroom as part of your teacher preparation program, prior to becoming a fulltime classroom teacher? (Includes all field experiences such as observations, practicum, internships, or student teaching)	-0.057	.021	-0.130	-2.751	.006
2	(Constant)	1.708	.168		10.174	.000
	Length of time in the field — Roughly, how much time did you spend in a PreK–12 classroom as part of your teacher preparation program, prior to becoming a fulltime classroom teacher? (Includes all field experiences such as observations, practicum, internships, or student teaching)	-0.049	.021	-0.114	-2.307	.022
	Variety of field experiences — Vary by grade level	-0.087	.070	-0.067	-1.243	.215
	Vary by school level	.056	.053	.054	1.059	.290
	Vary by school district	-0.002	.057	-0.002	-0.037	.971
	Vary by racial composition	.009	.104	.008	.087	.931
	Vary by SES	-0.031	.110	-0.028	-0.279	.781
	Vary by number of ELL students	.216	.068	.205	3.163	.002
	Vary by ability level of students	-0.039	.077	-0.036	-0.510	.610
3	(Constant)	3.396	.208		16.334	.000
	Length of time in the field — Roughly, how much time did you spend in a PreK–12 classroom as part of your teacher preparation program, prior to becoming a fulltime classroom teacher? (Includes all field experiences such as observations, practicum, internships, or student teaching)	-0.023	.019	-0.053	-1.208	.228
	Variety of field experiences — Vary by grade level	-0.060	.061	-0.046	-0.975	.330
	Vary by school level	.035	.047	.033	.741	.459
	Vary by school district	-0.007	.050	-0.007	-0.141	.888

		B	SE	Beta	t	Sig.
	Vary by racial composition	.003	.090	.003	.033	.974
	Vary by SES	-0.075	.096	-0.068	-0.777	.437
	Vary by number of ELL students	.175	.059	.166	2.950	.003
	Vary by ability level of students	-0.012	.067	-0.011	-0.174	.862
Program characteristics	My program articulated a clear vision for teaching and learning	-0.138	.046	-0.158	-2.968	.003
	My program placed a lot of emphasis on teaching in rural schools	.000	.028	.000	.007	.994
	My program placed a lot of emphasis on teaching in high-poverty schools	-0.082	.027	-0.158	-2.993	.003
	My program had a strong sense of coherence among courses	-0.073	.037	-0.115	-1.956	.051
	My program had a strong sense of coherence between courses and field experiences	-0.073	.040	-0.107	-1.809	.071
	I heard similar views about teaching and learning across courses	-0.036	.044	-0.047	-0.820	.413
	I felt part of a larger group of people who all shared common values with respect to teaching	-0.102	.040	-0.134	-2.575	.010
4	(Constant)	2.976	.226		13.182	.000
Length of time in the field	Roughly, how much time did you spend in a PreK-12 classroom as part of your teacher preparation program, prior to becoming a fulltime classroom teacher? (Includes all field experiences such as observations, practicum, internships, or student teaching)	-0.016	.019	-0.038	-0.874	.382
Variety of field experiences	Vary by grade level	-0.056	.061	-0.043	-0.925	.355
	Vary by school level	.014	.047	.014	.307	.759
	Vary by school district	.012	.049	.011	.241	.810
	Vary by racial composition	-0.007	.090	-0.007	-0.081	.935
	Vary by SES	-0.083	.095	-0.075	-0.881	.379
	Vary by number of ELL students	.158	.059	.150	2.700	.007
	Vary by ability level of students	-0.009	.066	-0.008	-0.132	.895
Program characteristics	My program articulated a clear vision for teaching and learning	-0.136	.046	-0.156	-2.930	.004
	My program placed a lot of emphasis on teaching in rural schools	.003	.027	.006	.120	.905
	My program placed a lot of emphasis on teaching in high-poverty schools	-0.070	.027	-0.134	-2.568	.011

(Continued)

Table 8.5. (Continued)

Model		Unstandardized Coefficients		Standardized Coefficients	t	Sig.
		B	Std. Error	Beta		
	My program had a strong sense of coherence among courses	-0.074	.037	-0.117	-1.977	.049
	My program had a strong sense of coherence between courses and field experiences	-0.050	.040	-0.074	-1.242	.215
	I heard similar views about teaching and learning across courses	-0.038	.043	-0.050	-0.892	.373
	I felt part of a larger group of people who all shared common values with respect to teaching	-0.063	.040	-0.082	-1.565	.118
Quality of placement and cooperating teacher	My cooperating teacher was an excellent teacher	-0.124	.056	-0.194	-2.214	.027
	My cooperating teacher provided me feedback that improved my instruction	.005	.068	.009	.080	.937
	My cooperating teacher provided me feedback that improved my classroom management	.004	.065	.006	.055	.956
	My cooperating teacher taught in ways that were quite similar to methods I was learning in my courses	.127	.044	.237	2.886	.004
	I held similar ideas about teaching and learning to those espoused by my program	-0.048	.045	-0.085	-1.073	.284
	Someone from my program was available to talk with me when I had questions or concerns about teaching	.008	.041	.012	.191	.848
	I was observed on a regular basis by someone from my program	.020	.039	.033	.522	.602
	Someone from my program gave me useful feedback on my teaching	.024	.049	.037	.488	.626
	My student teaching allowed me to try out the strategies and techniques I was learning in my classes	.082	.041	.127	2.025	.044

Note: a. Dependent Variable: Preparedness composite.

does significantly predict preparedness, $t = -2.75$, $p = 0.006$. However, in terms of the practicality of that prediction, length of time in the field only explained about 1.7 percent of the variance of early career teachers' sense of preparedness.

Variety of Field Experiences

When variety of field experiences was added to length of time in the field, the predictive power of the model increased to 5 percent of the overall variance of early career teachers' sense of preparedness (table 8.4). The cluster of items pertaining to the variety of the field experiences during the teacher preparation program contributed only 3.3 percent to the explanatory model ($F_{change} = 2.154$, $p_{change} = 0.037$). Among this cluster of items, only the item indicating a presence of English language learners (table 8.5) was significant ($t = 3.163$, $p = 0.002$). In other words, field experiences that varied by grade level, racial composition, SES, or ability level did not have a significant effect on the preparedness of early career teachers.

Teachers who reported having field experiences during their preparation programs that included ELL students, tended to report being more prepared for teaching. In this model, length of time in the field remains a significant predictor ($p = 0.022$).

Program Characteristics

Model 3 included length of time in the field, variety of field experiences, and teacher preparation program characteristics. Together, these three predictors increased the predictive power of the model to 30.3 percent ($F_{change} = 22.060$, $p < 0.0001$). Adding program characteristics into the model rendered length of time in the field as nonsignificant in the model ($p = 0.228$). The importance of providing field experiences that include ELL students, however, still remained a significant predictor ($t = 2.950$, $p = 0.003$). Within program characteristics, only three of seven characteristics contributed to the model. These included "program articulated a clear vision for teaching and learning" ($t = -2.968$, $p = 0.003$), "program placed a lot of emphasis on teaching in high-poverty schools" ($t = -2.993$, $p = 0.003$), and "felt part of a larger group of people who all shared common values with respect to teaching" ($t = -2.575$, $p = 0.010$).

Quality of Field Placement and Cooperating Teacher

Finally, model 4 included all predictor variables: length of time in the field, variety of field experiences, teacher preparation program characteristics, and the quality of the field placement, including the cooperating teachers. This full model yielded an $R^2 = 0.350$ (Adj $R^2 = 0.312$), indicating that this linear combination of variables explained approximately 35 percent of the variance associated with the sense of preparedness of early career teachers ($F_{change\ 9,416} = 3.313$, $p = 0.001$, Durbin–Watson = 1.797). All of the variables that were significant in model 3 remained so in model 4 except the program characteristic "program had a strong sense of coherence among courses" was now significant ($t = -1.977$, $p = 0.049$).

Not all of the nine items that comprised the Quality of Placement variable were significantly added to the model. The two strongest predictive items pertained to the quality of the cooperating teacher: "cooperating teacher was an excellent teacher" ($t = 2.214$, $p = 0.027$) and "cooperating teacher taught in ways similar to . . . courses" ($t = 2.886$, $p = 0.004$). The third significant item in this cluster was "My student teaching allowed me to try out strategies and techniques I was learning in my classes" ($t = 2.025$, $p = 0.044$).

DISCUSSION

These findings of this study point to the dynamic and complex nature of the factors related to teacher preparation. Teacher preparation programs must articulate a clear vision of curriculum goals and the role the teacher plays in student learning. In addition, aligning curriculum across the program as well as aligning course content with field experiences serves to reinforce the connection from theory to practice above and beyond the time the candidates spend in the field.

The finding that teachers indicated the value of a student teaching environment that allowed them the ability to try out strategies and techniques they learned in their coursework points to two important factors in teacher preparation. Teacher preparation programs, faculty, and coursework must reflect the cutting edge of research and best practices to prepare candidates for the twenty-first-century classroom. In addition, the choice of cooperating teacher is a critical one for teacher preparation programs. More than meeting minimum requirements, an effective cooperating teacher must be able to not only mentor and guide but also provide a student teacher with the freedom to turn theory to action, practice to praxis.

The finding that new teachers specified the importance of quality cooperating teachers during their internships indicates a great need to identify the qualities of an effective cooperating teacher. This finding suggests future research to determine what specific characteristics of cooperating teachers are most helpful to teacher candidates? Once identified, teacher education program should systematically put policies in place to find and foster productive relationships with cooperating teachers with those characteristics.

The variety of field experiences yielded mixed results as predictors of teachers' sense of preparedness when considered together with program characteristics. This finding suggests that recent calls for clinically intensive teacher preparation models are not sustainable without further investigation. Decentralizing teacher preparation program curriculum and only embedding the content within the field experiences could undermine the program goals and cohesion of the content.

CONCLUSION

Overall, the results suggest that length of time in the field becomes secondary to a strong, cohesive, and mature program along with cooperating teachers who are exemplars of best practices. The results of this study support the findings of Caprano, Caprano, and Helfeldt (2010). When comparing the perceived competence of novice teachers, they found no statistical significance when factoring in length of time in the field.

The findings of these two studies do not necessarily negate earlier calls to extend field experiences and internships for teacher candidates. However, the results strongly suggests that length of field experiences loses importance when considered alongside program qualities such as cohesion of message, emphasis on special populations, alignment of course curriculum with field experiences, and placement of candidates with quality cooperating teachers.

High-profile national reports on the direction of teacher preparation have emphasized the importance of field experience and current calls for action indicate the need for longer field experiences. Unfortunately, there is little empirical support for these calls. The cost of implementing year-long internships would be unwieldy and unsustainable. Fallon (2006) took educational researchers to task for not empirically investigating and producing persuasive, trustworthy evidence around how to best prepare teachers. He concluded his article:

> Advocates of teacher education programs within institutions of higher education cannot promote them effectively with a predominance of logical propositions and moral argument. In the end, dependable relationships between the interventions of teacher education programs and the learning of pupils taught by teachers who have been subject to those interventions must be reliably demonstrated with convincing evidence. (p. 152)

The current study provides empirical evidence about the effectiveness of teacher preparation programs, specifically, the length of culminating field experiences/internships. The findings of this study suggest that while length of time in the field is somewhat important, it is overshadowed by the overarching teacher preparation program goals and curriculum. The difference between six-month and year-long internships is more than a factor of length; longer internships are more costly for teacher education programs, for teacher candidates, and for K–12 schools. When recruiting students, program faculty must justify why significant time in the field is necessary when potential teacher candidates could easily find a program with little to no internship requirements. Some teacher candidates might find the time and expense of year-long internships to be prohibitive.

Previous research has recognized the importance of the field experience and current calls for action indicate the need for more quality field experiences. However, rather than treating field experiences monolithically, this study provided closer scrutiny into the significant components that make the student teaching experience meaningful and effective.

This study was located in Arkansas because the state significantly exceeds the national average on teacher retention and teacher quality (Nolen & Clemmons, 2013; Ingersoll & Smith, 2003) and provides an intrinsically valuable case for investigation for the benefit of the national discussion on quality teacher preparation. By reflecting on what worked and what was effective in preparing early career teachers for the classroom, this study illuminates several important facets comprising quality student teaching experiences.

On a larger scope, research on teacher preparation needs to further deconstruct what is "quality teacher preparation" in order to build the most effective programs that will produce confident and effective teachers. All stakeholders in the debate about how best to prepare teachers need to know specifically what works that is grounded in empirical research, so that ineffective practices can be pruned and those that are most essential and valuable can be further developed.

REFERENCES

American Association of Colleges for Teacher Education (AACTE). (2010). *The clinical preparation of teachers: SA policy brief.* Washington, DC: American Association of Colleges for Teacher Education.

AACTE. (2013). *The changing teacher preparation profession.* Washington, DC: American Association of Colleges for Teacher Education.

Atiles, J. T., Jones, J. L., & Kim, H. (2012). Field experience + inclusive ECE classrooms = increased preservice teacher efficacy in working with students with developmental delays or disabilities. *Educational Research Quarterly, 36*(2), 62–85.

Ball, D., & Forzani, F. (2009). The work of teaching and the challenge for teacher education. *Journal of Teacher Education, 60*(5), 497–511. https://doi.org/10.1177/0022487109348479

Bergman, D. (2013). Comparing the effects of suburban and urban field placements on teacher candidates' experiences and perceptions of family engagement in middle and high schools. *School Community Journal, 23*(2), 87–112.

Caprano, M. M., Caprano, R. M., & Helfeldt, J. (2010). Do differing types of field experiences make a difference in teacher candidates' perceived level of competence? *Teacher Education Quarterly, 37*(1), 131–154.

Darling-Hammond, L. (2010). Teacher education and the American future, *Journal of Teacher Education, 61*(1–2), 35–47. https://doi.org/10.1177/0022487109348024

Darling-Hammond, L., Chung, R., & Frelow, F. (2002). Variation in teacher preparation: How well do different pathways prepare teachers to teach? *Journal of Teacher Education, 53*(4), 286–302. doi: 10.1177/0022487102053004002

Fallon, D. (2006). The buffalo upon the chimneypiece. *Journal of Teacher Education, 57*(2), 139–154. https://doi.org/10.1177/0022487105285675

Grossman, P., & McDonald, M. (2008). Back to the future: Directions for research in teaching and teacher education. *American Education Research Journal, 45*(1), 184–205. https://doi.org/10.3102/0002831207312906

Hollins, E. (2011). Teacher preparation for quality teaching. *Journal of Teacher Education, 62*(4), 395–407. https://doi.org/10.1177/0022487111409415

Ingersoll, R. M., & Smith, T. M. (2003). The wrong solution to the teacher shortage. *Educational Leadership, 60*(8), 30–33.

Lampert, M., Franke, M., Kazemi, E., Ghousseini, H., Turrou, A., Beasley, H., & Crowe, K. (2013). Keeping it complex: Using rehearsals to support novice teacher learning of ambitious teaching. *Journal of Teacher Education, 64*(3), 226–243. https://doi.org/10.1177/0022487112473837

Lee, J., Tice, K., Collins, D., Brown, A., Smith, C, & Fox, J. (2012). Assessing student teaching experiences: Teacher candidates' perceptions of preparedness. *Education Research Quarterly, 36*(2), 3–16.

Liakopoulou, M. (2012). The role of field experience in the preparation of reflective teachers. *Australian Journal of Teacher Education, 37*(6), 42–54. doi: 10.14221/ajte.2012v37n6.4

Mihaly, K., McCaffery, D., Sass, T. R., & Lockwood, J. R. (2012). Where you come from or where you go? Distinguishing between school quality and the effectiveness of teacher preparation program graduates. National Center for Analysis of Longitudinal Data in Education Research. Washington, DC.

National Council for Accreditation of Teacher Education (NCATE). (2010). *Transforming teacher education through clinical practice to prepare effective teachers: Report of the Blue Ribbon Panel on clinical preparation and partnerships for improved student learning.* Washington, DC: National Council for Accreditation of Teacher Education.

National Council on Teacher Quality (NCTQ), (2014). 2013 Arkansas Teacher Policy Yearbook. Retrieved from http://www.nctq.org/dmsView/2013_State_Teacher_Policy_Yearbook_Arkansas_Press_Release on March 7, 2014.

Nolen, A., & Clemmons, K. (2013). Deconstructing what works in student teaching: A state-wide analysis of early career teachers' experiences. A paper presented at the 2013 Annual Meeting of the American Educational Research Association, San Francisco, CA.

Otaiba, S., Lake, V., Greulich, L., Folsom, J., & Guidry, L. (2012). Preparing beginning reading teachers: An experimental comparison of initial early literacy field experiences. *Reading and Writing, 25*(1), 109–129.

Sampson, M. B., Linek, W. M., Raine, I. L., & Szabo, S. (2013). The influence of prior knowledge, university coursework, and field experience on primary teachers' use of reading comprehension strategies in a year-long, field-based teacher education program. *Literacy Research and Instruction, 52*(4), 281–311.

Silvernail, D. L. (1998). *Findings from an initial analysis of the New York City Teacher Survey.* New York: New Visions for Public Schools.

Solomon, J. (2009). The Boston Teacher Residency: District-based teacher education. *Journal of Teacher Education, 60*(5), 478–488. https://doi.org/10.1177/002248 7109349915

U.S. Department of Education. (2011). *Our future, our teachers: The Obama Administration's plan for teacher education reform and improvement.* Washington, DC: U.S. Department of Education.

Zeichner, K. (2010). Rethinking the connections between campus courses and field experiences in college and university-based teacher education. *Journal of Teacher Education, 61*(1–2), 89–100. https://doi.org/10.1177/0022487109347671

Chapter 9

Implementing Professional Development Days within the Elementary Methods Semester

Patricia Paulson, Geri Von Grey, Danny Swensen, Jay Rasmussen, and Katie Bonawitz

Teacher preparation has undergone criticism in recent years due to the stagnation of PreK–12 student scores on high-stake assessments as well as the high attrition rate of new teachers (Goldhaber & Cowan, 2014). University instructors continue to seek out strategies for moving away from the traditional methods courses to find the most effective means for preparing highly qualified teachers, who are able to meet the increasing demands of the classroom (Richmond, Bartell, & Dunn, 2016). In response to this research, over ten years a private university in the Midwest began to "block" the methods courses for elementary education majors in order to support teacher candidates' ability to connect pedagogical practices and theory.

The first block of ten credits included courses in literacy and educational psychology, focusing on the needs of the primary grade learners. The second block, focused on intermediate grade learners, began as an eighteen-credit full semester designed with methods courses in mathematics, language arts, social studies, science, educational psychology, art, music, physical education, and health. Both blocks included extensive clinical experiences. While the first block was successful, the number of courses in the second block quickly overwhelmed the teacher candidates.

The intermediate block was reduced to the core subjects of mathematics, literacy, social studies, science, and educational psychology, using an integrated approach of core content methods and pedagogy, classroom management, technology, and exceptionalities. The teacher candidates are in assigned classrooms at their clinical site every day for the first week of the semester, every day the last two weeks of the semester, every morning for half of the semester and every afternoon for the second half of the semester.

A gradual release model is used where the teacher candidates begin by observing, move to co-teaching, and finally to delivering lessons they have prepared for each content area. The teacher candidates are engaged in the methods courses on campus when they were not in their elementary classrooms. The methods instructors communicate frequently and are intentional regarding assignments attached to the clinical experience.

DESCRIPTION OF THE PROBLEM

Data for the teacher candidates at the university was collected, including data from edTPATM, Minnesota Teacher Licensure Examinations, and cooperating and supervisor evaluation. After analysis of the data, it became clear that the teacher candidates were exhibiting what Bransford et al. (2005) described as the struggle with perceived dissonance between theories and practices learned within the university classroom and the reality of daily classroom demands. Bransford et al. noted that as teacher candidates move between varied curriculum and methods courses, transfer of learning may not occur without intentional opportunities and planned coherence.

Empirical evidence has demonstrated that "teacher education programs that have coherent visions of teaching and learning, and integrate related strategies across courses and field placements, have a greater impact on the initial conceptions and practices of prospective teachers" (Darling-Hammond et al., 2005, p. 392). The methods instructors determined that increased intentionality within the semester block was needed to assist teacher candidates in making connections between theory and practice.

Three areas of concern emerged as troublesome to the teacher candidates: lesson design, assessment, and differentiation (Darling-Hammond et al., 2005). Instructors observed that teacher candidates seemed to function well within individual methods courses; however, they failed to synthesize effective practices overall. Teacher candidates perceived that they were being told *different things in different classes*. It was decided that the methods instructors would plan and collaboratively deliver three professional development days (PDDs) throughout the semester, modeling the inservice model for professional educators. The days were planned for Fridays when the teacher candidates were typically not at their clinical sites and designed to be authentically modeled after PDDs school districts conduct.

The PDDs have been modified over time, based on teacher candidate data, to the model presented in this paper. Three research questions posed to the teacher candidates informed these modifications:

- How has your understanding of the connections between educational theory and practice deepened as a result of the PDDs?

- How have you grown as an education professional as a result of the PDDs?
- How has your understanding of the function and value of community deepened as a result of the PDDs?

RATIONALE

While the methods instructors communicated frequently regarding curriculum and instruction, and believed they were teaching for transfer of concepts across the courses, program assessment data did not confirm the transfer of learning the instructors were seeking. As Hollins (2011) explained, "The level of coherence, strength in the representation of the organizing ideas for teaching, the quality of the epistemic practices that frame learning experiences, and the consistency in application determine the integrity of the program" (p. 407). It was hypothesized that PDDs, planned and delivered jointly by all the instructors, would assist teacher candidates in seeking meaningful connections between theory and practices.

Professional learning communities (PLCs) were implemented on each of the days to facilitate dialogue between the elementary teacher candidates and the instructors. PLCs have been shown to strengthen professional discourse within the community of practice to increase student achievement (DuFour, 2004). Danielson (2016) affirmed that "listening to colleagues, summarizing a discussion, acknowledging and building on others' ideas can assist teachers in problem identification and problem solving" (p. 23). She also pointed out the importance of an "infusion of expertise" when it is warranted.

THEORETICAL FRAMEWORK

The impact of effective teaching on student achievement is well recognized (Paige, 2002), and increasing demands on teacher preparation programs for providing high-quality teacher candidates continues to fuel research for innovative, effectual strategies. As Darling-Hammond (2008) stressed, "In order to help teachers enact good practices, close connections between theory and practice, coursework and clinical work are necessary, along with access to high-quality modeling, practical strategies, useful tools, and repeated opportunities for practice" (p. 1321). Grossman and McDonald (2008) described how teacher education must move from the cognitive demands of teaching that have dominated the field for the past twenty years to an expanded view of teaching as a practice that includes cognition, craft, and affect.

Novice teachers must be prepared for the relational aspects of teaching as well as for the intellectual demands. The cohesiveness of such connected knowledge must extend beyond the individual course design to the design of the entire program (Bransford, et al., 2005). The ability to move across the domains provides the opportunity for expertise to be developed in what Ericsson (2002; 2006) refers to as "deliberate practice."

Moving candidates from viewing themselves through the lens of a student to one of a professional requires a level of "adaptive expertise" to enable them to balance efficiency and innovation for improving student performance (Bransford et al., 2005). A practice-based teacher education program (Hollins, 2011) provides teacher candidates the opportunity to participate in dialogue with both peers and faculty to learn the discursive practices of the profession. Assisting their transition into the community of practice involves intentional partnerships with local districts to engage in such professional discourse (Rosaen & Forio-Ruane, 2008).

Teacher candidates often need to be taught how to engage in PLCs (Hollins, 2011) as they begin to form their sense of a professional identity. Using reflective practice as a "lens into the world of practice" (Loughran, 2002, p. 33) allows candidates to view their practice through their own lens as well as the lens of others. Hollins (2011) described how the professional community could enhance "professional identity and the ability to engage in self-directed professional growth and development, to recognize characteristics and qualities of professional communities in different contexts, and to work collaboratively with colleagues to improve learning outcomes for students" (p. 395).

Intentionality in planning, teaching, and assessing requires ongoing reflection and analysis; as Schultz and Ravitch (2013) explained, "Teaching is a complex and ever-changing activity that requires teachers to respond to their students and the curriculum strategically and in the moment" (p. 35). Johnston and Badley (1996) described reflective practice as the "acquisition of a critical stance or attitude toward one's own practice and that of one's peers" (p. 4). As discussion continues regarding the nature of reflection and the development of effective reflective practitioners, the dynamic interplay between thinking and action becomes more explicit, forming what Shulman (1987) termed the "wisdom of teaching."

Krebs and Torrez (2011) remind teacher educators, "In elementary teacher education, we must not forget the holistic nature of teaching and the importance of nurturing the whole preservice teacher as we help the beginning teacher become a teacher of children" (p. 79). As Darling-Hammond et al. (2005) further clarified, citing the work of Ball and Cohen (1999) and Lampert and Ball (1998), "Recent studies of learning to teach suggest that immersing teachers in the materials of practice and working on particular concepts using these materials has the potential to be particularly powerful for teacher's learning" (p. 401).

Current initiatives for performance assessments of teacher preparation such as the edTPA (Stanford, 2015) demand candidates synthesize theory and practice within the student teaching experience. Darling-Hammond and Hyler (2013) affirmed the appropriateness of such measurements to assess teacher preparedness, arguing that "teaching requires deep knowledge of how children learn differently and a sophisticated repertoire of skills deployed through professional judgment" (p. 12).

Methods courses disconnected from one another, with only marginal ties to field placements, must be replaced with a coherent, scaffolded and connected approach to teacher preparation. Purposeful integration of pedagogical content knowledge, best practices in teaching and learning, extended field experiences, and opportunities for professional discourse should intersect in the preparation of a teacher candidate ready to face demands of the twenty-first century.

PLAN

Three critical factors were considered as the PDDs were designed and implemented: (1) the need for teacher candidates to build meaningful connections between theory and practice related to lesson design, assessment, and differentiation; (2) the desire to build professionalism within teacher candidates; and (3) the desire to build community for teacher candidates. With these factors in mind, the five-person instructional team developed the basic framework for how each PDD would operate within a given semester.

- PDD 1—focused on lesson design and was held three weeks after the semester start.
- PDD 2—devoted to exploring assessment and was held three weeks after the first PDD.
- PDD 3—focused on differentiation and typically was held three weeks after the second PDD.

The three PDDs, which ran from 9:00 a.m. to 4:00 p.m., were frontloaded in the semester to allow teacher candidates maximum time to practice their new learning. In an effort to maximize community building and face-to-face instructional time, the majority of the content for each day was flipped through the use of narrated PowerPoint presentations, readings, videos, and reflective writing. Teacher candidates arrived at each PDD prepared to interact with one another and the content they previously studied either in methods courses or through individual preparation for the day.

The interaction for teacher candidates occurred within a five-to-eight-member PLC, which included an instructor, with the goal of modeling and preparing teacher candidates for professional discourse. Throughout the day instructors co-taught and led interactive learning experiences that extended the initial learning beyond the content shared in a flipped format.

METHODS

A qualitative approach was used in this research for a number of reasons. First, a qualitative approach aligns with the research objective of extending the reader's understanding of the phenomenon in question (Merriam, 2009) through producing a product that is *richly descriptive* (Patton, 2002). In addition, a qualitative approach allowed the researchers to examine the experiences of the participants through their narratives, which according to many researchers (e.g., Clandinin & Connelly, 2000) is one of the most effective ways to investigate complex phenomenon in educational environments. Moreover, a qualitative approach was appropriate in this case as the focus of the research is on individual experiences, rather than any products produced (Bogdan & Biklen, 2007; Merriam, 2009).

Data collected were a part of the normal classroom activities and collected anonymously so that no responses could be traced to individual students. Since feedback was sought as aggregate data on the effectiveness of the PDDs and not linked to individuals, IRB approval was not sought. The data were qualitative, using "exit" tickets at the end of each PDD and one spring focus group. The researchers used an action research approach, as described by Stringer (2013).

Exit tickets have been described as an effective means of determining the level of student understanding (Marzano, 2012). For this research, a one-page exit ticket ($n = 80$) was given to the teacher candidates at the end of the PDD day (i.e., fall 2014, spring 2015, fall 2015, and spring 2016).

Teacher candidates were asked to answer three questions on their exit tickets: What three things do you most want to remember/implement relating to lesson planning, assessment or differentiation? When reflecting on this PDD, what worked well for you as an educator? How could this day be improved for you as an educator? Teacher candidates were also asked to indicate on a Likert scale (1–5) how much they agreed with the following statement: "This day was valuable for me as an educator moving from being a student to being a teaching professional." The instructional team used the exit ticket data for formative feedback to modify and adjust the planning and implementation of subsequent PDDs.

Second, a focus group discussion was conducted (spring 2016). A neutral qualitative researcher was used to conduct the focus group discussion. The teacher candidates ($n = 14$) were asked each of the research questions:

- How has your understanding of the connections between educational theory and practice deepened as a result of the PDDs?
- How have you grown as an education professional as a result of the PDDs?
- How has your understanding of the function and value of community deepened as a result of the PDDs?

Teacher candidates were asked to reflect on each question independently in written form as a way to help them process their thoughts before oral sharing with the group. These written responses were not collected due to the fact that they were meant to act only as a processing tool for the focus group participants. After adequate time was allowed for this process, the candidates were asked to voluntarily share their written conclusions verbally with the group, one statement at a time. The facilitator then wrote down the candidate statements verbatim and then asked the group how many agreed with each of the statements. The shared responses and the number of candidates who agreed with each statement were consolidated into one document. The information was then shared with the instructional team.

RESEARCH FINDINGS

The research examined the impact of a series of three PDDs on preservice elementary candidates. The objective of the research was to determine the effects of the PDDs on the participants using the narratives of the teacher candidates. The research was guided by the three research questions: How has your understanding of the connections between educational theory and practice deepened as a result of the PDDs? How have you grown as an education professional as a result of the PDDs? How has your understanding of the function and value of community deepened as a result of the PDDs? The following section is organized according to the three research questions.

Connections between Educational Theory and Practice

The first question that was addressed was: "How has your understanding of the connections between educational theory and practice deepened as a result of the PDDs?" Darling-Hammond (2008) indicated that strong connections between theory and practice are an essential part of educators successfully incorporating suitable practices in their classrooms. The narratives of the teacher candidates collected in the research contained evidence to suggest that participants made meaningful connections between educational theory and practice as a result of participating in the three PDDs.

An important theme that emerged in the data was the emphasis on practical applications and on the connections to the various content areas (e.g., literacy, science, special education, mathematics, and social studies). This theme is illustrated in the focus group feedback where there was 100 percent agreement about the importance of "having the chance to connect content with practical applications instead of just memorizing information" and "it deepened understanding by practical connections to each content area." This theme also resonated in the narratives from the exit tickets:

- "It was very involved and applicable to real teaching."
- "Having us use real situations and experiences was so valuable."
- "High-energy activities are purposeful and applicable to my future classroom."

In each instance, the narratives underscore the value participants placed on experiences where the theory presented had strong connections and applications to the real situations in the classroom. Many participants recognized the strong value in having a current elementary teacher lead the discussion on the interpretation of the Northwest Evaluation Assessment data using authentic but unidentifiable data. The exit tickets data revealed that many teacher candidates ($n = 14$) found the use of real assessment data helpful and appreciated the opportunity to interact with data in the same way that a practicing teacher would.

A second theme that emerged was the value participants placed on the conversations and interactions with the instructors during the three PDDs. For instance, all the members of the focus group agreed that the perspectives shared by the instructors were essential in regard to better understanding the connections between educational theory and practice. A typical response was: "[I] enjoyed how each professor gave their own perspective on each topic so we could gain a broad perspective."

In addition to sharing various perspectives, the exit ticket data ($n = 81$) indicated that having an instructor as an integral part of each PLC was critical in terms of providing input, sharing wisdom, and giving examples. The following exit ticket comment was representative of many participant's perspectives: "Thank you for allowing quality conversations and fostering thinking." Clearly the participants valued the time they had to interact and collaborate with the instructors during the PDDs.

A final theme in relation to the first research question aligns with the work of Bransford et al. (2005), which emphasized the importance of considering overall program design in addition to isolated content. The focus group data relating to the connections between educational theory and practice indicated that the participants were in agreement that the PDDs "deepened understanding by practical connections to each content area" by "making connections within education as a whole as well as in specific areas like lesson planning, assessment and differentiation." Clearly, participants valued the connections between the various content areas and how each fit into larger educational contexts.

Overall, in relation to connections between educational theory and practice, the participants found the real-world experiences and activities meaningful. Participants also cited the collaboration and interaction with the instructors as a valuable aspect of the learning process. Finally, as a result of the PDDs, participants were able to deepen their understanding of important connections between content areas and the overall program. In the next section, the effect of the PDDs on professional growth is explored.

Professional Growth

The next question that we asked was: "How have you grown as an educational professional as a result of the PDDs?" Assisting teacher candidates as they transition from the role of a student to a professional educator is an important objective of the PDDs. Essential elements of professionalism include an in-depth knowledge of how students learn in different ways, use of professional judgment in approaches to teaching, and development of a professional identity through work in PLCs where participants are able to interact with peers and professors (Darling-Hammond & Hyler, 2013; Hollins, 2011).

The narrative data suggest that participation in the PDDs helped teacher candidates grow in their role as a professional educator in three significant ways: (1) working with others in PLCs; (2) deepening knowledge of approaches to teaching and learning; and (3) building confidence as an educational professional.

A critical theme that emerged from the narrative data was that collaboration with a community of educators shaped the participants' understanding of what it means to be an educational professional. This theme was evident in the exit ticket data as participants ($n = 81$) cited the impact of both group discussions and PLCs during the PDDs. Specifically, participants emphasized the benefits of the group discussions where the instructors were willing to share their wisdom and provide rich examples. This was also reflected in the narratives from the focus group as participants were in 100 percent agreement about the value of "collaborative skills practice" and the benefits of participants being required "to work with people with different learning styles and personalities."

Moreover, focus group participants indicated that they benefited from the professionalism gained through "application of community values and working toward a common goal" and being part of quality conversations that fostered deeper thinking. These thoughts were consistent with the comments on the exit tickets:

- "It helps so much to gain the sense of community with everyone and information we learn is always so important."
- "I couldn't have asked for more supportive, invested and inspiring professors who are so passionate about students and teaching."
- "I appreciated the level of dedication all of you have put into today! This has been such a great day of learning and interacting with fellow educators."

These comments align with the data from the focus group and reinforce the important role community plays in developing professional educators.

The narratives of the participants also indicated that learning about the educational needs of the students in their future classrooms was an important aspect of developing as a professional. The following statements from the focus group reflect this:

- "Provided me with a deeper understanding of the core tenets of the profession, such as differentiation, assessments, and lesson planning." (100 percent)
- "It provided me with a wider understanding of the needs of my students and the different ways I can meet those needs." (100 percent)
- "Mastery of theory in the field of education." (100 percent)

The ties between the PDDs and participants' future roles as professional educators were also evident in the exit ticket comments. One student's comment was representative: "The high-energy activities are purposeful and applicable to my future classroom." Overall, the narrative data showed that participants valued the connections between the PDDs and their work as educational professionals.

Finally, the narrative data suggest that the PDDs built confidence in the participants in relation to their role as educational professionals. For instance, all the focus group members were in agreement with the statement, "I have grown more confident in my abilities as a future educator." This sentiment was also revealed in the exit ticket data:

- "The growth I have seen in myself from PDD one is almost unbelievable. I so appreciate the atmosphere and care that make true growth possible."
- "This made me feel more like an equal educator versus a student. Thank you!"

This narrative data suggest that the PDDs played a crucial role in developing the participants' confidence as professional educators.

In the end, there was evidence in the narrative data that showed growth in the participants as professional educators. This was evident in the professional community aspect of the PDDs, as part of the interaction with materials that exposed participants to the educational needs of their future students, and in the activities that demonstrated ways to address those needs in the classroom. In the next section, the development of community as the result professional development is explored.

The final question we presented to the teacher candidates was: "How has your understanding of the function and value of community deepened as a result of the PDDs?" Essential objectives of the PDDs were the development of an understanding of what it means to be part of a professional community and the benefits of being part of the community. The narrative data relating to the building of a professional community were organized according to two factors: (1) collaborative components, and (2) the access to high-quality modeling of community (see Darling-Hammond, 2008). In terms of the first factor, the narrative data revealed the value of teamwork and collaboration in educational environments. This was evident in the focus group data:

- "We all need each other because raising the next generation is a group effort." (100 percent)
- "Teaching is a hard profession to be in and without the support of colleagues you will burn out. Seek out community and be intentional about growing and learning together." (100 percent)
- "Leadership is necessary but doesn't always have to be the same person and that was modeled." (100 percent)
- "A positive environment is necessary to learn and succeed in a community." (100 percent)

These statements reflect the benefits of being part of an educational community in relation to the job itself (i.e., raising the next generation) as well as the difficulty of the job. The narrative data from the focus group also indicated that the PDDs were opportunities for growth for participants in regard to understanding the function and workings of a successful community. The participants in the focus group agreed:

- "Our groups were different every day. Not stuck in clumps. We had to work with different people and be effective." (100 percent)
- "Finding my place and how I contribute to a team or cohort." (100 percent)

These statements reveal an understanding of the benefits of working with a variety of individuals and figuring out how to be a successful part of a team or community. The exit ticket data also revealed the value participants placed on opportunities to interact with peers and instructors ($n = 81$) and the time in PLCs ($n = 81$).

The narrative data also reflected the impact of and an appreciation for the modeling of community by the instructors. The focus group participants agreed (100 percent) that working as a professional community "was modeled by a team of professors who worked together for the good of the students (and it pays off)." The focus group also commented (100 percent) on the leadership aspect of professional communities: "Leadership is necessary but doesn't always have to be the same person and that was modeled." The narrative data from the exit ticket revealed similar findings. The following is a representative comment: "I appreciated the level of dedication all of you have put into today! This has been such a great day of learning and interacting with fellow educators." These statements make it clear that the participants were able to see and found value in the modeling of community by the instructors.

One aspect of the modeling of the community by the instructors was the atmosphere produced during of the PDDs. The narratives in the exit tickets reflected this:

- "The growth I have seen in myself from PD Day one is almost unbelievable. I so appreciate the atmosphere and care that make true growth possible."
- "This made me feel more like an equal educator versus a student. Thank you!"
- "I loved discussing with professors."
- "Thank you for allowing quality conversations and fostering thinking."

This same sentiment was revealed in the focus group data (100 percent): "A positive environment is necessary to learn and succeed in a community." These data suggest that the modeling by the professors, and more generally the opportunity to be part of the three PDDs, deepened the understanding and value of an educational community.

Finally, teacher candidates also indicated on the Likert scale (1–5) how much they agreed with the following statement: "This day was valuable for me as an educator moving from being a student to being a teaching professional." The data results on this portion of the exit ticket remained consistently strong. The mean scores across all four semester ($n = 80$) indicate that students self-report making progress on the continuum of moving from student to teaching professional:

- Lesson Design PDD mean score = 4.565
- Assessment PDD mean score = 4.507
- Differentiation mean score = 4.582

In the end, the narrative data were used to explore the impact of the three PDDs in relation to the connection between educational theory and practice, the growth as a professional educator, and the value and understanding of community.

LIMITATIONS

This study had certain limitations. First, the study was limited to two types of teacher candidate self-report data. Second, the data were collected over a limited amount of time—four semesters for exit surveys and one semester for focus group data. The number of participants completing exit surveys ($n = 80$) and/or focus group members ($n = 14$) was relatively small and limited to one private Midwestern university. Third, only elementary education teacher candidates were represented in the study. Finally, although the evidence presented suggests that teacher candidate understanding of the connection between educational theory and practice deepened, candidates grew as professionals, and that candidate understanding of the function and value of community deepened as a result of PDDs, there is no empirical evidence that the PDDs impacted PreK–12 student learning during teacher candidate time in actual classroom settings.

IMPLICATIONS

There are potential implications of this study for the five instructors who designed the three-day series of PDDs and for teacher educators in other settings. In terms of the five instructors involved in the study, the evidence presented suggests that the PDDs are of high value to the teacher education candidates and should be continued in the future. Continuing data collection in the form of exit surveys and focus groups should be a regular practice as means of understanding program impact on teacher candidate growth. At the same time, designing and implementing measures to assess the impact of the PDDs on PreK–12 student learning would be of value when considering a future research agenda.

When considering the value of this PDD model for teacher educators in other colleges and universities, it is important for instructors to consider the investment of time involved in making this model successful. Instructors must be willing to devote time to collaborative planning, co-teaching time associated with each of the three days, and time invested in building the learning experiences for the flipped instructional model. At the same time, it is necessary to build three PDDs into a full teacher candidate academic calendar. This may be difficult unless methods courses are blocked just previous to the student teaching experience.

DISCUSSION

A team of education instructors at a private Midwestern liberal arts university determined that change needed to occur in the format and delivery of the elementary teacher education program in order to improve and enhance teacher candidates' abilities to connect theory and practice within the university classroom and K–6 classroom setting. Research supported the notion that teacher candidates often struggle with perceived dissonance between theories and practices learned within the university classroom and the reality of daily classroom demands (Bransford et al., 2005) so the importance of program coherence is especially critical (Darling-Hammond et al., 2005; Hollins, 2011).

Through three collaboratively designed PDDs, teacher candidates engaged with content relating to lesson design, assessment, and differentiation jointly presented by the instructional team. In addition to increased confidence in connecting theory to practice, the goals of increasing professionalism and building community with teacher candidates were also accomplished through strategically designed PLCs that included instructors and teacher candidates for each PDD.

This education team organized important aspects of teaching (i.e., lesson design, assessment, and differentiation) into PDDs to assist teacher candidates in connecting educational theory to practice, as suggested by Hollins (2011), Darling-Hammond et al. (2005), and Darling-Hammond (2008). The evidence collected indicated that, as a result of the PDDs, teacher candidates were able to make meaningful connections between educational theory and clinical practice.

Having instructors within each PLC also assisted the candidates in making connections between education theory and practice through the inclusion of rich discussions mixed with the "infusion of expertise" provided as warranted (Danielson, 2016, p. 23). A final theme emerging in the category of connecting educational theory and practice links to education in the greater context. More specifically, teacher candidates provided comments suggesting that they experienced the connections of various content areas and their relationships to the greater context of education.

Teacher candidates experienced a greater sense of professionalism as a result of the intentional design that mimicked Professional Development in K–12 schools. With the unique structure of the PDDs, including the PLCs, teacher candidates were able to learn through a variety of modes while forming their identity as professionals (Darling-Hammond & Hyler, 2013; Hollins, 2011). Practicing collaborative skills with a diverse group of individuals was a key component of the experience, as was the opportunity to practice core elements of teaching (lesson planning, assessment and differentiation) as they prepared for their future classrooms. Hollins (2011) stated how PLCs can be a vehicle where candidates engage in professional growth and development. During the PDDs described in this study, the data were clear that teacher candidates experienced growth and development as education professionals.

Opportunities to build community through teamwork and collaboration were intentional in the design of the PDDs through PLCs. In addition to taking part in educational discourse within the PLCs, two PLCs were responsible for leading an opening activity at the start of each PDD. These opportunities helped develop a larger sense of community prior to investigating the content components of each PDD. Teacher candidates leading the daily opening activities built community as well.

The group membership of each PLC changed by topic, allowing collaboration between participants with differing learning styles and opinions. Instructors were intentional about modeling community as a team during each PDD, as suggested by Darling-Hammond (2008). Lunch and snacks were also furnished to provide teacher candidates and instructors unstructured time together—another important aspect of community. The data suggested that, as a result of the three PDDs, candidates expanded their understanding and value of an educational community.

CONCLUSION

Accomplishing the delivery of the three PDDs required significant effort on the part of the instructors. Close collaboration was required while planning the PDDs as well as continued and ongoing reflection and analysis following each PDD as suggested by Schultz and Ravitch (2013). The instructors became a more effective team during the formal presentations of each PDD as a result of this collaboration. The instructors often engaged in dialogue throughout the day, modeling co-teaching (Friend, 2008), which further demonstrated to teacher candidates how a given content discipline so easily intersects with other content, theory, and practice.

As a result of the PDDs, instructors are now more strategic about when they teach specific content in their individual courses to insure alignment with each specific PDD. The instructors have also become more consistent regarding the use of educational terminology as a result of the PDDs. While limited changes have taken place from the original design of the PDDs, small enhancements of each PDD have become norm in what has become an iterative process.

The goal of purposefully integrating best practices in teaching and learning across elementary curriculum and methods courses, with opportunities for professional discourse linking theory and practice during a period of intense clinical practice, was met through the PDDs described in this study. In conclusion, the research team found strong value in the PDDs for teacher candidates and instructors. Due to the significant benefits of this unique learning experience, exemplified by one student who stated, "PD days were a great way to dive really deeply into specific aspects of our teaching," the PDDs will continue to be a valued and integral part of the methods block of courses.

REFERENCES

Ball, D. L., & Cohen, D. K. (1999). Developing practice, developing practitioners: Toward a practice-based theory of professional education. In L. Darling-Hammond & G. Sykes (Eds.), *Teaching as the learning profession: Handbook of policy and practice* (pp. 3–32). San Francisco, CA: Jossey-Bass.

Bogdan, R. & Biklen, S. (2007). *Qualitative research for education: An introduction to theory and methods, 5th Ed.* Boston, MA: Pearson.

Bransford, J., Derry, S., Berliner, D., & Hammerness, K. (2005). Theories of learning and their roles in teaching. In L. Darling-Hammond & J. Bransford (Eds.), *Preparing teachers for a changing world* (pp. 41–87). San Francisco, CA: Jossey-Bass.

Clandinin, D. J., & Connelly, F. M. (2000). *Narrative inquiry: Experience and story in qualitative research.* San Francisco, CA: Jossey-Bass.

Danielson, C. (2016). Creating communities of practice. *Educational Leadership*, 73(8), 18–23. http://www.rethinkingschools.org/archive/27_04/27_04_darling-hammond_hyler.shtml

Darling-Hammond, L. (2008). Knowledge for teaching: What do we know? In M. Cochran-Smith, S. Feiman-Nemser, D. McIntyre, & K. Demers (Eds.), *Handbook of research on teacher education* (3rd Ed.) (pp. 1316–1323). New York: Routledge.

Darling-Hammond, L., & Hyler, M. (2013). The role of performance assessment in developing teaching as a profession. *Rethinking Schools*, 27(4). Retrieved from http://www.rethinkingschools.org/archive/27_04/27_04_darling-hammond_hyler.shtml

Darling-Hammond, L., & Hammerness, K., with Grossman, P., Rust, F., & Shulman, L. (2005). The design of teacher education programs. In L. Darling-Hammond & J. Bransford (Eds.), *Preparing teachers for a changing world* (pp. 390–441). San Francisco, CA: Jossey-Bass.

DuFour, R. (2004). What is a professional learning community? *Educational Leadership*, 61(8), 6–11.

Ericsson, K. (2002). Attaining excellence through deliberate practice: Insights from the study of expert performance. In M. Ferrari (Ed.), *The pursuit of excellence through education* (pp. 21–55). Malwah, NJ: Lawrence Erlbaum.

Ericsson, K. (2006). The influence of experience and deliberate practice in the development of superior expert performance. In K. A. Ericsson, N. Charness, P. J. Feltovich, & R. R. Hoffman (Eds.), *The Cambridge handbook of expertise and expert performance* (pp. 683–704). New York: Cambridge University Press.

Friend, M. (2008). Co-teaching: A simple solution that isn't simple after all. *Journal of Curriculum and Instruction, 2*(2), 9–19. doi:10.3776/joci.2008.v2n2p9-19

Goldhaber, D., & Cowan, J. (2014). Excavating the teacher pipeline: Teacher preparation programs and teacher attrition. *Journal of Teacher Education, 65*(5), 449–462. https://doi.org/10.1177/0022487114542516

Grossman, P., & McDonald, M. (2008). Back to the future: Directions for research in teaching and teacher education. *American Educational Research Journal, 45*(1), 184–205. https://doi.org/10.3102/0002831207312906

Hollins, E. (2011). Teacher preparation for quality teaching. *Journal of Teacher Education, 62*(4), 395. https://doi.org/10.1177/0022487111409415

Johnston, R., & Badley, G. (1996). The competent reflective practitioner. *Innovation and Learning in Education, 2*, 4–10.

Krebs, M., & Torrez, C. (2011). I love kids! Doesn't that mean I'll be a successful preservice teacher? *Curriculum and Teaching Dialogue, 13*(1 & 2), 69–81. doi: 10.5430/jct.v8n3p111

Lampert, M., & Ball, D. L. (1998). *Teaching, multimedia, and mathematics: Investigations of real practice.* New York: Teachers College Press.

Loughran, J. (2002). Effective reflective practice: In search of meaning about teaching. *Journal of Teacher Education, 53*(1), 33–43. https://doi.org/10.1177/0022487102053001004

Marzano, R. J. (2012). Art and science of teaching: The many uses of exit slips. *Educational Leadership, 70*(2), 80–81.

Merriam, S. B. (2009). *Qualitative research: A guide to design and implementation.* San Francisco, CA: Jossey-Bass.

Paige, R. (2002). Meeting the highly qualified teachers challenge: The secretary's annual report on teacher quality. In M. Cochran-Smith, S. Feiman-Nemser, D. McIntyre, & K. Demers (Eds.), *Handbook of research on teacher education* (3rd Ed.) (pp. 493–500). New York: Routledge.

Patton, M. Q. (2002). *Qualitative research and evaluation methods.* Thousand Oaks, CA: Sage Publications.

Richmond, G., Bartell, T., & Dunn, A. (2016). Beyond "tinkering": Enacting the imperative for change in teacher education in a climate of standards and accountability. *Journal of Teacher Education, 67*(2), 102–104. *doi:* 10.1177/0022487116628837

Rosaen, C., & Forio-Ruane, S. (2008). The metaphors by which we teach: Experience, metaphor, and culture in teacher education. In M. Cochran-Smith, S. Feiman-Nemser, D. McIntyre, & K. Demers (Eds.), *Handbook of research on teacher education* (3rd Ed.) (pp. 706–731). New York: Routledge.

Schultz, K., & Ravitch, S. (2013). Narratives of learning to teach: Taking on professional identity. *Journal of Teacher Education, 64*(1), 35–46. https://doi.org/10.1177/
0022487112458801

Shulman, L. (1987). Knowledge and teaching: Foundations of the new reform. *Harvard Educational Review, 57*(1), 1–22.

Stanford Center for Assessment, Learning, and Equity. (2015). edTPA. Retrieved
https://scale.stanford.edu/teaching/edtpa

Stringer, E. T. (2013). *Action research.* Thousand Oaks, CA: Sage Publications.

Chapter 10

EFL Teaching Experiences of Mainstream Preservice Teachers in an International Service-Learning Project

Burcu Ates, Yurimi Grigsby, Helen Berg,
and Soonhyang Kim

As the world is becoming more diverse, internationalization has become an integral part of strategic and curriculum planning initiatives across universities and colleges in the United States and around the world (Sharma & Phillion, 2014). Internationalization in higher education embodies the integration of international and intercultural dimensions into teaching, research, and service functions (Maringe & Fosket, 2010). Many universities have adopted a two-pronged approach to internationalization: "home-based (internationalization at home) and overseas-based (internationalization abroad)" activities (Maringe & Fosket, 2010, p. 5). Further, they "have begun to recognize the importance of developing teaching and instructional programmes that have both local and international relevance, both to recruit students in a global market and also to prepare all their students for lives in a globalized world" (Maringe & Fosket, 2010, p. 7).

Thus far, teacher education field has many more rooms to be internationalized (Alfaro, 2008; Cushner, 2007; Stewart, 2013). Some students may participate in international study or travel experiences; the faculty may conduct research outside the United States; or courses may exist in comparative, multicultural, or international education degree programs; however, rarely are these efforts fully integrated into teacher preparation programs. Strict course or state requirements for teacher licensure and student teaching demands leave little room for studying abroad, studying a foreign language, or taking internationally oriented courses as electives (Longview Foundation, 2008).

Children of immigrants are the fastest-growing student population in the United States. Even though the nation's students continue to increase in cultural and linguistic diversity, the teaching force has not kept pace. Predominantly, the mainstream classroom teacher (who is also a content area teacher in English language arts, social studies, mathematics, and science) in the United States is a middle-class, white female who is a monolingual, native English speaker (Neal, Sleeter, & Kumashiro, 2015).

As U.S. schools become increasingly diverse, state and national accreditation agencies, such as Council for the Accreditation of Educator Preparation, expect teacher candidates to demonstrate abilities to apply culturally responsive pedagogy in their classrooms (Gay, 2000; Ladson-Billings, 1995), focusing on cultural sensitivity and positive dispositions toward racial, ethnic, and language diversity and sociocultural/socioeconomic differences among students.

In preparation for working with diverse student populations, some of the recommendations for preservice teachers include "study a second language; develop knowledge of language learning and linguistics; understand the socio-political aspects of language use" (Fitts & Gross, 2012, p. 76), including studying abroad. More specifically, Phillion et al. (2009) stated that teacher education programs in the United States are developing study abroad programs and various field experiences to address two main challenges in the teaching profession.

These challenges are (1) how to prepare predominantly white, female, middle-class, and monolingual teacher candidates to work with a diverse student population in schools and (2) how to develop and increase global competencies among preservice teachers. Global competence is a set of skills and knowledge of world languages, cultures, and regions and thus means to value and respect people who are from different linguistic, cultural, ethnic, racial, and religious backgrounds (Zhao, 2010).

Supporting exposure to international experiences through study abroad, Stewart (2013) argued, few teachers in the United States have knowledge of the "world beyond our borders, speak a second language, or participate in education abroad programs" (p. 85). Teacher education programs are developing various international initiatives more so than before; however, these activities still remain decontextualized without helping students to develop a deeper and broader perspective on culture and diversity (Stewart, 2013). Study abroad programs can provide opportunities for the candidate to experience navigating as the *other,* like language-minority students in the mainstream classrooms must do, and we posit that they will be better equipped to appreciate this feeling of being the *other* in their future students through the firsthand experience.[1]

This study involves three mainstream preservice teachers from the aforementioned demographic and explores how an international service-learning

(ISL) experience—teaching English as study abroad program participants to students in a low-income neighborhood in another country—helped them develop a disposition that will facilitate meaningful engagement with their future culturally and linguistically diverse students.

LITERATURE REVIEW

Schwarzer and Bridglall (2015) argued that there are three experiences that commonly seem to help teacher education programs accomplish internationalization goals: (1) study abroad, (2) technology-enhanced learning, and (3) "glocal" (reflecting or characterized by both local and global considerations) experiences. They describe internationalization as a broad knowledge base and the dispositions that preservice and inservice teachers need to effectively interact with others from various cultures and countries. Within this chapter, we define internationalization as the intentional efforts and purposeful planning directed at increasing awareness of or access to a specific resource or service offered by one group to another.

Overall, traditional study abroad programs and ISL are similar, yet the major difference is that ISL emphasizes community-based activities in international settings. Study abroad programs in general are classified into three distinct categories: (1) an *island program*, where faculty lead a group of students in one- or two-week programs abroad; (2) *direct enrollment/ full immersion*, where students study at a university abroad for a semester or a year; and (3) *hybrid programs*, which have features of both island and direct enrollment/full immersion programs (Craigen & Sparkman, 2014; Porcano, 2011).

Service-learning programs provide students a learning opportunity outside the walls of the classroom by connecting coursework into the real world and adding a sense of "community context" (Prins & Webster, 2010). Through meaningfully planned curriculum, activities, and reflections, students are "challenged to become active citizens, not only in their own community and nation, but in the world" (Prins & Webster, 2010, p. 5). Bringle and Hatcher (2011) defined ISL as follows:

> A structured academic experience in another country in which students (a) participate in an organized service activity that addresses identified community needs; (b) learn from direct interaction and cross-cultural dialogue with others; and (c) reflect on the experience in such a way as to gain further understanding of course content, a deeper understanding of global and intercultural issues, a broader appreciation of the host country and the discipline, and an enhanced sense of their own responsibilities as citizens, locally and globally. (p. 19)

ISL programs can promote the value of responsible global citizenship. Individuals who embrace global citizenship are likely to interact with people beyond their home base, are geographically mobile, and are more concerned with the welfare and rights of distant people regardless of their residence or birthright (Ibrahim, 2012). Students who are involved in such programs generally report having increased empathy and awareness of their professional identity and expand their commitment to social justice issues and advocacy (Craigen & Sparkman, 2014).

While an extensive body of literature exists that highlights the experiences of students in general with such programs (e.g., Le, Raven, & Chen, 2013), fewer studies focus on the experiences of preservice teachers in study abroad programs (e.g., Rodríguez, 2011; Sivakumaran et al., 2011). An even smaller number of studies focuses on the experiences of preservice teachers who have been directly involved in international field experiences (e.g., Sharma, Rahatzad, & Phillion, 2013).

A review of studies on the experiences of preservice teachers who participated in a study abroad program indicates that study abroad provides them the opportunity to go beyond their own culture and involve themselves in cross-cultural experiential encounters they may not necessarily attain or have access to in their hometowns or college campuses (Palmer & Menard-Warwick, 2012; Pray & Marx, 2010; Rodríguez, 2011; Sharma, Phillion, & Malewski, 2011). Further, Cushner (2007) argued that study abroad may play a significant role in changing people's understanding of other people, as well as developing "an increase in self-confidence, adaptability, flexibility, confidence in speaking to strangers and gathering information in new and unfamiliar settings occurs" (p. 30). International cross-cultural experiences allow more space for individuals to question their own beliefs, practices, and ethnocentric worldviews and to create more awareness toward the self and the other (Sharma, Rahatzad & Phillion, 2013).

Pray and Marx (2010), using pre- and post-questionnaires, compared two groups of preservice teachers who were enrolled in an English as a Second Language (ESL) education course: nine preservice teachers who visited Mexican schools with bilingual education program in a study abroad program in Mexico and the other which enrolled in a traditional on-campus class taught by native Spanish speakers. The study specifically compared the preservice teachers' attitudes and beliefs about culturally appropriate language teaching. The findings revealed that preservice teachers who were part of a study abroad program gained a better understanding of the issues concerning language and culture.

In Palmer and Menard-Warwick's (2012) study in Texas, eleven preservice teachers from diverse backgrounds participated in a four-week, short-term study abroad program in Mexico and were enrolled in a second language acquisition class. They described the program as one in which the "students were presented with a wide range of experiences meant to challenge them, including field trips, films, speakers, readings, discussions, and immersion with local families" (p. 17). Using dialogue journals written by preservice teachers as their data source, they learned how preservice teachers were able to empathize with their future students, especially with children of immigrant families, as a result of this experience.

Reviewing the literature for short-term study abroad, we came across various faculty-led study abroad programs where preservice teachers were immersed in the local culture and context (Palmer & Menard-Warwick, 2012; Pray & Marx, 2010; Rodríguez, 2011; Sharma, Phillion, & Malewski, 2011). There are a few studies available on the experiences of preservice teachers and student teaching abroad/international practicum (Cruickshank & Westbrook, 2013; Doppen & An, 2014; Lu & Soares, 2014), though we have not come across any studies where an actual teaching practicum was specifically set up as part of preservice teachers' academic course work in a study abroad program.

This case study explores how an ISL experience helped support three mainstream preservice teachers' intercultural competence (Byram & Wagner, 2018)—their ability to work competently and confidently with others from different backgrounds—in working with their future diverse students. The research question for our study was: How does an ISL experience help mainstream preservice teachers develop intercultural competence and skills for working with others who have different backgrounds?

THE STUDY

The case study design for this study reflects the complexities of selecting an international context for service-learning as well as the setting situating the study in Naples where the larger percentage of the people completed only an elementary education. The following sections will discuss the site selection, a description of the setting, a discussion of the predeparture preparation, the setup of ISL, participants, data collection, and data analysis.

Site Selection as the Context for ISL

We selected Naples, Italy, as our site in part because we had a strong connection with a "cultural broker" (Pipher, 2003), a local contact person who has a strong connection with the local area, in the city. Our contact, an American named Kelly (pseudonym), was born and raised in the same state as our participants. Kelly was ideal because she had significant knowledge of and access to the local community since she had been living in the area for nine years. Having a contact who knew and was invested in the local community was extremely important for us in selecting Naples because we wanted the preservice and inservice teachers to have an in-depth understanding and authentic experience of the local context.

Prior to setting up the service-learning, we the program leaders traveled to Naples and conducted a needs assessment of the community. We explained that we were teacher educators who taught multicultural and teaching English to speakers of other languages (TESOL)-related courses and that we wanted our students to be truly exposed to and immersed within the local community. After multiple meetings with schools, principals, and youth leaders in the city of Naples, we identified and collaborated with one public school in an older part of Naples that served low-income children.

Description of the Setting

The school our preservice and inservice teachers taught in was at the heart of the historic center in Naples, a neighborhood where 86 percent of the population did not attain higher than an elementary education and where youth potentially become gang recruits, according to a newspaper article. These same problems were shared with us during our survey identifying the needs of the neighborhood. Based on the needs analysis, we created a program where we offered about three weeks of English classes to children in grades four, five, and six.

Most students in the neighborhood spoke Neapolitan as their first language rather than Italian. They spoke Neapolitan at home and learned Italian at school. According to Coluzzi (2008), Neapolitan is considered an "unsafe" (p. 220), or nearly endangered, dialect of Italian.

Predeparture Preparation

Before leaving for Italy, we held several informational meetings with the preservice and inservice teachers in which we provided detailed information about Naples and less-detailed information about the school and children they would be teaching. We purposefully did not share a lot of background information about the school and students because we wanted the preservice teachers to form their own opinions about the context upon experiencing it.

At the end of the spring semester, we set up two workshops that focused on EFL teaching methods and strategies, as the preservice teachers did not have any formal teaching experience yet, and the inservice teachers did not have experience teaching EFL. We shared articles on lesson planning, second language strategies and techniques, ISL, writing reflections, and co-teaching. We also discussed potential topics they could teach.

Setup of the ISL

A month before we arrived in Naples, three local teachers (one general classroom teacher and two English teachers) created a sign-up sheet for the "Summer Class in English" for interested students. They contacted the parents to encourage their children to be part of the summer program. As a result, close to seventy-five students signed up for the program, and six sections, with ten to twelve students in each class, were formed. The English classes ran from 9:00 am until 12:00 pm, Monday through Friday, for two weeks. This was about thirty hours of teaching for our preservice and inservice teachers.

Due to the preservice teachers not having prior teaching experience, we created a co-teaching model, pairing a preservice teacher participant with an inservice teacher who is a current practicing teacher. All inservice teachers were enrolled in a master's program that focused on TESOL. With this approach, preservice teachers were not in the classroom by themselves and could learn various methods from their co-teachers, and inservice teacher participants had an opportunity to mentor novice teachers. In this program, we asked preservice and inservice teachers to create their own lesson plans and classroom materials based on the proficiency and interest level of their students.

Participants

Nine preservice and inservice teachers participated in the ISL program in Italy. Five of them were undergraduate students who were early childhood through grade six (EC-6) preservice teachers, and four of them were master of education in TESOL graduate students who were inservice teachers. Out of the five preservice teachers, we selected three for our study because they fit the mainstream preservice teacher population characteristics: white, female, monolingual, and middle class. (These characteristics may increase the likelihood of generalizability for future studies.)

For ethical reasons, we used pseudonyms for our study participants (Lindsay, Tiffany, and Kate). Lindsay was twenty-three, Tiffany twenty, and Kate twenty. All had completed the prerequisite course "Multicultural Education" and were enrolled in a summer "Second Language Acquisition" course while in Italy. Tiffany had not left the United States or her home state until this experience. Kate had traveled outside of the United States, though only with her parents, and Lindsay had traveled abroad but only on cruise ships.

Data Collection

In this study, we used single-case design with multiple participants, since our participants shared many common characteristics and conditions (Merriam, 2009). Our initial data source was reflection journals written by the preservice teachers. The journals were an ongoing semi-structured reflection before, during, and after the program. The students completed it either individually or during the whole-group sessions that were facilitated by the faculty at the end of each day. They had the option of completing it as an e-journal or as a handwritten one. In all cases, the students provided detailed reflections on their feelings, personal and teaching experiences, and observations.

These reflections shed light on new viewpoints the students were becoming aware of and insight into themselves, formal education, and the complexities of social contexts both within and outside of the United States. Another data source was the in-depth, semi-structured interviews that were conducted two months after the program ended. All participant interviews were audio-recorded and transcribed.

Data Analysis

First, we read the reflection journals and interview transcripts without any coding, then we color-coded them. In order to make sense of the data, we identified the similarities and differences among participants, as well as quotes we thought were meaningful. We reviewed the data repeatedly until themes and patterns that answered our research question emerged (Strauss & Corbin, 1998). Secondary data sources were mainly used to triangulate the findings.

FINDINGS

The designed experience included an overseas (the international component) setting in which preservice teachers worked in a low-income public school with an opportunity to engage in meaningful community service (the service-learning component) and reflection. The research question focused on deconstructing the development of intercultural competence and skills for working with others from diverse backgrounds. Two major themes emerged from our data analysis: making connections with future students and understanding privilege as a universality.

Making Connections with Future Students

Teaching EFL for two weeks in an underfunded school in a low-income neighborhood introduced the preservice teachers to an unfamiliar world and helped them make connections to their future teaching and potential students they may have in their U.S. classrooms.

Lindsay stated she had never been placed in a similar situation before where she did not understand the language. Thus, she commented orally, "I definitely had *no idea* how that would make you feel insecure, very hesitant to want to speak." She said she gained a better understanding for why a student who is learning a new language would feel reserved and would not want to say anything or interact with others in group work in the classroom. She explained, "of course you [the language learner] don't want to say anything, you don't know how to say anything."

First, she thought that "they didn't understand, so I'm just going to keep teaching them in English, but no, it's completely different, because you're teaching them English in English and they do not know that, and you don't know how to tell them what you're saying in Italian." Having experienced no communication barriers before, Lindsay came to the realization that simply teaching in English is not sufficient. She knew issues relating to language barriers existed, but it was different when she experienced such barriers herself. She further commented she "knew [it] existed but it's like a wall, it's like a cement fence. It's solid, like you really have to keep pushing through, even if the events are minuscule for that day, like you really have to keep doing it."

As a result of this experience she learned ways to modify her lessons, for example, by incorporating strategies she learned from her co-teacher and from the faculty present. In one of her journal reflections, Lindsay noted:

> When reflecting upon this experience and the classroom environment, I feel as if I have been able to learn so much about my future classroom and the way culture is connected to language. This EFL experience has really opened my eyes to the challenges that both the teachers and the students face when learning. I know that by being on this trip I was able to see firsthand what works in the classroom and what does not, and that experience is truly invaluable. These students are trying to learn a language that is only taught to them behind the walls of the school.

Kate, who wants to be a special education teacher, was able to make connections to both ESL students and special education students. She stated, "Children that have special needs can't always communicate in the same way that children that don't have special needs can." She believed being in a classroom where she had to communicate in myriad ways definitively helped her in her future classroom practices. She added that through this experience she became more open-minded about differences and more conscious of the struggles her future ESL students might face. She further admitted:

> For me, being in Italy and not knowing any Italian but teaching Italian children English was an eye-opening experience. Because I felt as if in a way, I was

experiencing what an ESL student would feel. Because everyone around me was speaking Italian and I had no idea what they were saying. Some of the challenges included the language barrier. That was a challenge for me when speaking to the students occasionally. I would have to find different ways to word or say things, but I think that that is very useful because that is something I will definitely have to do in a classroom one day.

In one of her early journal reflections, Tiffany wrote this powerful entry:

When I first heard about this trip, I immediately was excited about the possibility of learning how a foreign school operates and which methods and strategies are successful/unsuccessful for teaching. In that regard, I would like to learn how best to communicate with students who are foreign to me and to be able to appreciate the differences that are in our classroom.

Because I have not been many places before, I initially wanted to learn more about other cultures. One reason is so that I can better understand my own and others' beliefs . . . [already] I understand myself and other cultures/people more than I did before I left [mentions her home state]. As a teacher, I hope to use this appreciation to relate to my students and to handle cultural differences in a professional and helpful manner.

Ultimately, from this trip I am taking back an appreciation and understanding of culture, foreign citizens, alternate religions, and other differences that people have from one another. Teaching English while in an environment in which I myself am a foreigner will give me a unique perspective into both the feeling of an immersion student and a teacher instructing ESL students. These are all practices that will become invaluable when in my own classroom setting.

With complete immersion to the local culture and educational setting, even though for such a short duration, Tiffany connected to her future students in the United States. In her last journal entry, she discussed how she incorporated various strategies in the classroom that she could also later implement with future ELLs. Tiffany emphasized the value of addressing the individual needs of her students by differentiating her instruction, saying:

My teaching will forever be affected by this service learning experience because I felt the effects of my teaching, altered it to accommodate the students, and then yielded product as I saw how the students learned. This opportunity was unparalleled in that it brought the course work alive and shown in an actual setting.

Overall, this field experience seemed to have helped the preservice teachers understand the struggles some students have who do not speak English as their first language, particularly with finding new or alternative ways to communicate when native languages were not the same. We posit that this experience demonstrated for them to experience the language barrier by some

ELLs experience in the United States in their English-dominant classrooms and academic settings.

Being told in an ESL education course that teacher candidates will need to exercise patience and a willingness to differentiate instruction for their ELLs without actual experience is quite different from having teacher candidates experience situations firsthand in which *others* might be exercising patience and differentiating in their ways of communication for *them*. Such an experience is an unparalleled way to learn what would be difficult to replicate through other experiences.

Understanding Privilege as a Universality

As faculty, we had a specific goal in placing the preservice teachers in a low-income public education setting for their teaching experience. We wanted them to understand that struggles for social justice exist internationally; the struggle for equality does not only exist in the U.S. context. Many social issues, such as poverty, for example, are more prevalent in other parts of the world. In the middle of Naples, an urban setting, students can struggle due to parental income inequalities, just as students can in the major cities of the teachers' home states.

At the beginning, the preservice teachers knew the students they were going to teach were at a disadvantage socioeconomically, but they did not know much more. In one journal entry we asked them to define the word "underprivileged" and asked if they thought the students they were teaching fit that description. Initially, Lindsay wrote, "Our kids do not appear to be in this category because the school has many resources that I have seen." Tiffany wrote, "They have a well-rounded understanding of their surroundings and do not exhibit signs of children who are in need of any type of resource. However, they do not often discuss their home lives with us." Kate wrote:

> I am not sure if the children are underprivileged. They seem at the school they receive a lot of help and care. Also just looking at their appearance they do not appear to be what I would think as underprivileged. However, I do not know too much about the school or area or their backgrounds to say if they are underprivileged.

Based largely on the appearance of the students and the resources they had in school, the preservice teachers did not think the students were underprivileged. After a week of teaching, we asked our main contact teacher to share some of the stories of the students in this school. This teacher explained that most of the clothes the students wore were supplied by teachers' donations, and the renovations in the school and the technology present were all made

possible by a new grant received from the government. After being exposed
to this information, the preservice teachers appeared to have a new perspective. Lindsay stated:

> Where you come from does not have to dictate where you go in life. These
> students show so much strength in themselves it is beautiful. I know that in my
> future classroom I will have students that may face issues that fall along the
> lines of those we saw in Naples. They may have different stories and different
> needs, but what I know now is to look past all of the things the students may
> "come from" and focus on what I can do for the students in or order for them to
> have the knowledge and tools to decide where they will "go."

After hearing more information about the background of the students, Tiffany
made connections to students in her home state:

> This school exhibits that fact clearly in that these children come in, some from
> rough family lives (some even bringing that roughness into the classroom),
> seeking affirmation, knowledge, and safety. . . . This situation for the [name
> of school] children is not unlike the circumstances of inner-city or low-income
> district students in [her home state]. In fact, there are children facing all kinds
> of poverty, abuse, neglect, emotional insecurity, hunger, etc. in all classes and
> grades. This is where a teacher must have such patience and understanding to
> realize that teaching the subject may not be the goal for some students. Some-
> times the goal is to be that person who will never give up on them.

Kate stated, "The information just reminded me that you never know a child's
background and what they are going through, so school should be a safe place
for them. And showing them you care is also very important."

As can be read through the words of the preservice teachers, what the local
teacher shared allowed preservice teachers to view privilege more critically
than before. Kate stated that while she was growing up, her school district
did not have low-income schools, and she admitted she had never been in a
school setting like this before. She further expressed, "I knew it was out there
obviously, but I just had never actually like been in it, and I wouldn't actually
mind working in a place like that just because I would like to help those kids."
During our interview, Tiffany shared somewhat similar sentiments:

> The same need is here, every school that we have here [referring to the US],
> I bet there are neighborhoods like that one in [insert the city the participants live
> later once the blind review is done], there's a lot of them, and being able to see
> that there kind of put it in front of me that there is that here too, and I don't know
> I would love to work with kids like that, it would be a lot more work but. . . .

Similarly, in her interview Lindsay reflected on the overall experience and
expressed this critical statement: "I liked it way better than if we had gone

to a school that had . . . I don't wanna say money, because people who have money do need help too, but . . . these kids really benefitted from what we were doing."

All three preservice teachers reflected on their perceptions and assumptions about the other (those who did not share a similar background as theirs), and all three acknowledged the commitment needed for teaching children who are less privileged. We saw this as the beginning stage of what hopefully will be a continuous process of critical inquiry and reflexivity within these teachers regarding their diverse students.

DISCUSSION AND IMPLICATIONS OF THE STUDY

As faculty, the main goal of our program was to support and develop preservice and inservice teachers' understanding of diversity, equity, social justice, and pedagogy on local and global scales through service-learning. It was important for the preservice and inservice teachers to recognize the school context and students' characteristics and teach the student population in Italy to meet their needs and eventually understand its international teaching experience implications for them as teachers of diverse students in the United States. We believe the way we structured the program, the course readings and materials, participants' written reflection journals, and end-of-day group reflections (where faculty and preservice and inservice teachers joined together) contributed to who they will be as future teachers and to the connections they make to their future students.

The goal of this study was to examine how the ISL experience would help preservice teachers gain skills for working with culturally and linguistically diverse students. With full immersion into the local culture of the host country, preservice teachers were able to understand issues pertaining to the local neighborhood, community, school, teachers, and most importantly, the students at an in-depth level, rather than superficially.

Providing an opportunity for preservice teachers to teach in an underfunded school in a low-income neighborhood was purposeful. As Alvarado and Carey (2013) argued:

> Simply sending pre-service teachers abroad and hoping they develop empathy and the ability to critically analyze privilege is not enough. The curriculum must work in tandem with the goals of a study-abroad or experiential learning activity so that pre-service teachers' experiences are maximized. (p. 69)

We wanted to go beyond what traditional study abroad programs might offer. Being fully immersed in the local community and in a global community resulted in the awareness that local and global are inseparable. The preservice teacher candidates made comparisons between social justice and equity struggles in the United States and outside of it. They connected their language and communication difficulties in Italy with the ones they might experience in the future with their ELL students in the United States.

Experiences in an ISL setting become a catalyst for global citizenship. We believe this experience fostered a sense of global membership in that the preservice teachers can now relate to teachers and students in global contexts other than their own and understand teaching as a global profession. We believe these types of experiences provide opportunities to develop and grow intercultural competence, the ability to effectively communicate with people of other cultures. Our findings demonstrated that throughout the experience, preservice teachers internalized a global membership when they saw similarities between American classrooms and Italian classrooms and connected their experiences with ELLs in the United States.

It is the responsibility of teacher preparation programs to provide the learning opportunities for preservice teachers to be successful in reaching their PreK–12 students. This means teacher education programs are charged with cultivating knowledge and growing skills that ensure an instructional learning environment with minimized stress and anxiety (Garrett & Holcomb, 2005) and lowered affective filter (Krashen, 1982). In order for preservice teachers to meet the needs of their diverse students, they must first recognize and understand the struggles these students will face.

We believe Lindsay, Kate, and Tiffany experienced this firsthand. As can be seen from their reflections, they were able to relate and make connections to their future ESL students and develop a more authentic understanding of what it feels like to be the other. They became the other and negotiated culture and language in order to survive. It is of immeasurable value that preservice teachers experience the hardship and challenges of adjusting to a new culture, knowing what it is like for a student when the dominant language spoken is not the student's first language. Teachers who have experienced this unsettling feeling themselves will be much more likely to respond appropriately to lessen those feelings of uncertainty within their students.

In addition to seeing tremendous gains in teacher knowledge, skills, and dispositions, the data also revealed how the preservice teachers developed a deeper and more critical understanding about what it means to be underprivileged. For example, Lindsay was able to make connections to the issues of privilege, socioeconomic status, immigration, language support, and social justice in the United States in her interview by stating:

> We have somewhat fine economy, definitely people who are privileged, people who make billions of dollars, but there are also people in [refers to the largest city in her home state] who definitely need assistance and don't speak English and people who come from the border that we need to assist. . . . Just because

parts of the country is pretty doesn't mean the entire place is. Again, just because it looks pretty from an outside view does not mean places that need to be assisted do not exist.

Overall, the findings of our study confirmed that carefully planned study abroad programs provide preservice teachers "an opportunity to apply classroom teaching to concrete situations and the conditions for reflecting on the role of historical and cultural processes that affect the schooling of minority, immigrant and other diverse children in U.S. American classrooms" (Phillion et al., 2009, p. 333). As teacher educators, we can help bridge the disconnect between theory and practice by exposing preservice teachers to such settings where they have the opportunity to connect social issues to teaching/practice (Westheimer & Suurtamm, 2009).

The findings indicate many benefits of international experiences. However, we also understand and agree with the opinions of some authors that participating in an experience abroad is costly and attainable by only a small number of students (Rahatzad et al., 2013). Certainly, these are valid criticisms of study abroad programs and international practica, particularly when such programs do not encourage reflective practice and a "re/positioning" of oneself as a member of the twenty-first-century "global village" (Reimers, 2013, p. 57). To allow a larger number of teacher candidates the chance to experience diverse cultures, we recommend local programming and community venues for the chance to engage and learn within a culture different their own.

The TESOL faculty could create local service-learning opportunities in schools or communities where there are a high number of ELLs. We strongly value the learning that can happen in one's own neighborhood. As faculty, we are involved in service-learning in our communities. According to Smith, Jennings, and Lakhan (2014), "Service learning both domestically and abroad offers students a unique experiential learning opportunity to address advocacy in a way that is culturally, developmentally, and issue appropriate" (p. 1209).

We also believe the context of Naples could be replaced with any community where the local community and schools and the teacher education faculty and students collaborate successfully, respecting each other's goals and needs. It is important to note that it would not be fair to create a dichotomy between developed (developed countries have under-resourced communities as well) and developing countries, local and global, and perpetuate the notion that one requires more attention than the other.

The connection between our minds and our experiences shapes how we relate to the world. Intercultural competence and global-mindedness is important as the world continues to become more mobile. In a broad sense, preservice teachers become representatives of their state, and in a larger sense, their nation. We believe it is of vital importance to allow them to shape their world by getting to know the other cultures in it and allowing others to get to know them.

With this notion also comes an important caveat: opportunities for critical reflection must be included in experiences like these so that views do not become essentialized, and knowledge gained through the study abroad does not become dogmatic, serving to limit the very students we wish to empower. Lindsay's statement summing up her experience well captures and reflects the goal we had for this program: "I was able to meet such amazing kids and a community of people that truly welcome you right into their homes. I came here to become a better teacher, but I left a better person, and that is something that I will treasure forever."

CONCLUSION

Westheimer and Suurtamm (2009) stated, "Teaching is not just about individual successes of students, but rather about preparing them to work together to create a more equal, just world" (p. 592). With careful and meaningful planning, study abroad and ISL opportunities can help facilitate an awareness of global and social justice issues (Stanlick & Hammond, 2016). They provide the power to get rid of stereotypes, false notions, and expectations that one group, community, or nation has of another one through interaction and engagement. In this way, naïve or simplistic assumptions about a people or culture could be dispelled and replaced with greater cross-cultural competence and a deeper understanding of one's own culture.

Having the opportunity to increase one's knowledge about the world and widening one's perspective of one's role within it, as well as gaining a sense of independence and resourcefulness, are reasons to provide more preservice teachers with this type of experience. Thus, through this program, we are enacting our own commitment to social justice, in that this opportunity should be available to all students, not just a privileged few.

NOTE

1. A portion of the text, 617 words in the first seven paragraphs, was published previously in *International Journal of TESOL and Learning (IJTL)*. Copyright release was granted February 2, 2021 to republish the portion of text in this chapter by *IJTL* and Untested Ideas (UI) Research Center.

REFERENCES

Alfaro, C. (2008). Global student teaching experiences: Stories bridging cultural and inter-cultural difference. *Multicultural Education, 15*(4), 20–26.

Alvarado, M., & Carey, A. (2013). Identity and social justice development of preservice teachers. In G. Miller & L. De Oliveira (Eds.), *Teacher education for social justice: Perspectives and lessons learned* (pp. 67–79). Charlotte, NC: Information Age Publishing Inc.

Bringle, R. G., & Hatcher, J. A. (2011). International service learning. In R. G. Bringle, J. A. Hatcher, & S. G. Jones (Eds.), *International service learning: Conceptual frameworks and research* (pp. 3–28); IUPUI Series on Service Learning Research. Sterling, VA: Stylus.

Byram, M., & Wagner, M. (2018). Making a difference: Language teaching for intercultural and international dialogue. *Foreign Language Annals*, *51*(1), 140–151. doi: 10.1111/flan.12319

Coluzzi, P. (2008). Language planning for Italian regional languages ("dialects"). *Language Problems & Language Planning*, *32*(3), 215–236. https://doi.org/10.1075/lplp.32.3.02col

Craigen, L. M., & Sparkman, N. M. (2014). The value and importance of international service learning programs: A model for human service education. *Journal of Human Services*, *1*(34), 126–130.

Cruickshank, K., & Westbrook, R. (2013). Local and global—conflicting perspectives? The place of overseas practicum in preservice teacher education. *Asia-Pacific Journal of Teacher Education*, *41*(1), 55–68. doi: 10.1080/1359866X.2012.753989

Cushner, K. (2007). The role of experience in the making of internationally-minded teachers. *Teacher Education Quarterly*, *34*, 27–39.

Doppen, F. H., & An, J. (2014). Student teaching abroad: Enhancing global awareness. *International Education*, *43*(2), 59–75.

Fitts, S., & Gross, L. A. (2012). Teacher candidates learning about and learning from English learners: Constructing concepts of language and culture in the Tuesdays' tutors afterschool program. *Teacher Education Quarterly*, *39*(4), 75–95.

Garrett, J., & Holcomb, S. (2005). Meeting the needs of immigrant students with limited English ability. *International Education*, *35*(1), 49–62.

Gay, G. (2000). *Culturally responsive teaching: Theory, research, and practice*. New York: Teachers College Press.

Ibrahim, B. L. (2012). Understanding service-learning and community engagement: Crossing boundaries through research. In J. A. Hatcher & R. G. Bringle (Eds.), *International service-learning as a path to global citizenship* (pp. 11–21). Charlotte, NC: Information Age Publishing.

Krashen, S. (1982). *Principles and practice in second language acquisition*. New York: Pergamon Press.

Ladson-Billings, G. (1995). But that's just good teaching! The case for culturally relevant pedagogy. *Theory into Practice*, *34*(3), 159–165. doi: 10.1080/00405849509543675

Le, Q. V., Raven, P. V., & Chen, S. (2013). International service learning and short-term business study abroad programs: A case study. *Journal of Education for Business*, *88*, 301–306.

Longview Foundation. (2008). *Teacher preparation for the global age: The imperative for change*. Retrieved from www.longviewfdn.org/files/44.pdf

Lu, H. L., & Soares, L. (2014). US elementary preservice teachers' experiences while teaching students in Taiwan. *Journal of the Scholarship of Teaching and Learning, 14*(1), 59–74.

Maringe, F., & Foskett, N. (2010). Introduction: Globalization and universities. In F. Maringe & N. Foskett, *Globalization and internationalization in higher education: Theoretical, strategic and management perspectives* (pp. 1–16). London/New York: Continuum International Publishing Group.

Merriam, S. B. (2009). *Qualitative research: A guide to design and implementation.* San Francisco, CA: Jossey-Bass.

Neal, L. V. I., Sleeter, C. E., & Kumashiro, K. K. (2015). Introduction: Why a diverse teaching force must thrive. In C. Sleeter, L. V. I. Neal, & K. K. Kumashiro. *Diversifying the teacher workforce: Preparing and retaining highly effective teachers* (pp. 1–16). New York: Routledge.

Palmer D., & Menard-Warwick, J. (2012). Short-term study abroad for Texas preservice teachers: On the road from empathy to critical awareness. *Multicultural Education, 19*(3), 17–26.

Phillion, J., Malewski, E., Sharma, S., & Wang, Y. (2009). Reimagining the curriculum in study abroad: Globalizing multiculturalism to prepare future teachers. *Frontiers: The Interdisciplinary Journal of Study Abroad, 18*, 323–339. DOI: https://doi.org/10.36366/frontiers.v18i1.269

Pipher, M. (2003). *The Middle of Everywhere: Helping Refugees Enter the American Community.* New York: Mariner.

Porcano, T. (2011). An analysis of a study abroad learning effort. *Journal of the Academy of Business Education, 12*, 85–100.

Pray, L., & Marx, S. (2010). ESL teacher education abroad and at home: A cautionary tale. *The Teacher Educator, 45*(3), 216–229. https://doi.org/10.1080/08878730.2010.488099

Prins, E., & Webster, N. (2010). Student identities and the tourist gaze in international service-learning: A university projects in Belize. *Journal of Higher Education Outreach and Engagement, 14*(1), 5–32.

Rahatzad, J., Sasser, H. L., Phillion, J., Karimi, N., Deng, Y., & Akiyama, R. (2013). Postglobal teacher preparation: Border thinking along the global south through international cross-cultural experiences. *International Journal of Multicultural Education, 15*(3), 76–96. doi:10.18251/ijme.v15i3.709

Reimers, F. (2013). Education for improvement: Citizenship in the global public sphere. *Harvard International Review, 35*(1), 56–61.

Rodríguez, E. (2011). What preservice teachers bring home when they travel abroad. Rethinking teaching through a short international immersion experience. *Scholar-Practitioner Quarterly, 5*(3), 289–305.

Schwarzer, D., & Bridglall, B. L. (Eds.) (2015). *Promoting Global Competence and Social Justice in Teacher Education.* Lanham, MD: Lexington Books.

Sharma, S., & Phillion, J. (2014). Introduction: Internationalizing teacher education for social justice. In S. Sharma, J. Phillion, J. Rahatzad, & H. Sasser (Eds.), *Internationalizing teacher education for social justice: Theory, Research, and Practice* (pp. xix–xxxv). Greenwich, CT: Information Age.

Sharma, S., Phillion, J., & Malewski, E. (2011). Examining the practice of critical reflection for developing preservice teachers' multicultural competencies: Findings from a study abroad program to Honduras. *Issues in Teacher Education, 20*(2), 9–22. https://doi.org/10.1177/1028315318816455

Sharma, S., Rahatzad, J., & Phillion, J. (2013). How preservice teachers engage in the process of (de)colonization: Findings from an international field experience in Honduras. *Interchange, 43*, 363–377.

Sivakumaran, T., Sutton, J., Todd, T., & Garcia, K. N. (2011). Transcending classroom borders: Determining student perceptions of study abroad programs in a teacher education program. *National Teacher Education Journal, 4*(2), 19–22.

Smith, M. D. M., Jennings, L., & Lakhan, S. (2014). International education and service learning: Approaches toward cultural competency and social justice. *The Counseling Psychologist, 42*(8), 1188–1214. https://doi.org/10.1177/0011000014557499

Stanlick, S. S., & Hammond, T. C. (2016). Service-learning and undergraduates: Exploring connections between ambiguity tolerance, empathy, and motivation in an overseas service trip. *International Journal of Research on Service-Learning and Community Engagement, 4*(1), 273–289.

Stewart, V. (2013). Succeeding globally: Transforming the teaching profession. *International Educator, 22*(3), 82–87.

Strauss, A., & Corbin, J. (1998). *Basics of qualitative research: Techniques and procedures for developing grounded theory* (2nd Ed.). Thousand Oaks, CA: Sage.

Westheimer, J., & Suurtamm, K. E. (2009). The politics of social justice meets practice: Teacher education and social change. In W. Ayers, T. Quinn, & D. Stovall (Eds.), *Handbook of social justice in education* (pp. 589–593). New York: Routledge.

Zhao, Y. (2010). Preparing globally competent teachers: A new imperative for teacher education. *Journal of Teacher Education, 61*(5), 422–431. https://doi.org/10.1177/0022487110375802

Chapter 11

Epilogue: The Importance of First Lessons in Learning to Teach

Patrick M. Jenlink

Teaching is an uncertain and increasingly complex undertaking. If the act of teaching were known and constant—a prescriptive template for teaching practice, so to speak—teachers could simply follow the dictates of researched-based generalizations and teacher educators would know exactly what teachers needed, performatively, to be successful.[1] However, such is not the case and the act of teaching does not follow a template nor is it known and constant. It is this singular point that speaks to the importance of understanding first lessons in learning to teach.

First lessons are perhaps some of the most important to the foundation of who we are as teachers and what our practices[2] are in the classroom. Teachers leaving preparation programs and entering school classrooms are faced daily and increasingly with "cultures in their classrooms to which progressivism, and/or constructivism would seem to be an appropriate basis of teaching and learning. However, teachers entering schools today all too often find a system of education structured around behaviorism, accountability, and compliance and control" (Bates, 2005, p. 233).

As entry-year teachers, former preservice students may indeed be "student ready" in their ability to interact with students in classrooms but may not be "teacher ready" in terms of cultural and political tensions and pedagogical disconnects. This requires, as Garcia et al. (2010) noted, that preservice teachers "must be given opportunities to explore and comprehend their own cultural and personal values, their identities, and their social beliefs" (p. 136). Importantly, first lessons come at different points in an individual's life. It is in understanding these first lessons that the individual grows and matures into a teacher, hopefully a quality teacher.

THE IMPORTANCE OF FIRST LESSONS

First lessons offer insight into the formation of a personal pedagogy of teaching and an evolving epistemological understanding of learning to teach. Teacher educators who understand Dewey's (1904) concern for the relation of theory to practice in turn understand that first lessons are crucial sources of learning that instruct current and future teaching practice.

With that in mind, it is critically important for teacher educators to understand that they serve as living examples of the very kind of pedagogical practices, which they seek to instill in prospective teachers. Likewise, it is equally important that preservice and practicing teachers understand the critical nature of responsibility that comes with serving as a living example in a classroom populated with young minds seeking to learn.

First Lessons in PreK–12 Schooling

An individual's first lessons in learning to teach come at a very early age and are situated along a continuum of twelve-plus years of schooling. As young students, they sit in classrooms and experience teachers, several teachers a year, some great at what they do and others not.

These experiences leave an early imprint of what teaching means and take the form of first lessons. Importantly, these lessons are a source for a future teacher's beliefs and values about what it takes to be a great teacher. Teaching beliefs are partly related to the preservice and novice teacher's own perspectives on learning to teach (Kremer-Hayon & Tillema, 2002) but also closely "connected to the affordances of their actual teaching practice; i.e., impacted by the teaching context in which they work" (Tillema & Kremer-Hayon, 2005, p. 204).

The question that these first lessons raise, simply stated, is as follows: "What might be the result if we rethink teacher preparation so that all students are encouraged to examine their past experiences, drawing into specific relief the perspectives that shaped students' earliest beliefs about teaching?" John Dewey advocated a similar pedagogical position in 1904 in an article on the relationship between theory and practice in teacher education. He asserted that the "greatest asset in the student's possession—the greatest, moreover that ever will be in his [or her] possession—[is] his [or her] own direct and personal experience" (Dewey, 1904, p. 258).

Dewey believed that "beginning students [of teaching] have . . . a very large capital of an exceedingly practical sort in their own experience" (p. 258). With this in mind, he recommended that students be encouraged to bring their personal experience to bear upon subject matter being taught—deconstructing personal experience in the context of learning to teach. Doing otherwise, he warned, prevented teachers from developing and using their own independent intelligence and reinforced their "intellectual subserviency" (Dewey, 1904, p. 258).

Dewey further advised that failure to allow students to explore their past experiences in light of theoretical constructs would produce only a mindless imitation of others' practice rather than reflection on teaching as an interactive process. He was referring to knowledge about teaching and learning that candidates bring with them as a result of having been students for many years.

Learning to teach takes place primarily through practice—practice in classrooms and with students engaged in well-structured learning experiences. First lessons in learning to teach are also situated in our teacher preparation programs and the partner schools where preservice teachers complete their clinical experiences. The lessons learned in teacher preparation programs are varied in quality and defined, in large part, by the experiences of teacher educators' instruction in courses and mentoring students. The knowledge and understanding of teaching, for teacher educators, has been developed through experience and scholarship of teaching; it is knowledge and understanding that is ideologically and pedagogically embedded with personal values and beliefs.

First Lessons in Teacher Preparation

Significant first lessons in learning to teach are also found in teacher preparation. These first lessons are, as Murray (2005) explains, "inevitably permeated by . . . practice and by individual ways of understanding the processes of teaching and learning. These ways of understanding, for the teacher educator, are in turn saturated by personal values, beliefs and biographies" (p. 71). Simply stated, for the preservice students learning to teach, the teacher educators who shape the first lessons experienced in teacher preparation "are engaged in teaching about teaching through the medium of their personal pedagogy" (p. 71).

Experiences of learning to teach draw forward memories from first lessons learned as a student in school—some good and others not—that unconsciously contribute to how the preservice teacher interprets situated learning experiences in teacher preparation. Important for teacher educators is understanding that first lessons, which preservice students bring into the teacher preparation experiences, meld with the personal pedagogy of teacher educators. This melding process creates a space[3] in which learning to teach under the guidance of teacher educators gives way to yet more first lessons, lessons grounded in prior experiences and new insights about the practice of teaching.

Teacher educators' as well as preservice and practicing teachers' attitudes and beliefs serve as filters for what they learn, what they teach, and how they mature in their teaching lives. With this in mind, it is important that teacher educators understand the importance of providing opportunities for preservice teachers to explore and comprehend their own cultural and personal values, their identities, and their social beliefs. It should also go without saying that teacher educators and practicing teachers alike would benefit greatly from this same exploration and comprehension.

Crafting first lessons of learning to teach requires that teacher educators reflect critically and act strategically upon the nature of their own pedagogical practices and the institutional contexts in which they work. Villegas and Lucas (2002) are instructive in their proposal that teachers develop a "sociocultural consciousness," recognizing that each individual's "perspective reflects his or her location in the social order" (p. 42).

Dewey's (1904) emphasis on prior experiences cited earlier points to the repertoire of personal knowledge that comes about through past actions and experiences and is generally no longer readily available to an actor's conscious awareness. The responsibility of teacher educators is to help preservice teachers move toward a greater consciousness that includes understanding themselves as individuals and teachers—understanding the deeply held values and beliefs about teaching that define their practice.

Understanding that one's prior experiences function tacitly to guide a one's present and future practice is of critical importance. Preservice and practicing teachers' action and practice are shaped, in part, by tacit knowledge derived from prior experience, while each new experience in turn shapes the repertoire of personal practical knowledge available and is necessary to guide practice and future action in the classroom.

First Lessons in Teacher Practice

First lessons thus far have focused on the individual's personal experience with schooling as a student and on experiences within teacher preparation. While Dewey's recommendation for drawing on prior experiences is valued in teacher preparation, perhaps the more important first lessons in learning to teach are those lessons learned in practice of teaching. The epistemological importance of these first lessons in learning to teach is inseparably bound to teaching as a context of self-learning for the teacher.

Understanding learning, for the teacher, is situated in the day-to-day act of teaching within the interface between teacher and student in classrooms. The classroom is the situated field of practice, a practiced place of teaching and learning, within which the practicing teacher matures, learns what makes he or her a quality teacher, a teacher who understands the critical importance of shaping first lessons students.

First lessons in teacher practice, lessons that are imbued with epistemological curiosity, are concerned with the distinction between practice and theory and with different ideas necessary to student learning. Popkewitz (1998) makes the point this way: "The different ideas provide a way in which to think, speak, see, feel, and act toward the child. The different ideas overlap in a manner that produces boundaries to what is possible in thinking and acting" (p. 29).

These first lessons are part of the scaffolding that constructs the teacher, giving life to teaching practice. Through understanding and drawing from first lessons, the teacher matures and the act of teaching is directed by an understanding that practice "does not stand outside of theory but is itself a theoretical concept that 'tells' one how the world is to be held together and reflected upon" (Popkewitz, 1998, p. 80).

Teachers who first enter the classroom are confronted with the cultural patterns of the school imprinted with the dominate ideologies, unbalanced by the asymmetrical nature of power and knowledge, and challenged by the issues of difference, equity, and injustice. Lessons learned by teachers who first enter the classroom are hallmarks that define a teacher's practice in the long term. Cochran-Smith (1991) appropriately argued the point that teachers need to know "that they have a responsibility to reform, not just replicate, standard school practices" (p. 280). Teachers must learn to *"teach against the grain"* (emphasis in original) which

> is also deeply embedded in the culture and history of teaching at individual schools and in the biographies of particular teachers and their individual or collaborative efforts to alter curricula, raise questions about common practices, and resist inappropriate decisions. (Cochran-Smith, 1991, p. 280)

First lessons learned upon entering the classroom, and those lessons learned along the way in subsequent years, challenge the teacher to develop and mature a sociocultural consciousness of the school.

Equally important, first lessons as well as those lessons that follow create an ever evolving social and epistemological space, a space within which teachers' learning is situated. It is in this space that teachers advance their teaching practice, understanding teaching to learn as an intentioned act of self-critical examination of the values and beliefs that define the teacher. First lessons in teacher practice require that teachers "understand and work both *within* and *around* the culture of teaching and the politics of schooling at their particular schools and within their larger school systems and communities"

(Cochran-Smith, 1991, p. 284, emphasis in original). Simply stated, the what, how, and why of teaching cannot be separated from the need to constantly examine, self-critically, the substance of teaching practice.

REFLECTIONS ON FIRST LESSONS

First lessons are active on several levels, simultaneously. First, such lessons are active in unconscious background of individuals entering preservice teacher education. Those earlier first lessons define how an individual interfaces with education on multiple levels. In particular, this point speaks to how prospective teachers interface with the learning to teach experiences presented in teacher preparation. It also speaks to memories that many individuals carry with them, and which serve as a basis of values and beliefs about teaching.

First lessons are active in the personal pedagogy of teacher educators. Learning to teach in higher education settings builds on prior classroom teaching experiences, but with an important twist. Teacher educators are learning to teach adults how to teach, rather than teaching young students to learn subject matter such as math or science in classrooms. The focus on how to teach becomes the curriculums for preservice students and draws into specific relief the need for new pedagogical skills and knowledge for teacher educators. The twist is that teacher educators must understand how to translate a personal pedagogy into an experience of learning to teach for preservice teachers.

First lessons hallmark the learning to teach experience preservice students have in preparation programs. This means that teacher educators need to reflect critically and act strategically upon the nature of their own personal pedagogy and their related practices and the institutional contexts in which they work. For teacher educators, the interplay of first lessons brought into the preparation program by students, and the first lessons that emerge within the program create an incredibly complex array of pedagogical challenges.

CONCLUSION

First lessons build upon a layered life of first lessons, drawing forward memories of teaching that transcend life as a young student in school, a preservice teacher preparation student, and a student of one's own teaching practice. The power of first lessons lies in the inexhaustible nature of new experiences building upon prior experiences and the need to continuously learn from past, present, and future teaching practices. It is important for teacher educators to begin to rethink personal pedagogy in such a way that first lessons become a defining element of pedagogical considerations for preparing future teachers, and in turn, for translating first lessons in learning to teach into a deeply integrated consideration, which defines teaching as a practice and profession.

NOTES

1. Maxine Greene (1995) says that there are no templates for future action; "we cannot predict the common world that may be in the making" (p. 43). Teachers are more likely to become actively committed to a learning process of their own choosing.

2. A conceptualization of learning to teach in practice expands beyond learning on site in school placements. "From this perspective, coursework and university-based experiences are critical arenas for to linking practice" (Klette, Hamerness, & Jenset, 2017, p. 4).

3. Maxine Greene, in her book *Dialectic of Freedom*, reconfigured Arendt's (1958) construct of common space as "multiplex and endlessly challenging, as each person reaches out from his/her own ground toward what might be, should be, is not yet" (Greene, 1988, p. 21).

REFERENCES

Arendt, H. (1958). *The human condition.* Chicago, IL: University of Chicago Press.

Bates, R. (2005). An anarchy of cultures: The politics of teacher education in new times. *Asia-Pacific Journal of Teacher Education, 33*(3), 231–241. https://doi.org/10.1080/13598660500298056

Cochran-Smith, M. (1991). Learning to teach against the grain. *Harvard Education Review, 61*(3), 279–310.

Dewey, J. (1904/1977). The relation of theory to practice in education. In J. A. Boydston (Ed.), *John Dewey: The middle works 1899–1924* (vol. 3) (pp. 249–272). Carbondale: Southern Illinois University Press.

Garcia, E., Arias, M. B., Murri, J. J. H., & Serna, C. (2010). Developing responsive teachers: A challenge for a demographic reality. *Journal of Teacher Education, 61*(1–2), 132–142. doi: 10.1177/0022487109347878

Greene, M. (1988). *Dialectic of freedom.* New York: Teachers College Press.

Greene, M. (1995). *Releasing the imagination.* San Francisco, CA, Jossey-Bass.

Klette, K., Hamerness, K., & Jenset, I. S. (2017). Established and evolving ways of linking to practice in teacher education: Findings from an international study of the enactment of practice in teacher education. *Acta Didactica Norge, 11*(3), 1–22.

Kremer-Hayon, L., & Tillema, H. H. (2002). "Practising what we preach"—Teacher-educators' dilemmas in promoting self-regulated learning: a cross case comparison. *Teaching & Teacher Education, 18*(5), 593–607. https://doi.org/10.1016/S0742-051X(02)00018-5

Murray, J. (2005). Re-addressing the priorities: New teacher educators and induction into higher education. *European Journal of Teacher Education, 28*(1), 67–85. https://doi.org/10.1080/02619760500040108

Popkewitz, T. S. (1998). *Struggling for the soul: The politics of schooling and the construction of the teacher*. New York: Teachers College Press.

Tillema, H., & Kremer-Hayon, L. (2005). Facing dilemmas: Teacher-educators' ways of constructing a pedagogy of teacher education. *Teaching in Higher Education, 10*(2), 203–217.

Villegas, A. M., & Lucas, T. (2002). *Educating culturally responsive teachers: A conceptually coherent and structurally integrated approach*. Albany: State University of New York Press.

About the Editor and Contributors

Patrick M. Jenlink is Regents Professor and has held the position of E. J. Campbell Endowed Chair in Educational Leadership, coordinator of the Doctoral Program, Department Chair, and professor of doctoral studies in the Department of Secondary Education and Educational Leadership, Stephen F. Austin State University. Dr. Jenlink's teaching emphasis in doctoral studies includes courses in ethics and philosophy of leadership, research methods and design, and leadership theory and practice. Dr. Jenlink' s research interests include politics of identity, democratic education, self-efficacy theory, educator clinical practice, and critical theory. He has edited and/or authored nineteen books and authored over ninety-five book chapters. As well, he has authored and published over 175 peer-refereed articles, and over 200 peer-refereed conference papers. His most recent books include *STEM teaching: An interdisciplinary approach* (Rowman & Littlefield Publishing Group), *Teacher preparation at the intersection of race and poverty in today' s schools* (Rowman & Littlefield Publishing Group), *Multimedia learning theory and its implications for teaching and learning* (Rowman & Littlefield Publishing Group), *A commitment to teaching: Toward more efficacious teacher preparation* (Rowman & Littlefield Publishing Group), *Teacher preparation and practice: Reconsideration of assessment for learning* (Rowman & Littlefield Publishing Group), and *The handbook of Dewey' s educational theory and practice* (Brill/Sense). Current book projects in progress include *Understanding teacher identity: The complexities of professional identity as teacher* (Rowman & Littlefield Publishing Group), *Teaching as a clinical practice profession: Research on clinical practice and experience in teacher preparation* (Rowman & Littlefield Publishing Group) and *Ethics and the educational leader: A casebook of ethical dilemmas* (Rowman & Littlefield Publishing Group).

ABOUT THE CONTRIBUTING AUTHORS

Burcu Ates is an associate professor of Bilingual/ESL Education in School of Teaching and Learning at Sam Houston State University. She holds a master' s degree in TESOL from Michigan State University and a PhD in Curriculum and Instruction with a focus on ESL/Multicultural Education from Texas A&M University. Her experience during two decades as an educator includes teaching ESL/EFL to children and adults in different parts of the world. Some of her research interests are culturally and linguistically responsive pedagogies, cultural narratives, online teaching, and international service-learning/study abroad. She led various ISL/study abroad trips to Costa Rica, Italy, Belize, and Mexico. She published her work in *Journal on Excellence in College Teaching, Journal of Praxis in Multicultural Education, World Englishes, Reflective Practice*, and *Journal of International Students*.

Courtney Lynn Barcus is a former instructional coach and special education teacher in both Chicago and St. Louis Public Schools. She has fifteen years of experience supporting teachers, schools, and districts across the Chicago area to implement effective instructional practices. Her research focus is on supporting special education teachers' knowledge development for teaching mathematics. She is currently a special education adjunct instructor and doctoral student at the University of Illinois at Chicago.

Anna E. Bargagliotti is a professor of Mathematics at Loyola Marymount University (LMU). Her areas of research are mathematics and statistics education, nonparametric statistics, and data visualization. She is an author of the American Statistical Association(ASA) Statistics Education of Teachers report, a co-lead author of the upcoming ASA Guidelines for Assessment and Instruction in Statistics Education report, and sits on the Joint ASA/NCTM K–12 Education committee.

Elizabeth M. Bemiss is an assistant professor in the Department of Teacher Education and Educational Leadership at the University of West Florida. Her research examines teacher identity construction, effective literacy teaching practices, and critical literacy practices with young children.

Helen Berg, native of Mexico City, is Professor of Education in the School of Teaching and Learning at Sam Houston State University. She received her doctorate from the University of Colorado-Denver and her Masters at Lesley University, Boston, Massachusetts. Her research interests are on international service-learning, bilingual/dual language education, social justice in teacher education, and educational issues related to Spanish-speaking students in U.S. schools. Her teaching interests are in the areas of bilingual education and teaching English to speakers of other languages (TESOL). She is a member of several professional organizations in bilingual education/TESOL. She published in *Journal of Latinos*, *The Review of Higher Education*, and *READ: An Online Journal for Literacy Educators*.

Katie Bonawitz is an associate professor of Education, Bethel University. She has twenty years of experience in the field of special education. She has presented nationally and internationally on the importance of collaboration between general education and special education.

Gina Braun is an assistant professor of Special Education at Rockford University in Rockford, Illinois. She teaches a wide range of special education courses, and her research focus is on supporting early career teachers' instructional practices for enhancing reading comprehension skills to students with autism spectrum disorder. Previously, she was an instructional coach for novice special educators as well as a special education teacher for Chicago Public Schools.

Karina R. Clemmons is an Associate Professor of Medical Humanities and Bioethics at the University of Arkansas for Medical Sciences. Dr. Clemmons has taught English Language Arts for English learners in middle school, high school, and abroad and taught graduate and undergraduate courses in Secondary Education. Her current research interests include teaching and learning in medical education, teacher education, the learning environment, and content literacy. Recent publications include a 2013 book chapter titled "Constructing community in higher education regardless of proximity: Re-imagining the teacher education experience within social networking technology" and a peer-reviewed journal article (2020) titled "Mobile spaced education in surgical education settings and specialties: A scoping review."

Stephanie G. Davis is a senior lecturer of Literacy Instruction at the University of North Carolina at Greensboro in the Teacher Education and Higher Education Department. Her research examines adaptive teaching, literacy instruction, and teacher education.

Yurimi Grigsby is a professor of ESOL Education in the Department of Teaching, Learning, and Diversity within the College of Graduate Studies, at Concordia University Chicago. She received her PhD from the University of Tennessee, her home state. Her teaching expertise and research interests include ESL, Sociolinguistics, Intersectionality, and Digital Storytelling. She has published articles on implementing cultural narratives and digital stories in the classroom. Some of the journals she published in are *Journal of Praxis in Multicultural Education*, *Reflective Practice*, and *Journal of International Students*.

Laura J. Hopkins is an assistant professor in the Education Department at Houghton College in Western New York State. Her scholarship addresses literacy teaching and teacher education, with a specific focus on how teachers navigate contextual resources and constraints to design high-quality, responsive literacy instruction.

Soonhyang Kim is TESOL director and an assistant professor at the Department of Teaching, Leaning and Curriculum at the University of North Florida, Jacksonville, Florida. She has been working in U.S. higher education, teaching a wide variety of subjects, including TESOL, bilingual education, and general teacher education courses. Her recent research interests are second and bilingual language/literacy development, academic oral classroom discourse, preservice/inservice teacher preparation, non-native, English-speaking teacher issue, and online teacher education.

Erin M. McTigue is an associate professor and research fellow at National Reading Centre of Norway, University of Stavanger, Stavanger, Norway. Her research interests are comprehension of informational texts, multiple representations within texts, reading motivation, and science literacy.

Diane M. Miller is an assistant professor of Literacy in the Department of Urban Education, College of Public Service, University of Houston-Downtown, where she teaches literacy methods courses for future and current educators. Her twenty years of K–12 educational experience and six years of university experience inform her research interests of content-area literacy instruction, bridging research to practice, and mentoring.

Amanda L. Nolen is a Professor of Educational Psychology in the School of Education at the University of Arkansas at Little Rock. Her research interests include how instructors use assessment of learning to make empirically sound choices about curriculum design and student learning. These interests have led her to explore these phenomena in STEM contexts, specifically in engineering education and academic medicine. Her work has appeared in Educational Researcher, Routledge's *Theory into Practice, Educational Psychology Review, American Journal of Pharmaceutical Education,* and *The Journal of Acoustical Society of America.*

Amanda A. Olsen is an assistant professor of Measurement and Statistics in the College of Education at the University of Texas at Arlington. As an applied quantitative methodologist, she engages in a variety of topics relating to educational policy, equity, and quantitative methods such as causal inference, multilevel modeling, program evaluation, and complex survey design and analysis.

Patricia Paulson is a professor of Science Education, Bethel University. She has taught at both the K–12 and university levels. Prior to becoming professor of Science Education, she served as a district science curriculum coordinator.

Marliese R. Peltier is a doctoral candidate at Michigan State University in the Curriculum, Instruction and Teacher Education Department, specializing in language and literacy. Her research examines teacher learning, teacher education, and family literacies.

Jay Rasmussen is a professor of Education, director MA in Education, coordinator of Faculty Development, Bethel University, and has over thirty-five years of experience in K–12 and higher education.

Roya Q. Scales is a professor of Literacy Education in Western Carolina University's School of Teaching and Learning. Her research interests include teacher visioning, preparing teachers to teach literacy, and adaptive teaching. She currently serves as an associate editor for *Reading & Writing Quarterly: Overcoming Learning Difficulties*.

W. David Scales is an assistant professor in the Psychology Department at Western Carolina University. His research interests include the application of advanced psychometric techniques in education and psychology, including teacher education, small-sample equating, cognitive diagnostic modeling, and gender equity in research psychology.

Roberta J. Scholes is a retired teaching professor from the College of Education at the University of Missouri at Columbia. She has over twenty-plus years of experience in the education field, specializing in measurement. Her research interests include charter schools, teacher development, and K–12 education.

Chyllis E. Scott is an associate professor of Literacy in the Department of Teaching and Learning at the University of Nevada, Las Vegas. Her areas of teaching expertise include graduate-level courses in content-area literacy and disciplinary literacy, literacy assessment, and literacy research seminars. Her research interests include content-area and disciplinary literacy, academic writing, and mentoring practices for preservice and inservice teachers and students in higher education.

Courtney Shimek is an assistant professor at West Virginia University in the Department of Curriculum and Instruction/Literacy Studies. Her research interests include reading education, teacher education, and nonfiction children's literature.

Danny Swensen is Professor of Education, Bethel University. He has areas of interest that include innovative approaches to teaching mathematics, effective use of educational technologies, and culturally-relevant pedagogy.

Rory P. Tannebaum is Assistant Professor of Education at Merrimack College in North Andover, Massachusetts. Prior to starting this position, Dr. Tannebaum attended Clemson University where he received his PhD in Curriculum and Instruction with a focus on social studies education. His research interests focus on the development of reform-oriented preservice social studies teachers through powerful teacher education.

Marie Tejero Hughes is a professor of Special Education at the University of Illinois at Chicago. She teaches graduate courses in literacy, which are designed to assist teachers working in urban communities meet the needs of students struggling with literacy across the curriculum and directs several projects designed to enhance the leadership skills of educators in the field of special education. Her areas of expertise include teacher education, comprehension instruction for students with learning disabilities, and students struggling with reading comprehension, and Latinx family engagement in education.

Ann Van Wig is an assistant professor at Eastern Washington University in the Department of Education. Her research interests include culturally responsive pedagogy, teacher education, and struggling readers.

Geri Von Grey is an instructor in Education, Bethel University. She enjoys working with future educators on creative and innovative ways to engage students in thinking and learning. Her areas of interest include teacher preparation, reflective practice, and elementary social studies education.

Erin K. Washburn is an associate professor in the Reading and Elementary Education Department at the University of North Carolina, Charlotte. Her research interests include teacher knowledge relating to teaching literacy, literacy teacher preparation and professional learning, and the efficacy of school-based literacy interventions for striving readers and writers.